P9-DXJ-388

30
Energy-Efficient
Houses...You Can Build

30 Energy-Efficient Houses...You Can Build

by Alex Wade

photographs by Neal Ewenstein

 **Rodale Press,** Emmaus, PA

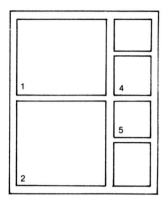

Front Cover

1. Wright House
    Sea Ranch, California
    Architect: David Wright
    Photographer: Harry Estes

2. Rice Studio
    Barrytown, New York
    Designer: Dustin Rice
    Photographer: Neal Ewenstein

3. Terry House
    Santa Fe, New Mexico
    Architect: David Wright
    Photographer: Karen Terry

4. Shingleton House
    Hilton Head Island, South Carolina
    Architect and Photographer: Alex Wade

5. Gummere House
    Duxbury, Massachusetts
    Architect and Photographer: Alex Wade

Back Cover

Page House
New Hampshire
Architect and Photographer: David Howard

Mackey House
Tinmouth, Vermont
Architect and Photographer: David Howard

Copyright © 1977 Alex Wade and Neal Ewenstein

All rights reserved. No part of this publication may be reproduced or transmitted in any form or by any means, electronic or mechanical, including photocopy, recording, or any information storage and retrieval system without the written permission of the publisher.

Printed in the United States of America

10 9 (Hardcover)

10 9 (Paperback)

Library of Congress Cataloging in Publication Data

Wade, Alex.
    30 energy-efficient houses . . . you can build.

    Includes bibliographical references and index.
    1. Dwellings—Energy conservation—Amateurs' manuals.
2. House construction—Amateurs' manuals.
I. Ewenstein, Neal, joint author. II. Title.
TJ163.5.D86W3   690′.8   77-22069
ISBN 0-87857-203-1 (Hardcover)
ISBN 0-87857-191-4 (Paperback)

Inside Photo Credits:

Models of Kotajarvi and Pergola houses and Fennell exterior
    by David Borenstein

Models of Dowling-Miller and Replogle houses
    by Eric Van Horn

Pictures of Steinberg guest houses
    by David Howard

Skylight picture on page x
    by Richard M. Gummere

Photos of remodeling of Blume house
    by Howard Blume

Contents

Acknowledgments

Neal and I wish to thank all of the families whose houses are shown in this book for letting us intrude so that their work can be examples for others.

I also wish to thank editors Carol and Mike Stoner for their hard work and guidance. Very special thanks go to Iain Mackenzie who helped an inexperienced writer get started and gave generously of his time with preliminary editing and many suggestions.

Finally, I wish to thank J. C. Brotherhood, Eric Van Horn, and Dave Borenstein for their help with models of houses not yet completed.

A. W.

Introduction

Getting Started

Several months ago, a set of sketches from Montana arrived in the mail. These drawings were roughly based upon a house design for which I had made working drawings available. The plans had been published in a small quarterly newsletter. My first reaction to the sketches was despair; the new plans didn't fit the structural arrangement of the house. The clients were trying to push the plan beyond its intended limits. Later, I studied it and discovered that the structure could easily be changed to accommodate the new plan. This, I realized, was an entirely new house design. Compared to the original, the only similarities were the overall exterior dimensions. The ideal design process was working. The clients had taken my basic idea and completely reworked it to fit their own needs. Then they sent it back to me and I refined it to work as an integrated structure. I hope that more people will respond to their housing needs in a similar fashion—taking an idea and reworking it to suit them. The intent of this book is to give people the background to make these kinds of modifications.

A recent article in the *Wall Street Journal* indicated that small houses as well as small cars are not selling well. Major tract housing builders are said to be canceling their construction plans for small houses because "they" (the buyers) don't want just a little box. Maybe the builders should take a closer look at what is happening to the auto industry. Recently introduced, heavily advertised compacts from Detroit have sold poorly. The manufacturers try to excuse poor sales by saying that the public doesn't want small cars. Yet, well-designed, properly engineered and reasonably priced foreign cars are selling so well that there are even waiting lists.

The parallel is quite striking. The very few builders who have responded to the energy challenge are swamped with orders. R. B. Fitch of Chapel Hill, North Carolina, builds well-designed, energy-conserving houses

People who live in small houses can afford to relax.

David Howard, Architect

with heavy insulation, compact plans, and water-saving fixtures. His houses are selling very well. David Howard of Alstead, New Hampshire, who designs and prefabricates small efficient post and beam houses has a two-year backlog of orders. Our local non-union contractor who builds post and beam houses which people can afford has so much work he is starting to turn down jobs. At the same time, the local union hall hasn't had a job opening in almost a year; the unions are screaming for government programs to put their men back to work, presumably building more inefficient and unsaleable houses. It is obvious that the public wants both cars and houses that do their job well and has become increasingly critical of those that don't.

Unfortunately for the prospective home buyer, the above examples of with-it builders are very rare. There are no Honda Civics for home buyers. The Honda is carefully designed to provide the most transportation capability with the least amount of space and fuel. We desperately need houses which are designed with similar standards. Both our housing and automotive industries have tried to take the quick, easy way out by cutting down on the size of existing models rather than spending the time and money to engineer efficient new ones. In this book, I offer a wide range of small houses that use space and materials wisely. They range in size from minimum-sized, basic living units for one or two people to full-sized family houses. All are thoroughly engineered to do the most for the least.

Design inefficiency has contributed to waste of materials and energy which, with inflation, has pushed the commercially marketed house out of reach for 85 percent of the people in our country. Cost-saving techniques, common in other industrialized nations, have been shut out by a combination of pig-headed unions and absurd building codes. Sharp increases in energy costs may possibly drive some present homeowners to sell their houses because they can't afford to maintain them. The designs in this book reduce costs dramatically and put private houses back within reach of most people.

Architects in this country tend to design houses for themselves and other architects without regard for the tastes or preferences of their clients or the general public. Competitions for design awards are almost always judged by panels of architects. The awards invariably go to sterile white boxes which are sometimes nice sculpture but rarely nice houses. The architects then cry that the public doesn't care about architecture and the result is that the average citizen has to live in a very badly designed house. In my own practice, I try to work with clients as an advisor rather than force my designs down their throats. I find it much more of a "happy" challenge to take someone else's ideas and organize them into a good building than to simply start with a vague set of requirements for a house. There are no "projects" or architects' dreams in this book.

I hope that architects in this country will respond to new trends and learn to help people by consulting rather than demanding a large fee for handling all the design and construction details. One of the reasons that architects' services cost so much is our silly division of the architect from the builder. In more advanced countries, the architect is directly involved in the building process as are most of those I have included in this book. David Howard makes a deal with his clients. He goes on the job and teaches them to build an efficient Rumsford fireplace. In return, they agree to teach two more people to build their own fireplaces. I hope that this attitude will spread and prosper.

I had the pleasure, a couple of years ago, of contributing to a book edited by Eugene Eccli called *Low-Cost, Energy-Efficient Shelter* (1976).* The book's objective was to give people information to help them design their own houses and save money in initial and operating costs. I included a couple of my sketches for simple post and beam structures and my address for ordering complete plans. The results were amazing. Many people ordered plans, often sending a sketch requesting extensive modifications. Others wrote, asking me to design new structures for them. Gradually, a collection of houses emerged, similar only in their common roots of post and beam construction, compact layout, and economical use of materials. These designs have formed the nucleus for the energy-efficient houses presented in these pages. Examples of "passive" solar-tempered houses by various other designers whom I respect and houses totally designed and built by their owners round out the book.

My book is primarily directed to those of you who want to build something more reasonable than what is commonly offered on the commercial market. If you are like the average person, you must untangle the intractable mess of the housing industry if you are to realize the American dream of owning your own home. Hopefully, I can help you. In this book, I demonstrate examples of what can be done to make construction simpler and cheaper, while still providing handsome accommodations for you and your family. I selected houses that I think will appeal to a wide variety of tastes and needs. Since the principles involved in designing compact, energy-efficient houses are different from those used in planning a conventional house, I outline the most important concepts here. Although not all the houses employ every concept, these guidelines will enable you to study the plans with a much more critical eye.

The first and most obvious principle is to not waste space, either in the house or on your site. Built only as much house as you need. If possible, build your house two or more stories high. Plans which are square or nearly so use much less wall area than long, rectangular ones. Thus, you will require a smaller plot or can have more ground area left for vegetables, recreation, woodlot, or whatever your fancy.
Use every inch of interior space you have. Most houses waste space. The sloping area under the roof is taken up by useless trusses in most houses. In early settlers' homes, this valuable space was used for sleeping lofts. But consider other possibilities for this upper-level space as well—a play area for the children, extra storage, space for a solar hot-water heater, or even space for a small auxiliary furnace. Use your

The individual house had no place in American culture anymore.

A comment made by John Dinkerloo, a partner in one of the major architectural firms in this country at a jury awards meeting for *Progressive Architecture*.

Giving awards to houses is like giving awards to toys instead of the real things.

Sara P. Harkness, a partner in Architects Collaborative. (This comment was made at the same jury meeting.)

Make Use of Every Inch

*Rodale Press, 33 East Minor Street, Emmaus, PA 18049.

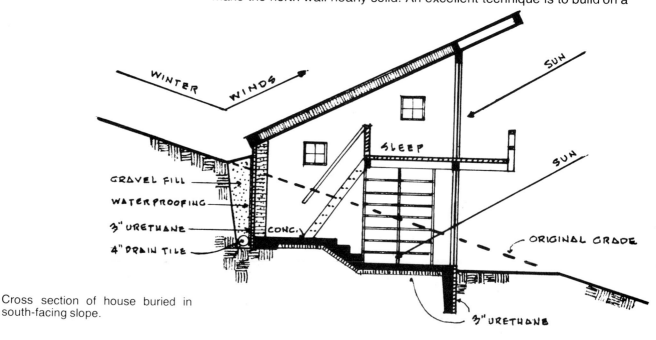

Tiny second-floor room was made bright and spacious by removing a low ceiling (originally on the bottom of the beams) and adding skylights. Sleeping loft is at left.

imagination. Let spaces flow together vertically or horizontally to visually increase their apparent size. In a loft, leave out part of the floor between the loft and the areas below; both spaces will seem considerably larger. For children's bedrooms and play areas try having small sleeping cubicles open off a central play space. (See the Holbrook House, Number 3.) Living, dining, and kitchen areas should always be combined, making use of the entire space more flexible. Open planning also provides better air flow, making it easier and cheaper to design heating and cooling systems. One important trick to compact planning is to make interior spaces usable with skylights. Long, inefficient rectangles are initiated by designers who don't understand skylights, and who therefore design stretched-out houses to provide adequate daylight.

Careful use of built-ins will enable you to design smaller rooms and save on furnishings. Beds are naturals to be built in. Foam rubber makes excellent mattresses and cushions. If you buy foam rubber in bulk, without a cover, and place it on a wooden base, you can have a fine bed for less than a quarter of the price of an ugly monster from the furniture store. The foam on wood is also much better for your back than a conventional mattress and box spring. As an added bonus, use the space under the bed for storage. Build in some used chests of drawers, or, for out-of-season storage, hinge the bottom boards under the mattress. Although most beds are built too low for useful storage, there is no logical reason why your bed can't be three or four feet off the floor, making the space underneath usable and allowing you to design a smaller room if you wish. The couch is another big candidate for building into place. Since new couches can range upwards from $500, this can be a big savings. Here, too, you can use the space under the couch for storage. If you put the couch in an alcove (as in House Number 30) it can also double as a guest bed.

Use your site effectively. Turn your back on the north winds. If possible, make the north wall nearly solid. An excellent technique is to build on a

Cross section of house buried in south-facing slope.

steep, south-facing slope, burying all or most of the north wall into the hillside. Not only are you saving heat from less exposure to the cold north winds, but you are also tempering the inside of your house by using the constant temperature of the earth. Since tract builders are usually distressed by slopes, you can frequently pick up this property at cut rates. Make sure, however, that it isn't solid rock, since blasting can be very expensive. To avoid glare from the south-facing glass, balance your lighting with skylights and high strip windows along the north wall. But study chapter 4 before deciding on this type of design; it requires special attention to insulation, waterproofing, and the design of the underground walls themselves. (See the sketch for a cross section of this type of house.)

Make your house store its own heat. Use as much masonry inside your house as possible. If you are building into a hillside or on a flat site, always build your floor of masonry right on grade. Uninformed people may tell you that brick or concrete built right on the ground will be cold. On the contrary, the slab will be warm in winter and cool in summer *if* it is very thoroughly insulated around the perimeter. (See the working drawings in chapter 12 for proper details.) If possible, build a masonry chimney, but whatever you do, *don't* place it on an outside wall. Place the chimney so that sun from south-facing glass hits the masonry. It will store a lot of heat. (See the Perlberg House, Number 24 for an excellent example of this technique.)

Solar greenhouses and/or large areas of glass should be used on the south wall to take maximum advantage of the sun's free heat. Many of the best designs in this book incorporate solar greenhouses. Industry giants such as Exxon and Portland Cement Association are trying to convince the public to eliminate windows to save energy. The engineers who advise them to make these recommendations are invariably victims of poor training in a very different era. They are known as "textbook engineers." Simple observations, such as the heat one feels from the sun when standing near a south-facing window are completely beyond them. The standard mechanical engineering texts which they studied treat all glass areas equally in terms of heat loss, regardless of orientation. In order for heat gained in the daytime from south-facing glass not to be lost at night, provide a means of covering the glass with an insulating material. Several good methods were described in *Low-Cost, Energy-Efficient Shelter*. There are additional ideas in the working drawings in chapter 12 as well as in chapter 7 which cover windows, doors, skylights, and insulating flaps.

Your very ability to survive in your house in the next few years may depend upon your ability to heat it. Cost and availability of fuels are going to create major problems for us all in the near future. Choose your heat sources carefully, making sure that you have a backup system if either the electricity or fossil fuel source, or both are interrupted. Most furnaces regardless of fuel source require electricity for their controls. At the very least, shop carefully and buy one of the new furnaces with an efficient European burner (oil-fired only). The big oil companies successfully kept the efficient burners out of this country until very recently. They go under the trade name of "Blue-flame." Intensive research is

An engineer's principal purpose as an engineer is to create obsolescence.

Elisha Gray II, Chairman of the Board, Whirlpool Corporation

Maximize Heat Efficiency

underway to approve efficiencies of all fuel-consuming appliances, so check very carefully before you buy. Keep in the back of your mind that it takes three times as much fuel to generate electricity as it does to get an equivalent amount of heat from fuel burned right in your home. The power companies do not have any magic ways of defeating the laws of physics, so don't let them tell you otherwise.

It is vital to reduce the heating load to a bare minimum. Insulation and sealing against air infiltration are very important. All of the rest of the cost-saving techniques will be for nothing if you don't pay attention to this aspect of building. While many different types and thicknesses of insulation can be used, I personally recommend the following: use 12-inch fiberglass or equivalent in all roofs and suspended floors; use 6-inch urea-formaldehyde in exterior walls (to do this you should use 2 × 6 framing members spaced 24 inches apart). Urea foam is a bit expensive and must be applied by a commercial applicator. If you are in a remote area or on a really tight budget, use 6-inch fiberglass instead. A contractor friend just built a house using the 12-inch and 6-inch fiberglass insulation with framing members spaced 24 inches apart. He reports that it actually costs less for the heavier walls and insulation than for conventional construction. This is one case where better quality is actually cheaper; it just takes a bit of creative design. The reason that it is cheaper is that labor costs for installing the materials were much less because the wider spacing of the framing members meant that fewer pieces of material had to be installed. Obviously, if you do all of your own work, the insulation will cost a bit more. But, if you hire others, don't let some contractor charge you more for "better" insulation claiming that it costs more; it simply doesn't. For slabs-on-grade and concrete-grade beams, I recommend a minimum of 3 inches of polyurethane foam board, applied directly to the outside face of the concrete. (See details in chapter 12.)

Post and Beam Construction

Most of the houses in this book are of post and beam construction which are cheaper and quicker to build than conventional houses. Many architects, engineers, and contractors are unfamiliar with this type of construction. Most will try to convince you that it's more expensive than conventional construction. Those of us who have actually built such structures know better. Pat and Patsy Hennin of the Shelter Institute of Bath, Maine, built an 1,100-square-foot, well-insulated, post and beam house for less than $4,000. A post and beam structure with exposed framing will not only save in initial construction costs, but will save a lot in heating costs in the years to come. It actually takes 25 percent less wall to enclose this type of house. (See the sketch which shows how this is possible.) The simple logical arrangement of the framing system makes these houses very easy to build. The Householder House, Number 18 was my first post and beam house, built over 20 years ago. Two men framed up all three levels of the house starting from the slab in just two-and-a-half days. They had never seen a post and beam house before.

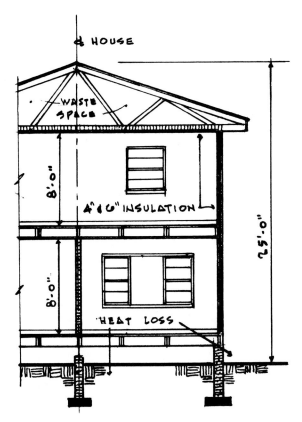

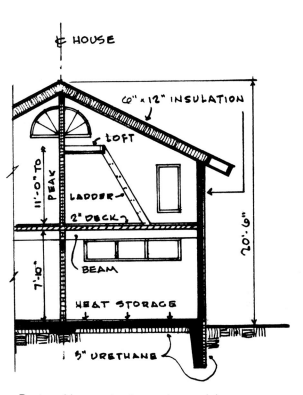

Conventional framing wastes space and materials—in the crawlspace, attic, and between floors.

Post and beam structure set on a slab saves space and materials. Loft under sloping roof is added bonus.

Design Ecologically

Use native materials where possible. remember that it takes oil to transport materials and others require excessive amounts of energy to manufacture. One reason that tract houses have become so expensive is that they use great quantities of energy-intensive materials which also happen to be ugly. Wherever possible, reuse materials which have already used up energy to manufacture (excellent examples are bricks and plumbing fixtures). Really think ahead and make sure that your house suits you and your site. Stake out the house on your site and mentally walk through it. Go through a typical day in your house. Think about where every window and door and room will be. Where will the sun and the winds be? What will you actually see through that large glass window?

Get Involved in the Design and Building

You should gain enough information from the houses shown in this book to design and build your own. If you are not up to actually building at least make a crack at working up your own design. Remember, all sites and family requirements are different, so modify any design to suit your own needs.

Until the mid-1800s, it was standard procedure for each family to build its own house. True, houses were smaller and simpler in those days. In fact, many were similar to some of those included in this book. Except for my father, every generation of my family has built its own house. This goes all the way back to my great-great-grandfather Jacques who built his 18 × 20-foot log house on land granted him by King George of England back in the 1780s. The house still stands and is in use as a barn. My aunt recently chased away NBC when they wanted to buy it for a Bicentennial special.

If you do not have the time or inclination to build yourself, you will have to shop very carefully for young, progressive workers who are willing to try new ideas. They are out there; it just takes time and effort to find them. You will, of course, make mistakes; some may be expensive. When you are all done, however, you will have the satisfaction of knowing that you have tamed a recalcitrant system and made it work for you. You will also have set an example for others to follow.

This is a very personal book. The products, materials, and construction methods represent those which I have found by trial and error and 20 years of experience make the most sense. Some of you may disagree with me, but I feel that I have included those ideas which produce the best house for the least money—houses that are suited to today, and the years ahead.

For those of you not familiar with construction terms, I give you this short glossary. This is by no means a list of all the words dealing with design and construction—only those that I have found to be the most puzzling to people not in the house building business. I suggest that you look it over before you read any further.

"Small houses and rooms strengthen the mind; Large ones weaken it."

Leonardo da Vinci

Glossary

Batten—Narrow strips of wood used to cover joints or as decorative vertical members over plywood or wide boards.

Cantilever—Any structural member extending from a support at one end but unsupported at the other end.

Conduction—A process of heat transfer whereby heat moves directly through a material.

Convection—A heat transfer created by the motion of air resulting from a difference in temperature and the action of gravity.

Fascia—Vertical trim boards at edge of roof or overhang.

Flashing—Sheet metal or other material used in roof or wall construction to protect against water seepage.

Footing—A masonry section, usually concrete in a rectangular form, wider than the bottom of the foundation wall it supports.

Furring—Strips of wood or metal applied to a surface to even it and usually to serve as a base for finish material.

Glass Types:

Insulating Glass—Factory-sealed, double-paned glass with an air space in the middle. Edges are fusedwith additional glass or a metal edge. Ranges from ½- to 1-inch thick; ⅝ inch the most common.

Plate and Float Glass—Clearer quality than sheet glass, and can be made thicker and stronger. Plate glass can often be picked up secondhand at bargain prices. Thickness ranges from ⅛ inch to 1 inch but ¼ inch is most common.

Sheet Glass—Double-strength (⅛-inch thick) is the most useful. Single-strength ($3/_{32}$ inch) breaks easily. Also made in $3/_{16}$-inch and $7/_{32}$-inch strengths.

Tempered Glass—(Also known as safety glass). Can be made from all of the above except single-strength sheet glass. The glass is heat treated to become over three times stronger. It cannot be drilled or cut, for it will disintegrate into small pieces. It is much safer when broken since pieces do not have the jagged edges of regular broken glass.

Wired Glass—Glass with embedded wire mesh. It is sometimes required in codes for safety purposes.

Grade—The slope of the land.

Grading—Adjusting the slope of the land to new contours.

Heat Pump—A heating and cooling unit that operates like a normal air conditioner in summer but in winter operates in reverse ejecting warm air indoors.

Jamb—The side and head lining of a doorway, window, or other opening.

Jig—A device for holding pieces in place for assembly. Very useful for making repetitive items.

Lintel—A horizontal structural member that supports the load over a window or a door.

Masonry—Stone, brick, concrete, etc., bonded together to form a wall or mass of any sort.

Penny—A measure of nail length. It is abbreviated as "d."

Pier—A column of masonry, usually rectangular, used to support other structural members.

Pitch—The incline slope of a roof, or the ratio of the total rise to the total width of the house: e.g., an 8-foot rise and a 24-foot width are a ⅓ pitch roof. Roof slope is expressed in inches of rise per 12 inches of run.

Plumb—Exactly perpendicular; vertical.

Rabbet—A continuous slot in a wood member into which another wood member will be placed to create a mechanical joint.

Sash—A light frame containing one or more panes of glass.

Screeding—Leveling off wet concrete to produce a uniform surface.

Sheathing—Structural covering, usually boards or plywood, used over the studs or rafters of a structure.

Sill—The lowest member in the frame of a structure, resting on the foundation and supporting the floor joists or the uprights of the wall. Also the bottom of a door or a window.

Slab-on-Grade—Method of building in which the floor and foundation are one unit installed directly on ground level.

Soffit—The underside covering of an overhanging cornice.

Solar-Tempering—A design process using windows and masonry within a house to partially solar heat the structure.

Terne—A durable steel sheet coated with lead to make it last a long time. (The original terne roof is still in place on Monticello.) It is used in a variety of roof flashings and roofings, e.g., standing seam, batten seam, or flat pan.

Thermal Wall—A masonry wall used to store heat from the sun. The heat is stored at a time when there is more than enough (such as noon) and then given off when the temperature falls after sunset.

Truss—A beam made up of small, light pieces and used rather than a heavy beam as a means of spanning long distances.

U.S.G.S.—United States Geological Survey. This government agency makes maps on a large enough scale to identify individual houses. Maps show topography, tree masses, roads, and other features which can be identified from aerial survey. Though the maps are very accurate, they may be out of date.

Window Types:

Awning—This window has its hinges at the top so that it swings out at the bottom. There may be one or any number of sashes.

Casement—A window attached to its frame by means of hinges at the sides similar to a door.

Clerestory—A window placed vertically in a wall above one's line of vision to provide natural light. Usually at an intersection of two offset roof planes.

Double-Hung—A window that has an upper (outside) sash that slides down, and a lower (inside) sash that slides up.

Fixed Sash—A window that doesn't open.

Operating Sash—A window that slides or pivots open.

Skylight—A clear or translucent panel set into a roof to provide natural light.

All of the plans and sections in this book were drawn to a scale of 1/8 inch=1 foot. I have drawn all of them exactly to size so that you can scale all of the dimensions.

Since many of these houses are built into the ground, I have numbered the floors rather than attaching labels such as "basement" or "first floor" as these could be confusing. Number 1 is always the lowest living floor.

Rather than use conventional graphics with just heavy black lines for the walls, I have used standard construction indications for materials so that you can actually tell how various parts of the building are constructed.

In order to give a sense of scale to the plans, I have shown a minimum amount of furniture. The various furniture indications are included with the materials legend which follows:

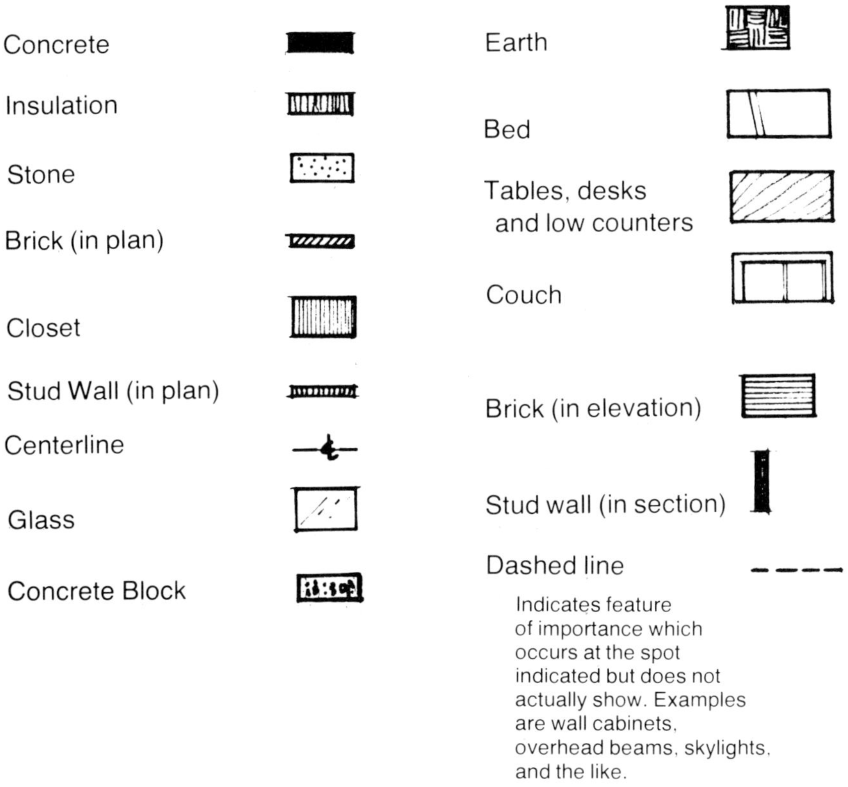

Legend for Plans

Concrete	▬	Earth	
Insulation			
Stone		Bed	
Brick (in plan)		Tables, desks and low counters	
Closet		Couch	
Stud Wall (in plan)		Brick (in elevation)	
Centerline			
Glass		Stud wall (in section)	
Concrete Block		Dashed line	– – – –

Dashed line Indicates feature of importance which occurs at the spot indicated but does not actually show. Examples are wall cabinets, overhead beams, skylights, and the like.

Technical Data

Each set of plans is accompanied by a set of technical data which will help you to evaluate the houses.

The efficiency ratio (ER) represents the ratio of the exposed area of the house to the usable floor area. Under this formula, large houses achieve a higher number than small ones. Consider any small house which approaches .50 as very efficient. The small Replogle house even exceeds .50. Since buried walls and floors on grade actually store heat (if properly insulated) I have assigned a zero loss to these areas. Suspended floors over crawlspaces and sod roofs are assigned half value. These comparisons assume that all of these houses are equally well insulated which could occur if you follow my recommendations.

Part I

**30 Houses and
the Stories behind Them**

Chapter 1

Family Houses—How to Build to Suit *Your* Needs

This chapter talks about the ideal way to build a house: Get right in there and build it yourself! As skilled labor gets more and more expensive, many people will discover that the cheapest way to get a new house is to build it yourself. There is also the added factor of pride in personal achievement. When you do it yourself, you will do it right and not skimp on that last corner when the caulking ran out.

Even if you don't have all the necessary skills, you can still build it yourself. You may have to subcontract some of the major elements of the work, but it is still possible for you to do all of the shopping for materials, to compare subcontractors, and to get the best workmanship for the price. It may take a bit longer, but the final results are well worth the extra effort. Remember, you'll probably only do this once in your life, and your labor contributions can actually be worth more than double the dollar value of the professional labor which they replace. This savings is due to the fact that you won't have to pay outright for someone else to do the work and because you won't have to pay the extra interest on a larger mortgage. This second point becomes quite significant when you consider that the interest will usually exceed the amount of the principal during the term of the mortgage. Therefore, every dollar which you don't have to borrow is two or more dollars actually saved.

It may amaze many people, but it is still possible to build an elegant small house for less than $5,000. Several of the houses in this book were constructed for that price or even less. Of course, that represents the extreme case of doing all your own work and shopping very carefully for materials.

Be very careful that you don't run afoul of building codes; they can throw a monkey wrench in your plans. Building codes are widely regarded as protecting health and safety. I suspect that their purpose is

Malfunction of a major nature occurred in 50 percent of the units installed. . . . Most of them resulted from such things as air locks in water pipes, improper fittings, putting circulator pumps in backwards, miswiring, setting timers so the unit worked only at night, equipment breakdowns and leaks in the pipes because of inadequate insulation.

From a *New York Times* article describing a test of solar water heaters. (Compared to a full active solar heating system, solar water heaters are simple. Just imagine what would have happened if the same workmen had tried to install a full system. The article was used to show that solar energy isn't what it's cracked up to be. I read it as 50 percent of the plumbers were incompetent. Do it yourself, then you know it's right.)

to protect overpaid and inefficient union building trades workers. They have worked hard to lobby codes into existence in rural states such as Montana so that they can effectively shut out the use of ecological materials and unskilled labor. If the nasty building code requires an automatic heating system capable of maintaining 70°F., as many do, you are effectively prevented from using wood heat or solar-tempering to heat your house. If someone had come around trying to enforce such a code in my grandfather's day, he would have picked up the offending gentleman by the collar and the seat of the pants and deposited him in the nearby creek. Indeed, one unfortunate Republican politician did wind up there.

The Republican was running for sheriff and was so impressed that my grandfather had thrown him in the creek that he came back and made him an offer. "If you will come campaign for me, I'll get a bridge put in and take that road out of your front yard." (The road led to a shallow place where the creek could be forded.) So, for the first and only time in his life, my staunch Democrat grandfather went out and campaigned for a Republican. Since my grandfather's opinion was highly valued, the Republican won. And the road was moved and the bridge built.

Building it yourself lets you take maximum advantage of using recycled materials. If you are your own boss, you can feel free to make changes in the plan to accommodate that fine old arched window which turned up after you had finished the shell and had the rooms laid out. If you were paying labor costs to a contractor, you couldn't dream of making the change. You can also spend spare time pulling nails from old applewood floorboards which the ordinary contractor would immediately burn in the trashpile. Your six trips to various scrapyards to find fittings to hook up the old marble sink just wouldn't be tolerated by the union plumber who wants to hook up the sink at a set time (for $32 per hour).

Obviously, setting forth in uncharted waters for such a major undertaking as building a whole house can be a bit scary. In the houses which are shown in this chapter, I show you several approaches which make building your own easier. Before doing anything else, do your homework thoroughly so that you know what you are getting into. The best book on the market for actual construction is a new book put out by the Shelter Institute. It is called *From the Ground Up* (1977) by John N. Cole and Charles Wing.* It is quite a valuable reference for such essentials as sizing and bracing of structural members and basic approaches to construction itself. You also might want to read *Basic Construction Techniques for Houses and Small Buildings Simply Explained* (1972) by the United States Navy.† While a bit dated, it will give you a very thorough background in conventional construction methods and is of particular value when dealing with contractors. A careful reading will familiarize you with common construction terms and methods. There are some areas in which we disagree, so read both books carefully and take your pick.

---

*The book is available from Little, Brown & Company, 34 Beacon Street, Boston, MA 02106 or The Shelter Institute, 72 Front Street, Bath, ME 04530.

† Dover Publications, Incorporated, 180 Varick Street, New York, NY 10014.

The Shelter Institute is known all over the world for its pioneering work in teaching people to build their own houses. If you are a bit nervous about launching in after only a bit of reading, by all means go to Maine and take one of their courses.

The first house included here belongs to the founders of the Shelter Institute, Pat and Patsy Hennen. This house almost perfectly illustrates all of the principles which I advocate in this book. It is aesthetically pleasing, and houses a family very comfortably at a very reasonable cost. It was built by a crew of two people in two months in 1975. It cost $3,800 to build. Land cost was $800 for six acres.

Number 1: The Hennen House

Pat Hennen is a strong advocate of careful planning: "Build it all on paper prior to construction and make absolutely no changes." I can't second this strongly enough. Many people look at the open frame of a house and decide that it is too small and start trying to enlarge the house before seeing it enclosed. This is a serious mistake. Sometimes you may want to change sizes or shapes of windows or doors or add a few built-ins as you go, but take your time and refine your design thoroughly before you start; then follow the plans faithfully.

Southwest view of exterior. Note solar shower on the corner of the house.

Pat believes in very heavy insulation with reflective foil and air space to radiate heat back into the livingspace. Outside walls are designed so that no framing members penetrate through the wall to break up the effectiveness of the insulation. Pat's insulation consists of 10 inches of fiberglass plus a 2-inch air space for the ceiling; 8 inches of fiberglass

View from the children's loft. Parents' sleeping area is top center.

View of kitchen from living room. Upper level is reached by steep, space-saving ship's ladder. Bunks for children are on the upper level behind the wall with the Mexican hanging.

plus a 2-inch air space for the floor; and 6 inches of fiberglass plus a 2-inch air space in the walls. The exterior doors were built on the site and are 5 inches thick. The result of Pat's attention to insulation and construction details is that the entire 1,000-square-foot house can be heated with one Jøtul woodstove with a capacity of 20,000 Btu's. The Jøtul is supplemented by the south-facing glass wall with enough mass built into the floor to absorb what is collected. The nice open plan makes for good air circulation, providing easy heating and cooling. Pat comments: "Very cozy, warm. A house you can clean in 10 minutes. Very cool in summer. Easy to change air through venting." (What he means by this last statement is that the windows are designed to create a pressure differential so that the house can be quickly ventilated.)

At present, the plumbing consists of an indoor hand pump, and a privy. A Clivus Multrum composting toilet (see chapter 8 for more information on this and other composting toilets) is sitting in the yard, a fascinating monster lying on its side so that the inner workings show. It is to be installed shortly. A small leach field with a capacity of 10 gallons per day per person has been installed to handle the greywater from the balance of the plumbing system.

Double-decker bunks for children are fitted neatly under the sloping roof.

The foundation of the Hennen house is made of pressure-treated telephone poles embedded into the ground below frostline, placed on concrete footings sized for the soil. These support a platform upon which the house proper is constructed. The frame of the house itself consists of eight 8 × 8 posts attached to the platform. The structural members are hemlock; some of the beams are hand-hewn. The exterior siding is roughsawn pine. All construction work including built-ins was done at the site.

The Hennen house has a very simple open plan. The first floor is one sweep of open space except for the enclosed study which forms a very different private environment. It is carpeted and has more refined finishes which contrast nicely with the rustic character of the rest of the house. The second floor consists of a U-shaped balcony reached by a ship's ladder. The children have built-in bunks on one end of the house; the parents' bedroom is located on the other. Both floors of the house

Patsy at the pump, "Just love it. It gives a psychological feeling of space; it's open."

Study is the one enclosed, totally private space in the house. With its carpeted floor and book-lined walls, it is in stark contrast to the open rustic feeling of the rest of the house.

Other structures which were constructed by Shelter Institute staff and students. The top is a yurt built by the staff. The bottom is a large shed-roofed house. Windows are triple-glazed with small standard-sized panes of glass.

borrow space from each other through the large well in the center. The flow of space is further enhanced by the lack of railings at the second-floor level.

Graduates of the Shelter Institute have built many houses; a few of them are illustrated here.

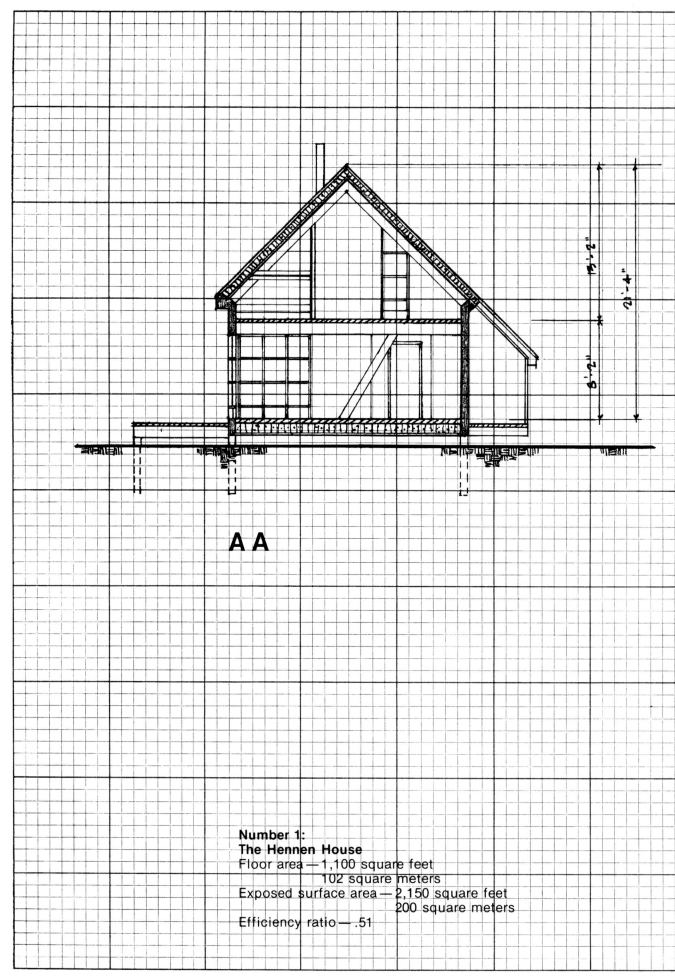

AA

Number 1:
The Hennen House
Floor area — 1,100 square feet
                102 square meters
Exposed surface area — 2,150 square feet
                            200 square meters
Efficiency ratio — .51

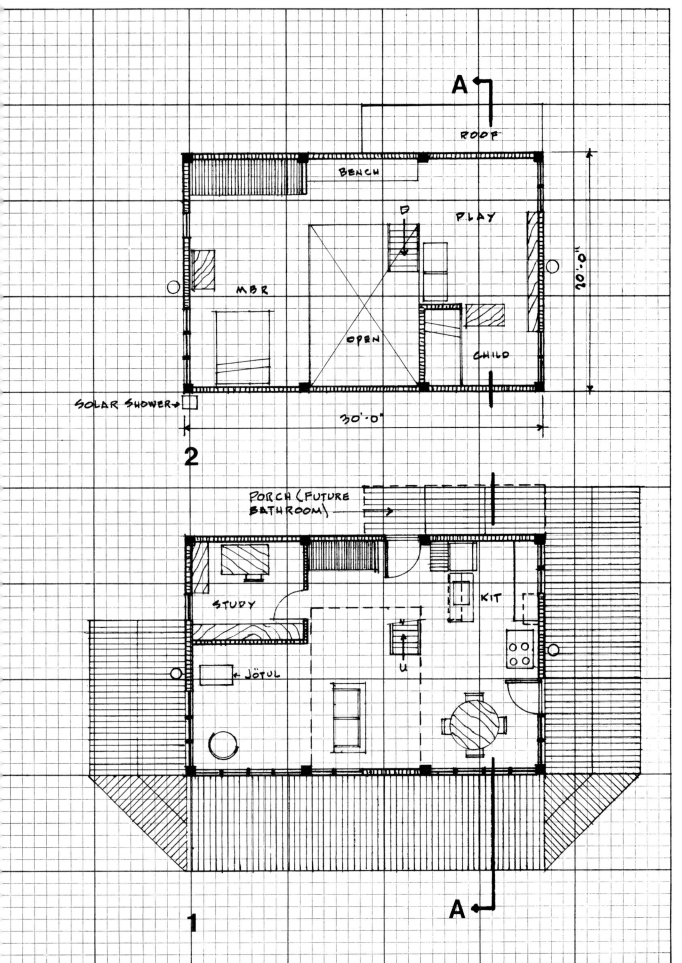

A

ROOF

BENCH

PLAY

MBR

OPEN

CHILD

SOLAR SHOWER→

20'-0"

30'-0"

2

PORCH (FUTURE BATHROOM)

STUDY

KIT

JÖTUL

A

1

9

Number 2: The Kenyon House

This house belongs to David and Pam Kenyon of Dresden, Maine. It was built by Pam with help from some of the other students from the Shelter Institute. There was a showstopping picture on the front of the local newspaper, showing Pam building her own house—actually, getting in there and putting up the frame of the house.

Don't feel bound by the traditional stereotypes of our rather silly society that women can't do construction work. Just because all of the construction unions try to keep them out doesn't mean that a woman isn't as well or better qualified than a man for this work. She may have a disadvantage in that she didn't have the opportunity to take a shop class or to work on other construction projects, but there are ways to make up for these. She can take a course in shopwork or a course in construction such as the one the Shelter Institute offers. This is what Pam did. Since her husband was fully occupied with his law practice, Pam handled most of the work on the house.

I've seen situations in which it's better for a couple not to try to work together on carpentry work, but rather branch out and do different

South elevation shows fixed insulating glass with openable plywood flaps for ventilation.

tasks. There is just so much information that any one person can absorb in a reasonable length of time and not make a lot of mistakes. If you feel that there might be friction between you and your husband or wife on the carpentry phase of construction, one or the other of you should brush up on another expensive, yet vital trade. Such special skills as plumbing, electrical work, or plastering offer excellent opportunities for making a major contribution without getting into hassles about who can make the better fitting joint in carpentry work. Just from my own personal experience, women, once they have a bit of experience, are usually more careful in their work than men. So maybe the wife should do the finish carpentry work while the husband does the plumbing and electrical work. On the other hand, the wife may not want to try to learn to work with power tools and may prefer the more complex tasks of the mechanical work.

One example from my past experience will serve to illustrate. When we were building a friend's house, a number of the guys pitched in one weekend shortly before a rainstorm and did a rush job on a double-coverage asphalt roof. Five or six of us jumped in and had the roof on in a couple hours. Much to our chagrin, we came back the following weekend to find a new roof, installed by the women in our group. It seems that in our haste we had neglected to let the strips of roofing flatten out, and when the sun struck the freshly applied roof the next day, it just wrinkled up like potato chips. So the ladies proceeded to remove the ruined roofing and take their time to replace it properly. Their job came out perfectly.

Pam's house faithfully follows most of the teachings of the Shelter Institute. It is a two-story shed configuration with a very open plan. The only closed areas are the bath-sauna on the first floor and the children's bedrooms on the second. The master bedroom is on a balcony overlooking the living room. The open plan allows both floors to borrow space from each other, making the house seem quite large. Actually, it is one of the largest houses in the book, almost 2,000 square feet. Yet it was built for only $15,000.

Materials are low-cost, and native to the area whenever that was possible. Exterior walls are designed with framing exposed on the inside so that heat isn't conducted through the wall by the framing members. Insulation is applied on the outside of the wall with the sheathing spaced out to provide a dead air space. Fiberglass insulation is used with 6 inches in the walls and 12 inches in the roof. Siding is reverse board and batten, a handsome variation on standard board and batten which provides yet another air space and also allows the boards to air dry nicely if they must be put up green. All structural material is hemlock. Siding is native roughsawn pine. The roofing material is double-coverage roll roofing which makes a fine durable roof at very low cost.

Heat is provided by a Jøtul woodstove with electrical backup provided in the areas where there is piping. A Clivus Multrum composting toilet handles human wastes.

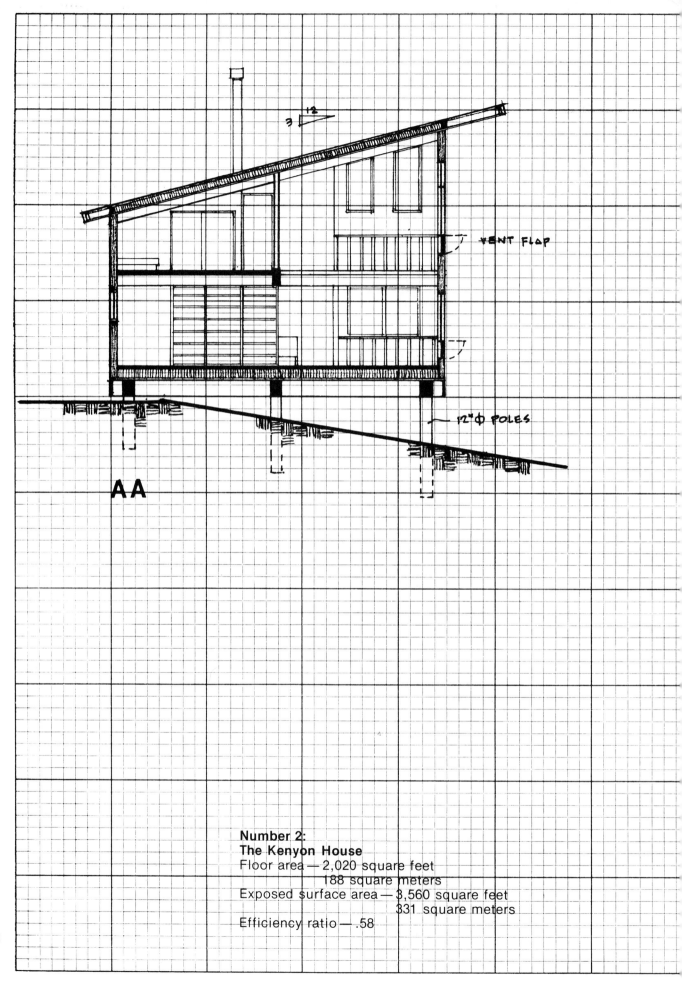

3 | 12

VENT FLAP

12" φ POLES

AA

Number 2:
The Kenyon House
Floor area — 2,020 square feet
188 square meters
Exposed surface area — 3,560 square feet
331 square meters
Efficiency ratio — .58

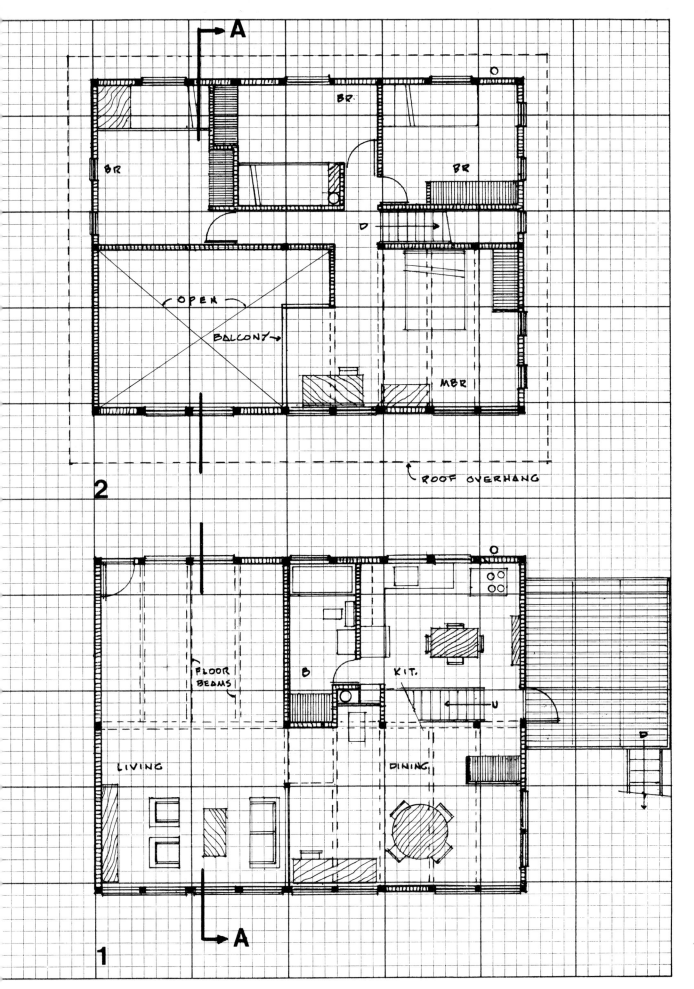

A

BR

BR

BR

OPEN

BALCONY→

MBR

ROOF OVERHANG

2

FLOOR BEAMS

B

KIT.

LIVING

DINING

1

A

13

Since neither Pam nor David had ever done any construction work before, their house is quite an achievement. However, it is not at all unusual for the Shelter Institute. To date, over 250 houses have been constructed by their graduates, many of them completely unskilled when they began construction.

By the way, Pam became so interested in construction that she went to school, took a drafting course, and went to work for the Shelter Institute doing details for the houses they build.

This plan is for an efficient saltbox house and was published in *Low-Cost, Energy-Efficient Shelter*. Bennett Holbrook of Bowdoin, Maine, was one of the first people to write to me for plans. He started construction of his saltbox in August of 1976. These pictures were taken in November. He hoped to have the house completed by early spring of 1977 in time for the arrival of his new baby.

Bennett has done virtually all of the work on his house by himself in his spare time. He has kept accurate records and can recite all of the figures. His site is quite remote and this has caused its share of problems. After investigating the cost of running power lines, he opted for his own Honda generator. With the premium rates charged for his remote location, Benett figures that he can pay for the generator in six months.

Excavation and road work are the biggest items in the budget. The combined costs of the septic system, road, and the excavation for the house proper totaled $3,000. The lumber for the shell of the house cost $2,662; much of it was native hemlock.

Two significant changes were made in the plans. First, a masonry chimney was added and placed in the center of the house. A Morsø

Number 3: The Holbrook House

Living room with loft above. A typical Shelter Institute-type plan with all rooms open except bath and children's bedrooms.

woodstove is connected to the chimney as the primary source of heat for the house. Bennett wrote to me during the early part of construction requesting my suggestions for a backup heating system for occasional periods when the house might be left unattended for a day or two. After examining several alternates, Bennett decided to install an 80-gallon, gas-fired hot-water heater with a small loop of baseboard radiation to provide heat to the bath and kitchen where the piping is located.

The second change to the plans was a step-down living room to follow the contours of the site and also to provide a bit more area for south-facing glass. As you can see from the pictures, Bennett has taken advantage of horizontal girts to provide nailing surfaces for vertical siding and horizontal application of Sheetrock. Bennett's house contains 960 square feet plus a 140-square-foot loft for a total of 1,100 square feet. He expects to spend about $12,000 plus a lot of hard work for his house.

Frame of the house from the southwest. Large openings will admit the sun through insulated glass. Note second-floor overhang for shading bedroom windows.

Bennett standing in front of the main entrance to his new house. Note the 2 x 6 horizontal girts which span the main structural posts. These permit easy installation of vertical siding and horizontal sheets of Sheetrock. Skylight is at upper right.

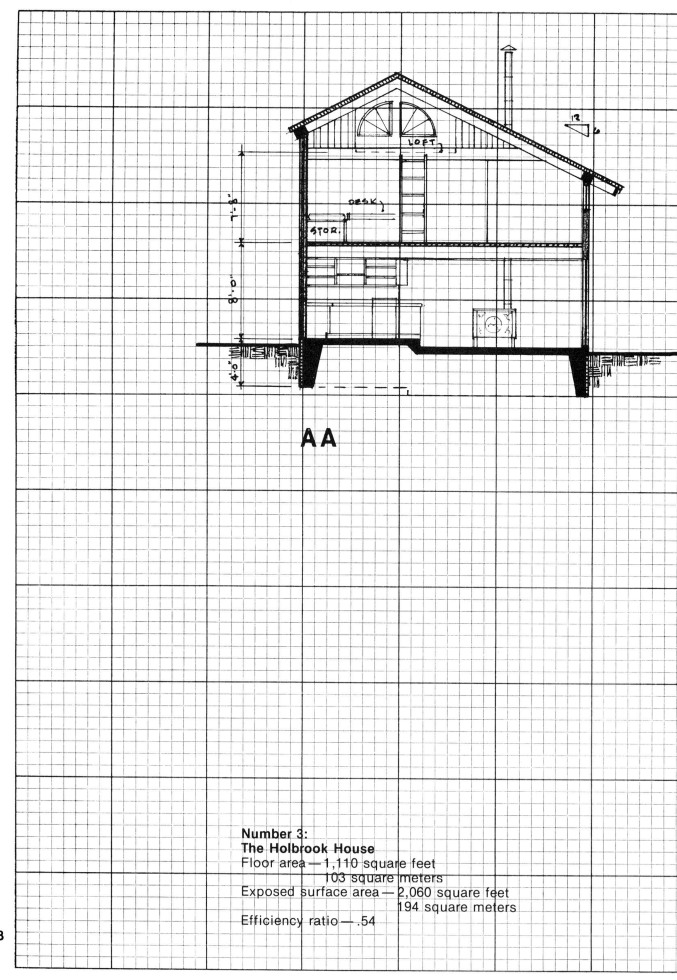

Number 3:
The Holbrook House
Floor area—1,110 square feet
          103 square meters
Exposed surface area—2,060 square feet
          194 square meters
Efficiency ratio—.54

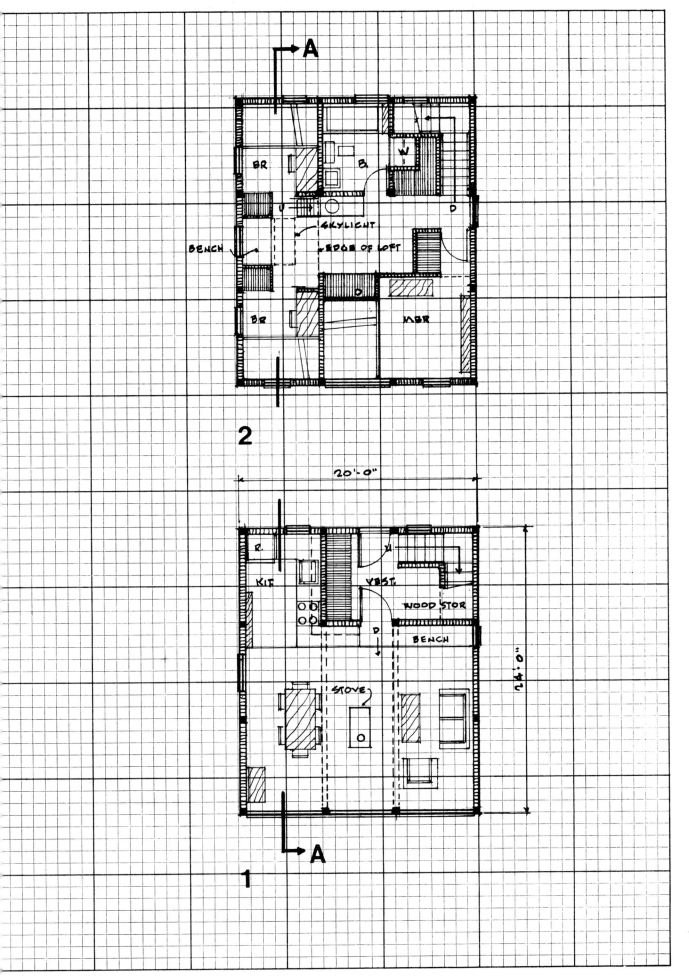

A

BR

B.

W

SKYLIGHT

BENCH

EDGE OF LOFT

D

BR

MBR

2

20'-0"

R.

KIT

VEST.

WOOD STOR

D

BENCH

STOVE

24'-0"

A

1

Number 4: The Kotajarvi House

Frank and Jeanie Kotajarvi have bought a 40-acre farm near Thayer, Missouri. They are expanding the saltbox plan into a farmhouse, enlarging the basic 20 × 24-foot saltbox to 24 × 24 feet and adding a small wing containing mudroom and a large pantry to the first floor. This adds 200 square feet to the main house plus another 190 in the mudroom for a total of 1,490 square feet. Frank and Jeanie are building as this is being written. They are milling much of the lumber for the new house themselves from native oak right on their farm. By doing all of their own work and using native wood, they hope to stretch their $5,000 savings to build the house and thus not have to go through bank hassles.

Frank and Jeanie make their living doing art glass windows. The living room will double as studio space until they can afford outbuildings. Heating for the house is supplied by a Jøtul stove. A Clivus Multrum is

The front of this house faces south. The tall, narrow stained-glass window is in the stairway.

The smaller, stone side of the north of the house provides space for the farm kitchen stores and a small back porch. The protected entrance here off the porch will be used in winter.

planned as a later addition. For now, an outhouse will be used. The bathroom has been moved downstairs in this version so that the plumbing can be more concentrated for winter weather.

Since construction has just started, we have built a model of this house to show how it will look finished. Note that the orientation is completely changed from the Holbrook house in that what was the west elevation is now south. Large windows have been added to this side to help with winter heating. A dark-colored, well-insulated concrete slab is used to store heat from the sun. Insulating shutters are provided for heat conservation at night.

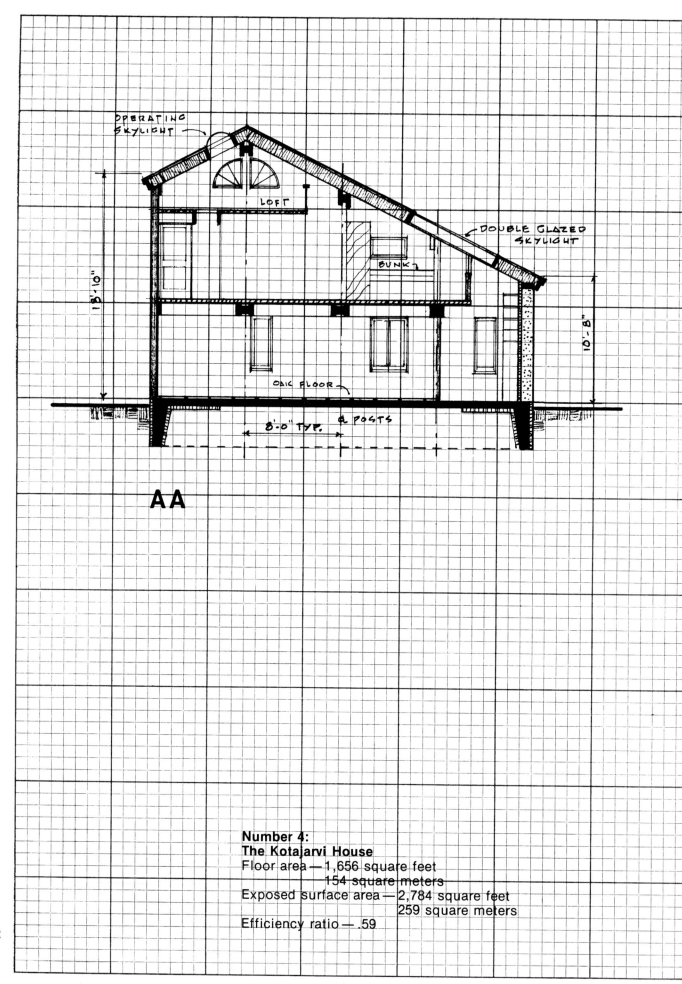

OPERATING
SKYLIGHT

LOFT

DOUBLE GLAZED
SKYLIGHT

BUNK

18'-10"

10'-8"

OAK FLOOR

8'-0" TYP. @ POSTS

AA

Number 4:
The Kotajarvi House
Floor area — 1,656 square feet
154 square meters
Exposed surface area — 2,784 square feet
259 square meters
Efficiency ratio — .59

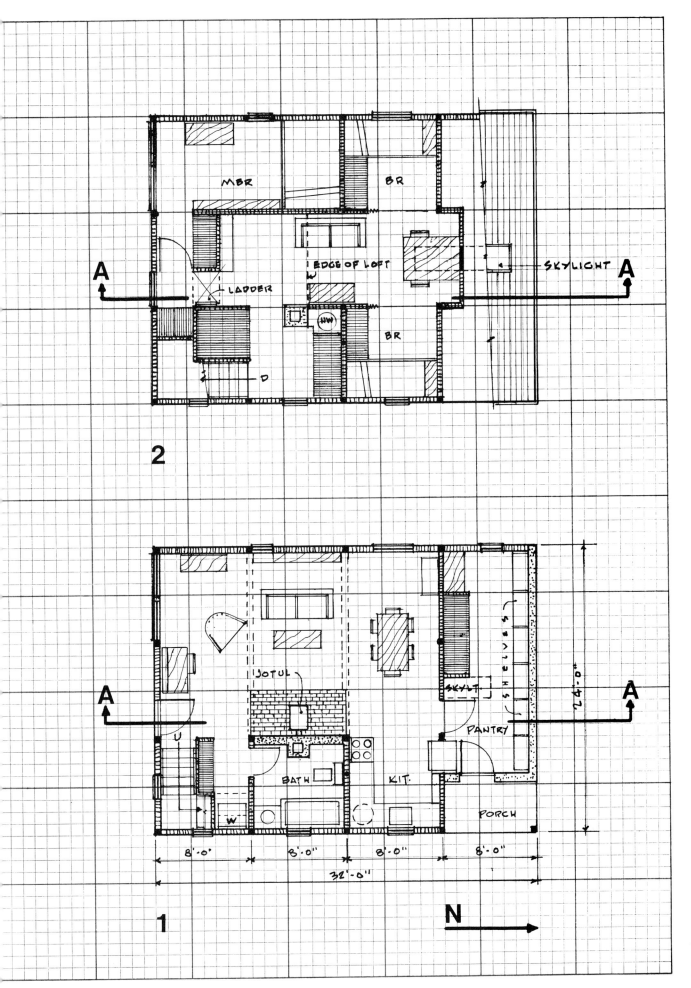

2

MBR

BR

A ──→ A

EDGE OF LOFT

SKYLIGHT

LADDER

HW

BR

D

1

JOTUL

SKYLT

SHELVES

A ──→ A

PANTRY

14'-0"

U

BATH

KIT

W

PORCH

8'-0"   8'-0"   8'-0"   8'-0"

32'-0"

N ──→

Number 5: The Page House   This house is one of the largest in the book. The reason for this is that it is built into a hillside so that the basement opens out to grade and is used as livingspace. The total area is 1,900 square feet. This is a very steep hillside which had long been passed up by others, so the land was a bargain.

The house is built around a solid-oak-braced frame designed and pre-fabricated by David Howard of Alstead, New Hampshire. Howard's frame is a bit expensive, but it provides a precise, accurate guide for the amateur builder. (I talk more about David Howard when I describe his house, Number 12, in chapter 2.)

David provides the frame for his houses either as a kit with instructions, or completely erected by his own crew. Detailed instruction books are provided for all phases of construction. Since the plans are compact and the houses very well insulated, David encourages his clients to use wood heat, usually a Rumsford fireplace plus a Defiant stove. (See chapter 9 for more on these.)

Nick and Elaine in front of their nearly completed new house.

The used pink house trailer in the foreground; new house to the rear. The Pages invited us to a nice trailer bonfire when their house is completed.

Number 5:
The Page House
Floor area — 1,376 square feet
128 square meters
Exposed surface area — 2,392 square feet
222 square meters
Efficiency ratio — .57

(technical data for next page)

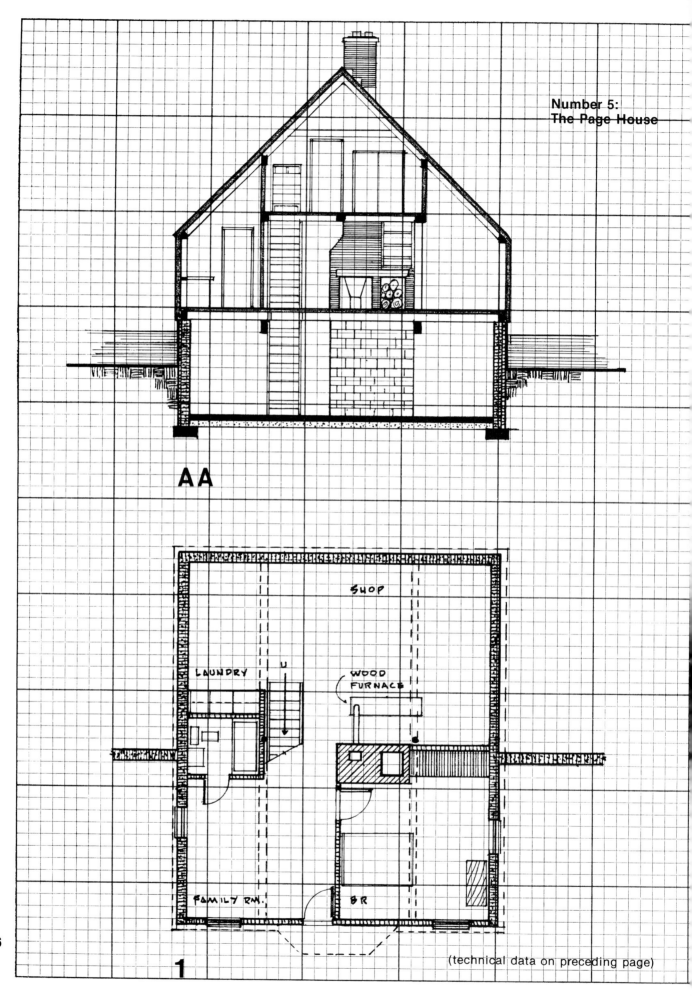

Number 5:
The Page House

AA

SHOP

LAUNDRY

U

WOOD
FURNACE

FAMILY RM.

BR

26

(technical data on preceding page)

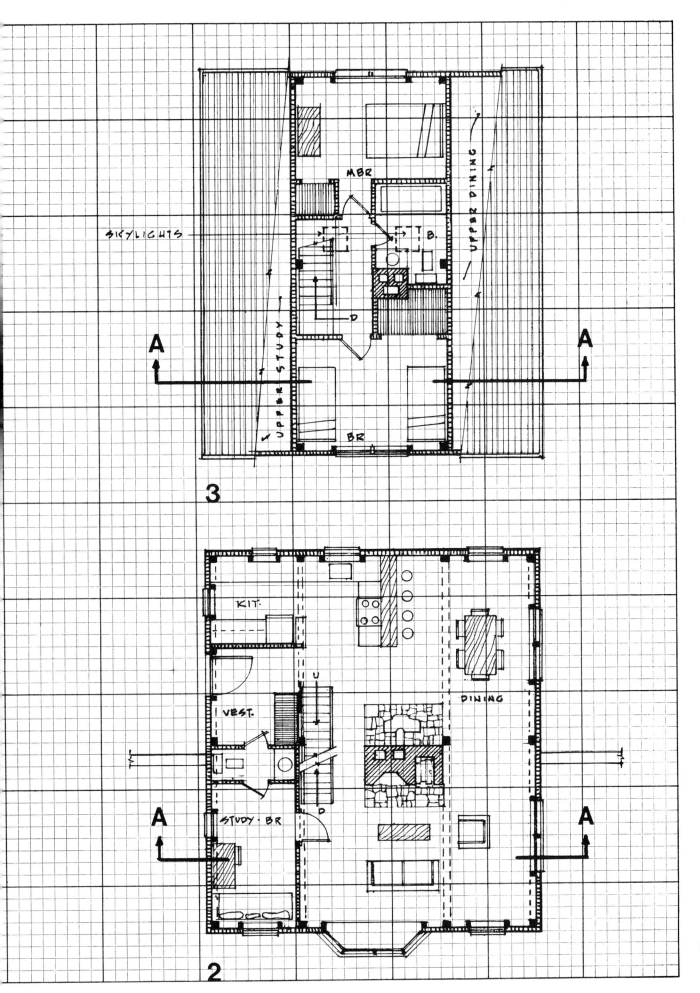

3

SKYLIGHTS

MBR

UPPER DINING

B.

D

UPPER STUDY

A · · · A

BR

2

KIT.

VEST.

STUDY · BR

DINING

D

A · · · A

The family dog guarding Nick's special heating system. On the day of our visit the temperature in the partially buried house was above 60°F., despite very cold weather, proving that Nick's "wood furnace" works well.

Nick Page is building this house entirely himself. Nick is a machinist and has been living on his property in a small trailer for several years saving money to build a house for his family. The house is 28 feet square and shows how flexible David Howard's framing system can be. The center of the house is a two-story, 12 × 28-foot frame. Eight-foot-wide wings are provided by extending the roof slope on each side of the main frame. In this manner, a large 28-foot-square first floor is created with a two-bedroom second-floor area in the center. This particular house also has a full living basement. In this basement, Nick has built a large wood-burning furnace of his own design that will accept large logs so that much cutting and stoking is avoided.

This basic frame which is illustrated in its fullest extension can be used to create a very wide variety of houses. The center core of the house can be used alone as a small two-story house, or it can be extended eight feet on one side or the other to create a saltbox design. One of the small saltboxes is discussed in chapter 2; it's House Number 12.

Nick's project provides an excellent illustration of how to get the most house for the least money. He has approached the problems step-by-step, paying for each step as he went rather than spending a lot of money paying interest to a bank. By making sacrifices and living in a small trailer for a few years, he was able to get a much larger and more elegant house than he could have afforded by borrowing and then building as is usually done. By having living quarters next door, he is able to take his time and do all of the work on his house himself without paying outside labor.

Number 6: The Fennell House

This one belongs to Bob Fennell. His wife, Cynthia, has worked very hard also, but there is no question that it is Bob's house. He has set out to closely duplicate an old Dutch stone house for as little money as possible. So far, he has spent $2,200 and 900 hours of hard labor. The two-foot-thick stone walls are completed except for the fireplace, and the roof is underway. Massive oak beams from an old barn support the floors. Flooring and miscellaneous framing members were salvaged from an old house which Bob purchased for $5. A friend helped with the dismantling in return for doors, windows, and hardware. Cynthia, who does cabinetwork as a hobby, is building authentic reproductions of old Dutch doors and windows and operating, functional shutters for their new house. She is a bit concerned at the detail work involved in making all of the delicate sticking for the casement windows. These are very unusual in old Dutch houses, but were used in a house that Bob and Cynthia both admire.

Bob swears up and down that he has had no training in laying up stonework. "Just lots of time spent observing the old Dutch houses and a bit of experimenting with stone drywalls in my present front yard." Be that

The hole in the massive stone wall allows space for a Rumsford-type fireplace. Authentic Dutch-style dormer at right provides space for second-floor bath.

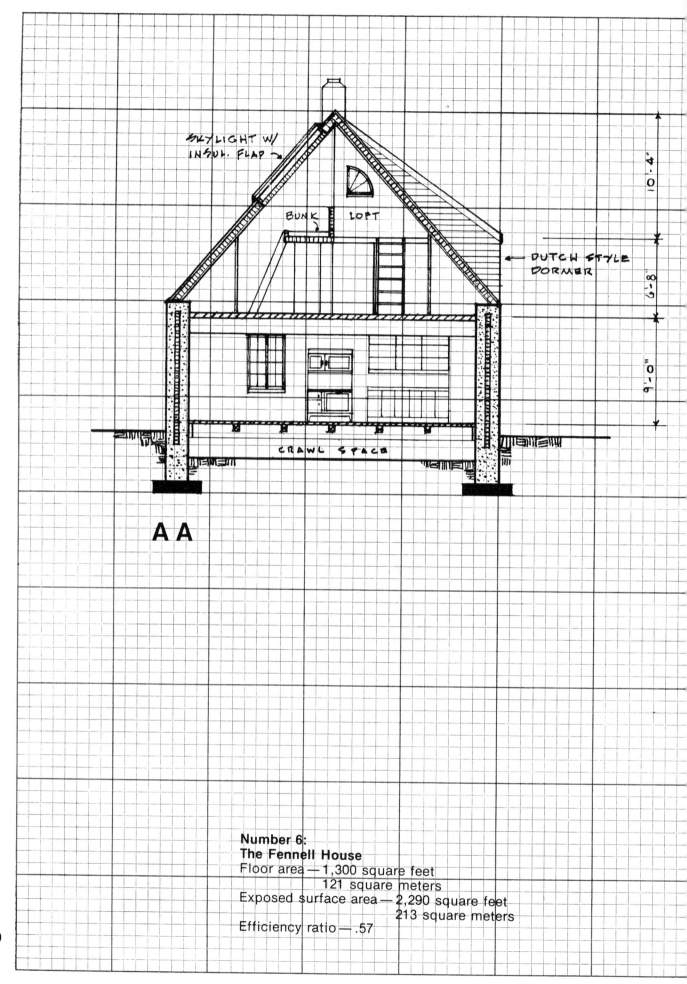

SKYLIGHT W/
INSUL. FLAP

DUTCH STYLE
DORMER

BUNK   LOFT

10'-4"

6'-8"

9'-0"

CRAWL SPACE

A A

Number 6:
The Fennell House
Floor area—1,300 square feet
          121 square meters
Exposed surface area—2,290 square feet
          213 square meters
Efficiency ratio—.57

30

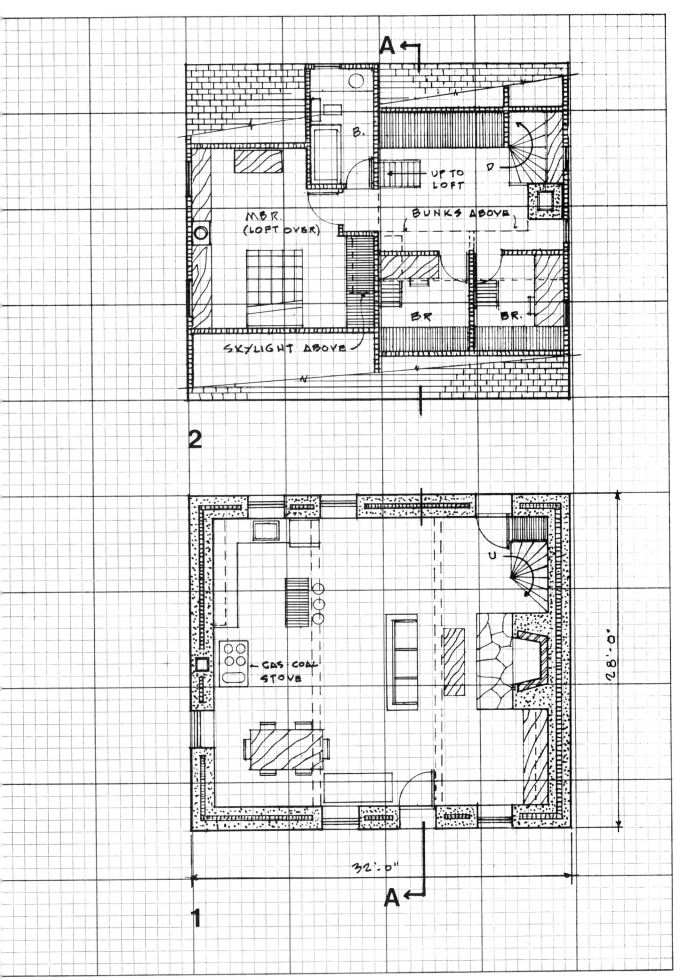

A

B.

UP TO
LOFT

BUNKS ABOVE

D

MBR.
(LOFT OVER)

BR.

BR.

SKYLIGHT ABOVE

N

2

U

GAS COAL
STOVE

28'-0"

32'-0"

A

1

31

as it may, he has done a job much superior to that of most professional masons. This is probably because he accurately copied the old techniques rather than using the inferior ones taught to contemporary masons.

Bob is using house building as an escape from a dead-end job. He and Cynthia plan to sell the house which they now own and use the proceeds to live on while Bob finds another line of work.

Although the house is only 28 × 32 feet (24 × 28 feet inside), Bob has managed to squeeze in ample room for a family of five. This was made possible by clever planning and efficient use of space. One trick was to use one of those little winding stairs which uses little space on either floor tucked in next to the fireplace. This is just one advantage of living in an area with no building code. Building codes do not allow authentic old stairways, preferring wide, straight, space-wasting ones.

Cynthia is installing a cedar-shake roof. The shakes were salvaged from leftover materials from other roofs.

The very steep $^{12}/_{16}$ roof is aimed south for future installation of solar collectors. This steep roof allows enough height to slip in a standing-height loft for the kids. One disadvantage of the plan is that you have to walk through the children's area to get to the master bedroom and bath. This could be solved with a conventional stair located in the center of the house, but Bob prefers the authentic one which provides much more space on both floors.

The Fennell house, looking up through the framing of the steep roof.

Bob started the house in October 1973, and has worked on it in his spare time since. The evolution of the heating system is interesting. When Bob started, he was planning to use electric heat. After electric rates soared, he enlarged the root cellar to allow space for an oil-burning furnace. Since oil prices have also climbed out of sight, he is now planning to heat with wood. A massive Rumsford-type fireplace graces the living room, with a woodstove of as yet undetermined type for the kitchen. The massive walls permitted the installation of the kitchen flue right inside the wall itself.

Number 7: The Schoolhouse

This one illustrates another unique approach for the owner-builder. Strictly speaking, it is not a new house, but a renovation. Since there are a great many abandoned one-room schools and churches of very similar size available, I have included it to show what imaginative planning can do. The big advantage to this approach for the builder is that the actual shell of the building is erected. While the construction of a building shell is not actually that hard, it is frequently a major psychological barrier for the beginning builder.

Janine is an account executive for an advertising agency in Rochester. Joe is a writer. Together they set out looking for an old house to remodel. Months of looking turned up nothing—except for an old falling-down, one-room schoolhouse. It sagged badly and the sun shone through holes in the roof. The floor beams had rotted away and bums had burned out much of the floor in the fireplace. Many people had looked at the place over the years and sadly turned away deciding that the building was too far gone. A previous owner had gone so far as to start construction of a massive foundation in front of the building.

Joe and Janine came knocking on my door one snowy morning to ask my advice. Were the locals right? Was it too far gone? Of course not, I said, it just needs lots of work. This is where the owner-builder aspect comes in. I advised that the building would require much hard hand labor, but that it was basically sound. The old floor had to come out to replace the floor beams. Three layers of flooring were installed during the years from 1840. Janine took them up with care while Joe started on the three layers of roofing which had to come up to replace roof boards.

Both the floor and the roof required unusual solutions. The original ceiling was removed to allow space for an upper-level sleeping area. This exposed a magnificent roof structure. The problem was, of course, insulation. How do you provide insulation for a northern climate and still expose the old structure? On earlier projects, I had sprayed polyurethane-foam insulation between the beams. A second spray application of plaster is used for fireproofing and to produce a pleasing surface finish. As both labor and material costs had escalated considerably since my earlier uses of this system, the first estimate was staggering. Besides requiring considerable labor masking the beams which were to be exposed, we would be covering the old weathered roofing boards.

The foam contractor suggested an alternate. Put the foam on top of the roof boards and spray an acrylic roof coating right over the foam, thus getting insulation and roofing all in one quick, easy application. A layer of 1-inch-thick rigid insulation board was nailed over the existing roof boards as a base for the foam insulation. This insulation board serves several purposes. It is fire retardant to protect the foam and its dark brown color hides the cracks between the old roof boards which had been widely spaced for the wood-shingled original roof. The foam averages 4 inches thick and provides excellent insulation, preserving the beautiful old beams and boards.

The insulation contractor did a number of other jobs while he had his equipment at the schoolhouse. By the time he came on the job, Janine had completely removed the old floor. The foundation was dry-set stone and there were numerous cracks right through to the outside. The entire inside face of the foundation and the main pipe to the well were encased in polyurethane insulation. Since the insulation is in a completely encased crawlspace about one foot high there is little danger from fire. The exterior walls were also insulated. In this case, both the interior and exterior surfaces were intact and no one wanted to tear them apart. Small, easily plugged holes were drilled between the studs and urea-formaldehyde foam was installed. This is a superior type of insulation which insulates so well that the walls actually feel warm to the touch in

South face of the schoolhouse. In the foreground is new deck. The door was salvaged from an old courthouse and fits the front nicely.

winter. Its one slight limiting factor is that it is fluid for the first several minutes and needs to be contained within a cavity, but this property makes it an excellent choice for insulating old walls as it will thoroughly fill all cavities and seal small cracks and holes. This insulation is expensive, but the cost is offset by the savings made by not having to tear off and replace finish materials in good condition. This material costs about twice as much as fiberglass, but I would still recommend it for new construction if your budget can stand it.

The solution to the problem of flooring was equally unusual, but not as successful as the roofing. Hopes of salvaging part of the original floor faded when we discovered that the original floor beams were all dry rotted. Also, we needed to replace one of the main sills next to the aforementioned massive foundation (the foundation had trapped water and snow against the front of the building, causing the main sill to rot away). Janine removed the floor with much tender loving care so that good parts of it could be reused. The bottom layer was used as fuel in the fireplace; the second layer was used to floor the loft and the top layer was used for the study partition and closets. The original beams were spaced approximately 4 feet apart, posing a problem if conventional flooring materials were used as a replacement. (Since common flooring materials only span 2 feet on center at most, we had to be creative for our floors.) Also, most conventional flooring materials were not suitable for the character of the old building. Others were much too expensive. Finally, roughsawn native pine planks 2 inches thick were selected. We tried to find lumber which had been air dried for several weeks to minimize shrinkage.

New floor beams were installed in the old locations and the fun began. Many days of fighting with crowbars, hammers, and the like were required. Grooves had been cut into the edges of the planks so they could be splined together, minimizing warping. The problem was that the semigreen planks had a mind of their own. The contractor who had been hired to install them gave up in disgust. Amateur labor was hired and Joe helped with the lengthy job of installation. The planks were anchored to the beams with countersunk wood screws and the holes filled with dowels. When the floor was finally installed, it was sanded and finished with satin polyurethane. The wood was still too green to sand adequately and the resulting job is rather rough. Despite all of the diffi-

The heat-circulating fireplace is the major source of heat for the building. A small extra sleeping loft is located above the bathroom at the right.

culties, the floor is so unusual that many visitors admire it and ask if it is the original.

Since the wall height of the schoolhouse is 11 feet, it easily accommodates a sleeping balcony. The balcony itself was constructed from beams which originally supported the ceiling. The floorboards were the well-worn applewood boards from the second layer of the original floor.

Simple ladders and straight-run stairways can be easily home-built to provide access to lofts. The ladder shown in the sketch is made of 1 × 4s with 1-inch dowels for the steps. Simply tack the two side pieces together, lay out the proper tread spacing (if it is a ladder, not a stair, space the steps about 15 inches apart; too close is dangerous for ladder rungs), drill holes through both pieces and then insert the dowels, glueing them in place. You can even make the ladder portable if you wish.

The budget for the schoolhouse was about $10,000. Almost half of this budget went for a septic system and other mechanical systems. Another large chunk ($1,300) went to the insulation contractor. Many house of discussion went into deciding what to do about heating the house. Since oil prices were soaring, it didn't seem to make sense to throw $1,500 or more into an obsolescent system. Solar collectors were too expensive and would have to be placed in a location remote from the building. But the building already had a large heat-circulating fireplace and we had insulated thoroughly. Maybe they could give it a try for one winter with the fireplace.

An electric heater was installed as a backup for periods when the house was unoccupied. A second, auxilliary heat source is the Glenwood combination wood-coal-and-gas cookstove. Its ability to burn coal provides insurance against wood shortages which are bound to occur as most people switch from more expensive fuels. In 0°F. weather a temperature of 64°F. was easily maintained just with the heat-circulating fireplace. Of course, this isn't 72°F. and there is no thermostat, but it's nice to know that you are not dependent upon the whims of gas, oil, or electric companies for your source of heat.

Before I moved into the schoolhouse I had bought two houses—one really more of a cabin—that I liked very much. It had never occurred to me to change them at all, despite their minor shortcomings. It was, therefore, a new experience to live in something designed for today's conditions—i.e., the energy crisis.

A writer lives in a house more like a housewife without children or a job. He needs to be comfortable to work and he also craves distractions, meaning what most folks call chores. The fireplace was already there, but the architect's insistence that a combination gas- and wood-burning stove be installed and that there need be no furnace created the constant diversions of woodcutting, buying, stacking, carrying, and burning. Really just enough to give a restless typist frequent opportunities to let the brain idle for 15 minutes while attending to warmth. Finally, installation of an electric radiator means that the fire need not be tended on a 40° to 50°F. day if one doesn't feel like it and that extended absences are possible while the house stays at about 45°F. for one's return.

The design focused on a main livingspace related to the fireplace, which left my working space at the south and elevated end of the house. This means that in winter I can type without artificial light, get warm sunlight in the afternoon, and glance out the window for the "long view." In extremely cold weather, I work in front of the hearth and then appreciate the architect's forethought in having two electric plugs installed in the floor there so that the livingspace-office doesn't become a tangle of extension cords.

The two skylights keep one in much closer touch with the weather and the seasonal and daily changes in sun angle than do conventional windows. Waking in the middle of the night on the sleeping balcony one looks up to the wheeling constellations, snowflakes, clouds, rain, treetops undulating in a night wind. Comforting those, in the small hours when thoughts tend to turn on what's wrong with life.

In six months I have had only one close call anent stepping into the ladder-stair space while on the balcony and have only bumped my head mildly a couple of times. These seem a small price to pay for the warmth of sleeping where the warm air migrates and for the extra livingspace downstairs. I have found, however, that an under-the-bed potty makes me more tolerant of having the bathroom on another level (and, at night, a colder one).

The kitchen seems ideal for a bachelor. The working space adjacent to the sink was built high for tall people—like me. When guests come and help cook, there's plenty of room for two to do things, unlike New York City corridor-type kitchens.

I've already mentioned the wood half of the stove, and there's a special satisfaction on a cold night in cooking dinner over the wood fire and giving the propane tanks a rest.

I've had a few problems with the water pipe under the floor (there's only about a foot of crawlspace and it's bloody cold down in there) and with the shower-bath drain (a special problem peculiar to the schoolhouse), but in what I've been told was the coldest winter in the history of the nation I've been comfortable virtually all the time (with sweaters).

As this is written, it's getting toward the end of February, and I'm pretty certain that by the end of March I'll have heated a 750-square-foot house since November for under $300. What more can I say?

—Joe

The basic big room was supplemented by a large sleeping loft with room for a small bedroom on either side of the stairs. **Janine decided to leave the loft open as one space.**

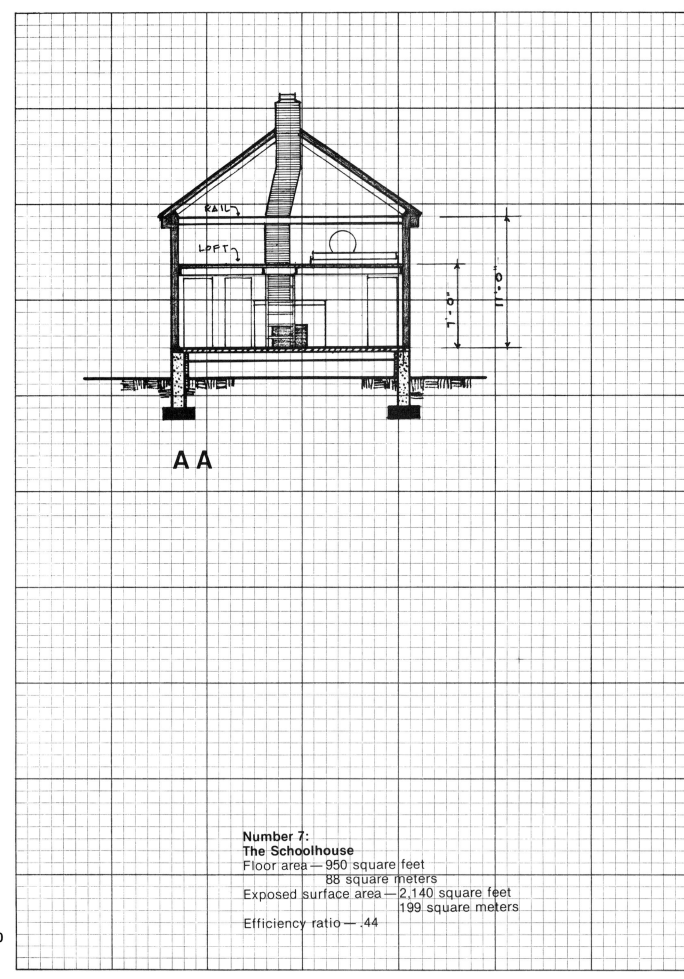

RAIL

LOFT

7'-0"

11'-0"

A A

Number 7:
The Schoolhouse
Floor area — 950 square feet
　　　　　　　88 square meters
Exposed surface area — 2,140 square feet
　　　　　　　　　　199 square meters

Efficiency ratio — .44

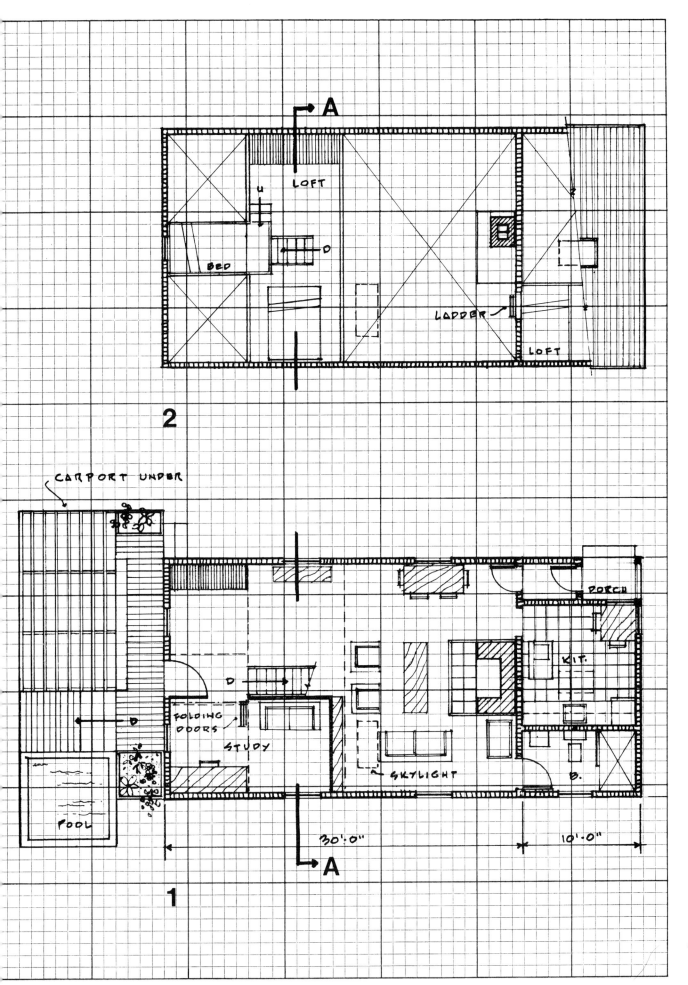

A

LOFT

BED

D

LADDER

LOFT

2

CARPORT UNDER

PORCH

D

FOLDING
DOORS

STUDY

D

KIT.

SKYLIGHT

B.

POOL

30'-0"

10'-0"

A

1

The small efficient kitchen contains a Glenwood combination wood-gas stove which helps provide heat in very cold weather.

After the main house had been renovated, we turned our attention to the horrible gaping pit resulting from the start of an ugly addition. Should we just take a bulldozer and fill it in? That would be the easiest solution, but we decided to recycle the pit into useful space. A series of stepped platforms was devised. A vine-covered trellis covers a parking space for the car—sort of a noncarport. One leftover corner at ground level became a pool. A variety of levels, textures, and planting spaces was used to break up the uninteresting expanse of the foundation. The parking space and much needed storage area were added bonuses.

I have devoted a great deal of space to describing this particular house as I feel that it offers a fine housing solution at low cost. If there had not been a very expensive septic system, costs would have been even lower. Also, since Joe and Janine could only work weekends, much labor was hired. This particular building was in poor condition and required more work than most. Our countryside is dotted with literally thousands of similar one-room schools and churches which are not in use. Instead of wasting resources building a new house, why not rehabilitate one of these gems? By using lofts and skylights, the interior can be bright and spacious without adding expensive additions. Finally, these buildings are usually small enough to be heated with one woodstove—a very major consideration these days.

This house was designed down to the last tiny detail by the owners. Mrs. Barnett had studied post and beam houses for years. She particularly admired one by a West Coast architect and wrote inquiring about the house. The architect replied that it had cost $250,000 and certainly wasn't suited to the mountains, saying, in effect, "Go away; don't bother me." Since the Barnetts had a budget of only $20,000, the post and beam house seemed hopeless. Undaunted, Mrs. Barnett got out her pencil and drew a small version of her dream house. The conservative contractor she approached threw a fit: "A bunch of sticks; it will fall down! A whole wall of glass facing south; you'll freeze to death and the heating bills will be astronomical. I won't build it; you're crazy."

Number 8: The Barnett House

Mrs. Barnett cast about for a solution. She had heard that the architect's office in town had recently hired a new architect just out of school (me) and she called and asked if I would review her drawings. I was delighted. Her design was of such high quality as to embarrass a great many "professional" architects. The only items missing from her plans were details for the post and beam framing members. Indeed, the frame did need some bracing, so we added a solid panel on the front of the house. Aside from that, her plans were practically perfect. The plan was divided down the middle by an east-west bearing wall. The large master

This simple shed-roofed house has a wide overhang which shelters the porch and shields the 10-foot plate glass windows from the summer sun while admitting the winter sun.

bedroom, living-dining areas and front vestibule faced south. The baths, kitchen, stairs to basement and guest bedroom faced north. Very simple, very elegant. Every detail was accounted for. The kitchen consisted of one long custom-built stainless steel counter with the sink and rangetop built into it. Fixed glass came right down to the counter. Small operating vents were placed up against the eaves to provide for natural ventilation. Kitchen storage and the refrigerator were built into the full-height wall to the rear of the work counter. The storage consists of full-height, shallow shelves, a concept which is so sensible that I have encouraged its use ever since.

In the meantime, Jim Barnett was also busy. Using the sun as a source of heat was virtually unheard of in 1958. He had carefully calculated the front overhang to provide shade for the 10-foot-high plate glass on the front of the house. It was designed in such a way that the house gets ample low rays of the sun in winter for heating, but no sun penetrates to the glass in the summer. Since the Barnetts had built way out from town on a little dirt road, no curtains were planned to obstruct the magnificent view through all of that glass.

After 20 years, the house looks almost the same as it did when it was first finished. The Barnetts did all of their own finish work and the care still shows. Oh yes, the heating bill. The heat bill for the entire winter of 1959 (their first in the house) was $22. Needless to say, it has gone up a bit since, because of the higher prices for fuel. But in fact, it is due to drop to just about zero for next winter. Jim has not lost his interest in the sun. His firm has given him unlimited access to their laboratories for solar research. He has a couple of very interesting items in an advanced stage of development. The first is a solar curtain with liquid-filled filaments which, when hung in front of the south-facing glass, absorbs heat from the sun in the daytime. At night, insulating curtains are drawn behind the solar curtain and the heat which was absorbed during the daytime is radiated into the room.

Jim's second invention is a low-cost, highly efficient focusing-type solar collector. An amusing incident occurred on the first day that he had his prototype installed at his laboratory. While he was at home for lunch, a hysterical secretary who had been assigned to record temperature rise called to report excitedly "something is terribly wrong; it's making funny noises and the water tank is jumping up and down." Jim told her to throw a blanket over the collector and went back to lunch. The collector was actually so extraordinarily efficient that it had started the water boiling in the storage tank. Jim figures that three of these efficient units can heat his entire house. We wish Jim well with his collectors and curtains. I hope he gets them onto the market soon; we need them.

Large living-dining area is brightly lit by extensive glass area. Jim handmade the massive door at left from scraps of siding used for the exterior.

North-facing guest bedroom has vent windows located under the eaves to provide excellent natural ventillation.

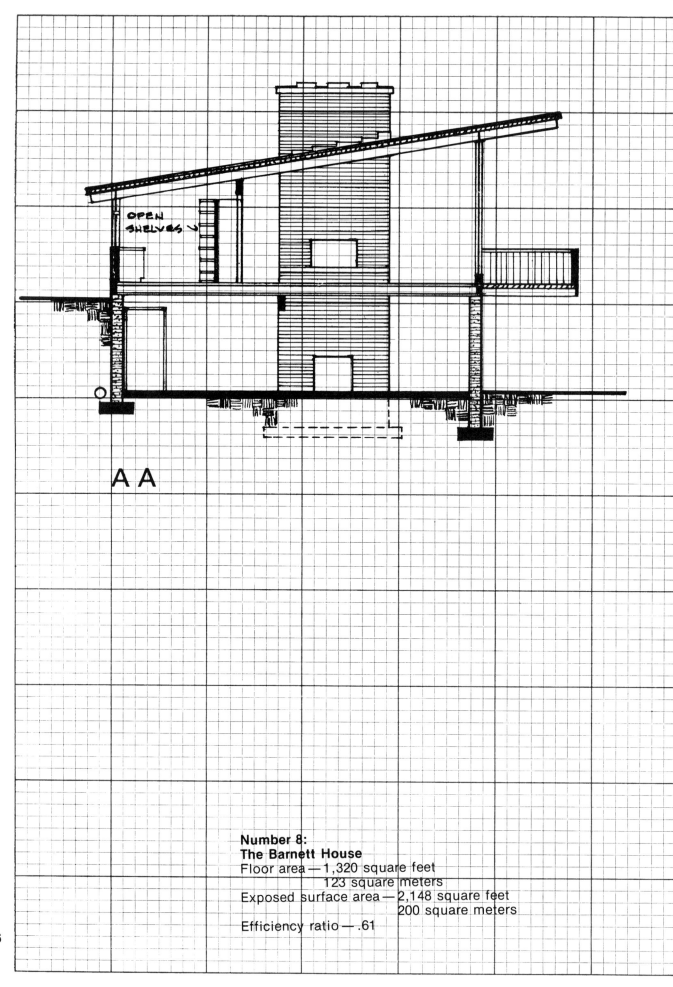

OPEN
SHELVES

A A

Number 8:
The Barnett House
Floor area — 1,320 square feet
123 square meters
Exposed surface area — 2,148 square feet
200 square meters

Efficiency ratio — .61

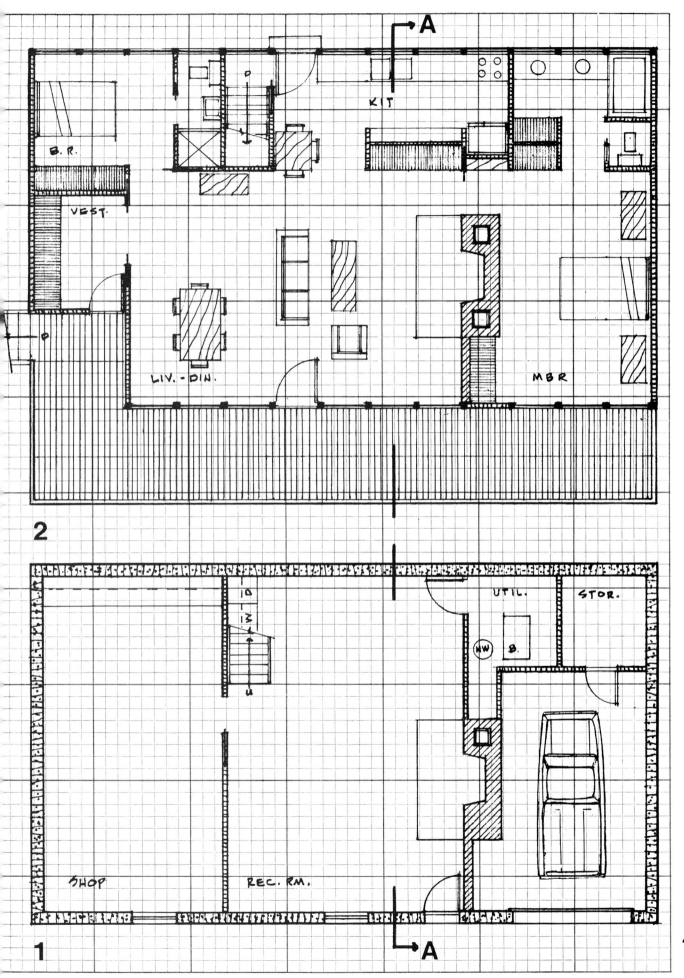

A

KIT

B.R.

VEST.

LIV.-DIN.

MBR

2

10
13

UTIL.

STOR.

HW   B.

SHOP

REC. RM.

1

A

Number 9: The Gummere House

The Gummere's house is almost a textbook case of all of the things which can and sometimes do go wrong when building a house. Seven or eight years ago, my good friends, the Gummeres, started talking about building a retirement house in Duxbury, Massachusetts. Mrs. Gummere's father had left her a piece of property, expecting that she would build a house upon it. Several years and many, many sketches passed. A design was agreed upon and plans prepared. As the house was to be built next to Duxbury Bay, the design showed pressure-treated posts as combination foundation and structural frame. This was done to avoid disturbing the natural contours of the land and affecting the runoff into the ocean.

I made a hasty trip across the country with the final plans to meet with the building inspector and get the building permit. The first of many nasty surprises reared its head—the deed for the property had not even been filed. It seemed that the lawyer who had been hired to file the deed had decided to go off and live in the Maine woods. Somewhere in his flight, he had even lost the original copy of the survey which had to be filed with the deed. The building inspector also expressed concern about our location for the house in that Massachusetts had just passed

A notch cut out of a traditional gable-roofed house allows two stories of south-facing glass. A large deck overlooks the ocean.

a Wetlands Act which might cause us some problems. We had the surveyor check the edge of the wetlands at the same time as he was making a new copy of the survey to replace the lost original.

The state Wetlands Act required that the house be set back 15 feet from the edge of the wetlands. We played it safe and set the house back 25 feet. The town officials came out and checked the layout and everyone was reasonably satisfied. We started construction immediately. A few

Tenants have moved the dining table to the living room so that they can enjoy the view. The table is a homemade copy of late 1700s tavern table.

Antique staircase was salvaged from an old house. Two-and-one-half-inch-thick solid oak door is at right.

days later we were stunned by a stop order from the Duxbury Conservation Commission. They charged that we were building the house on the wetlands. The young lawyer next door came rushing to our rescue: "What they have done is completely illegal; they haven't a leg to stand on."

Two years of court battles started. Judge after judge threw the case out of court. The lawyer for the town resorted to various dodges to have the case dismissed each time it got to court. Finally, the town hired a new lawyer, coincidentally the same lawyer who had testified for the Conservation Commission at our first hearing. We finally got the case into court. The two lawyers became so hostile that the judge whisked them off to his chambers for a private conference. During the conference, all of the parties were left together in the courtroom. We put our heads together and worked out a solution. The Gummeres agreed to move the house and the town made numerous offers of indirect financial aid. The town agreed to install the water line, let us install a small septic system, and use heavy equipment, and to make no further hassles of any sort provided we put the house back of the line established by the Conservation Commission. Then, we each took a lawyer to lunch to spoonfeed him the previously agreed-upon solution.

Next, we took a hard look at the house design. Building costs had escalated wildly during the two years since we had started construction. The energy crisis was on the horizon. The house had to be redesigned to make it as compact and efficient as possible. Again, many designs were sketched and then rejected. Since Peg Gummere is an artist, I was constantly bombarded with new ideas. Finally, we hit upon a design for a traditionally shaped house with a corner cut away to provide two-story glass facing south to the bay. This was a much more

Centrally located chimney allows back-to-back installation of Glenwood range and Franklin stove. Note extra woodstove on balcony at upper right.

The very compact kitchen shares a wall with bathroom for piping efficiency.

conventional-looking design and would hopefully appease some of the townsfolk who hadn't liked the earlier, more "modern" design. We always suspected that the real reason for the strange attack by the Conservation Commission was that someone in power decided that he or she didn't like the looks of the house after we started building it. I started to draw up the final plans.

Another disaster struck. I was severely disabled in an automobile accident and required delicate neurosurgery to fuse a disk in my neck. It would be many months before I could work again, if ever. Of course, the original band of workers who had started the house were long since widely dispersed around the country. I recruited two new workers to build the house, Jim, a young architect, and Bill, a young carpenter. Since the house wasn't nearly designed, Jim would have to finish the plans. The part of the house which had already been constructed would have to be moved to the new location. Estimates were gotten for moving the shell of the house. These seemed high and Jim and Bill persuaded me to tear the house down and rebuild it at the new site—a major mistake. Whereas it had taken us three days to erect the shell the first time (admittedly with a large crew) it took about three months to tear the house down and rebuilt it in the new location. Most of the problems centered around the lack of adequate plans.

Neither Bill nor Jim had the authority to make final decisions, so much time and money were wasted arguing over how the house was to be built instead of building it. Several irretrievable mistakes were made. A foot was added to the height of the house, requiring more materials than were on hand and also producing more space to be heated. A beam was incorporated into the window wall in such a way that it collects water and invariably leaks in a hard storm, no matter how carefully it is caulked.

Another problem was that the house was entirely foreign to Jim's own design concepts. He was, in effect, trying to read my mind and design a building to someone else's tastes. A very difficult task. Bill, a demon for work, became disillusioned and impatient with waiting for decisions and working around corners which had yet to be designed. Bill left, another blow, as his craftsmanship and experience were badly needed.

Jim worked frantically to finish off the house alone, helped along by his lady Nina. Fatigue and the rush to finish before the money ran out produced badly fitted windows and doors which leak air and water. Then money *did* run out and Jim and Nina packed up and left unhappily. The house did not suit Jim's aesthetic sensibilities and he felt unfulfilled leaving before it was completed.

By this time, I was able to do a bit of light work and the Gummere's son, Lish, and I set out to finish the house in time for summer tenants. Lish built the chimney while I built interior partitions, and installed the standing-seam terne roof. Both Peg and I are quite fond of these roofs. They are unheard of in the coastal Massachusetts area where all roofs are of cedar shakes. The natives still don't know what to make of it.

Opening skylight makes bed tucked under eaves bright and airy.

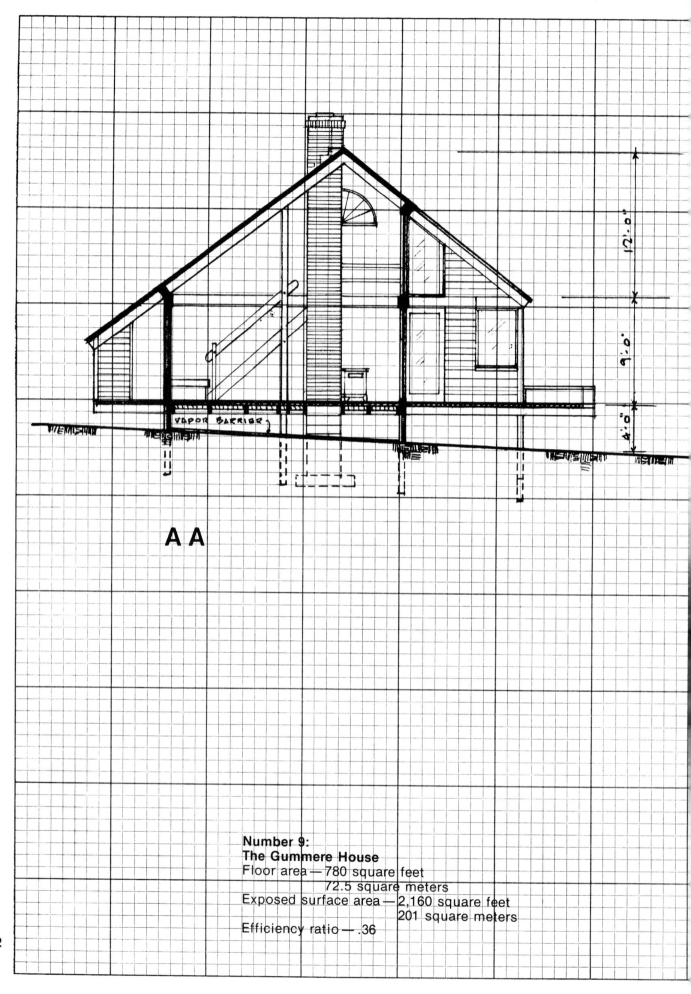

AA

Number 9:
The Gummere House
Floor area—780 square feet
                72.5 square meters
Exposed surface area—2,160 square feet
                      201 square meters
Efficiency ratio—.36

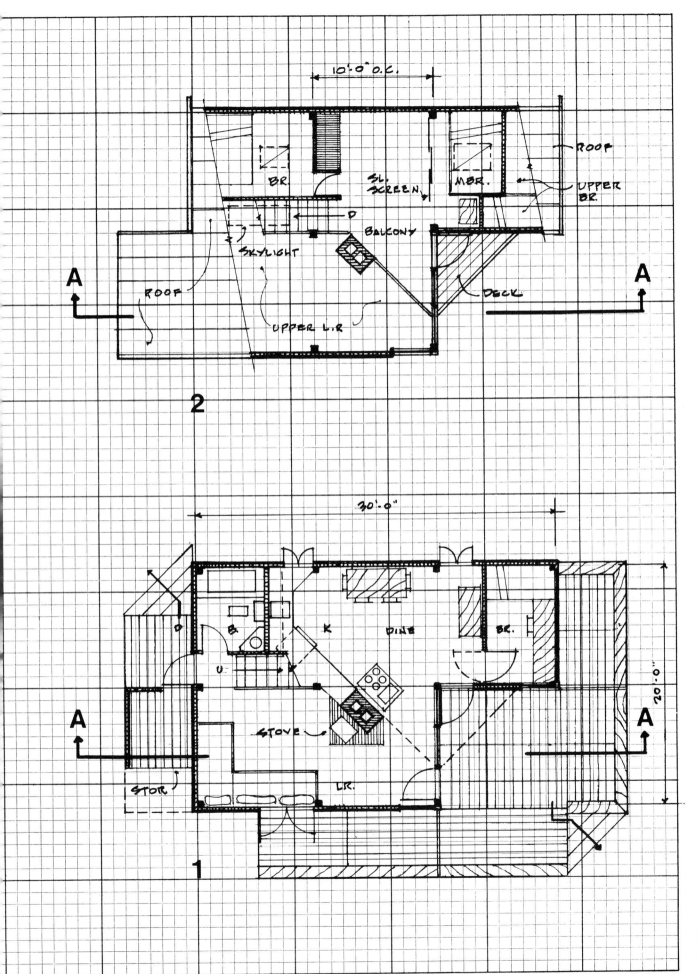

10'-0" O.C.

ROOF

BR.

SL.
SCREEN

M.BR.

UPPER
BR.

D

BALCONY

SKYLIGHT

ROOF

A

A

UPPER L.R

DECK

2

30'-0"

D

B

K

DINE

BR.

U

STOVE

A

A

20'-0"

STOR

L.R.

1

53

Since there was no money leftover to furnish the house, Lish and I built furniture from scrap. We made a copy of one of the old trestle tables from the Windsor House down the street. We did use new material, but it cost less than $20.

The house consists of one large lofty space with small sleeping areas opening off of it. The result is a seemingly large space which is actually quite small. Although the house contains just a bit over 600 square feet (the legal minimum in many places) it can easily sleep eight people. A crows' nest loft which is shown on the plan but has not yet been constructed would add two more sleeping spaces. One indication of how large the house seems was the reaction of our lawyer who said, "Alex, I want you to design us a summer place, but it doesn't have to be big like this."

Old cast-iron bathtub was sunk into the floor for an elegant effect at very low cost.

Maximum use was made of surplus and recycled materials in this house. All windows and doors except the two-story glass wall were purchased at a salvage yard. Likewise, the plumbing fixtures are all recycled. The kitchen countertop and the built-in desk were made of short scraps of the 2 × 6 decking which was used for the roof, finished with grey stain and numerous coats of polyurethane varnish. Lish constructed the chimney of used brick.

Instead of spending money on a central heating system, a massive Glenwood heating-cooking stove was installed. It can burn coal, wood, or gas. As a backup for severe weather and periods when the house is unoccupied, there is a small automatic, gas-fired circulating heater. As yet, nothing has been done to provide thermal barriers over the doors and windows, but these are badly needed. The south-facing glass absorbs lots of heat in the daytime, but loses it again at night.

The floor in the Gummere house deserves mention. Some of us love it; others hate it. The floor is constructed of 2 × 6 tongue-and-groove fir decking with a V-joint on one side. This flooring had been installed in the original house, but the flat face of the flooring was damaged by a catspaw when the house was dismantled. We turned the boards over and exposed the V-groove in the fashion of a ship's floor. This gives the floor a distinctive appearance, but makes it a bit hard to clean. Freshly sanded fir is bright yellow, but the combined effects of the weather and construction had produced a dark, mellow color in the floor. We simply cleaned it, hand-sanded badly soiled areas, and then applied several coats of Minwax antique oil finish. This finish is applied with a rag and must be hand-rubbed. Peg Gummere did most of the hard work on the floor. One visitor commented that the floor looked like it had been there for a hundred years. Since Peg doesn't generally buy anything less than 100 years old, I guess that's a compliment.

Number 10: The Shingleton House

This is a prefabricated post and beam house. If that sounds a bit like a contradiction of terms, I will explain. The skeletal frame and the roof were built at the jobsite while the interior and exterior walls were fabricated in a shop and shipped to the site.

For many years my friends, the Shingletons, had joked about having me design a new front stoop for their house. One day they called and said, "We just bought a lovely lot on Hilton Head Island and want you to design a house for us." This was one of those very rare jobs in which the clients wanted something entirely of my design, not a preconceived design of their own. I was free to design to my heart's content, or so I thought. Then the "deed restrictions" arrived in the mail. Fifteen pages of them. The Hilton Head resort had hired some sharpie lawyers from Yale to draw up a set of restrictions giving them ironclad control of every possible aspect of the design, construction, and use of the house. It further turned out that the management owned a piece of a prefab house-building outfit and slyly steered most prospective homeowners to their subsidiary. Buyers of lots were given a sales spiel which indicated that they could have a custom-designed house for about $20 per square foot.

Shortly after submitting my preliminary design to the Shingletons, I discovered that the "Design Review Board" had just rejected the design of a world-famous architect. They obviously wanted no competition for their quiet, understated California ranch-style prefabs. Just one outstanding house would make the natives restless. Since I was tied up as a supervisor on a large project, I hired a field man to visit Hilton Head and survey the lot, locate trees (required by the deed restrictions), check into local contractors, and generally get the lay of the land. Nothing in his report was encouraging: "Row after row of middle-class houses; tasteful, but dull." Fifty-two million dollars worth of building permits had been issued that year alone; contractors were not available. Waiting times of three to four years were common, even for the prefabs. But the Shingletons had sold their house and were waiting to move. The future looked bleak, but not nearly so bleak as what actually happened.

The Shingletons had bought one of the last available lots. It was a particularly handsome lot which dead-ended a road. It seemed rather odd that it had been passed up before. The reasons were soon to be-

Front entrance doors in the center of the picture are deeply recessed. The roofs slope steeply to provide full space on the first floor with just enough extra room on the second floor to reach the *required 2,000 square feet MINIMUM area,* as required by deed restrictions. Large square window provides lots of light in the small formal dining room without using up furniture space. The recessed area on the roof above the skylight contains a small private deck.

Inside the front doors one finds a brick "street" which divides the two halves of the house. We found the old brick in Charleston. They were "ballast brick" which came from England on ships which were sent to the colonies for goods manufactured here. (Each side has its own heating and cooling system.) The doors in the center fold to open the hall to the greenhouse beyond. The ceiling is carpeted for acoustic reasons.

The small greenhouse does double duty as a small enclosed porch. Doors at right open to living room.

Living room as seen from the stair landing. A large opening on the stairs allows one to look into the living room. It also allows light from the large skylight to illuminate the end of the room next to the stairs.

Exterior of house shows the end wall of the living room and the greenhouse. Outside brick terrace is at far right.

come obvious. A frantic call from the field rep: "That lot is part of the golf course. Tell them to get their money back." It seems that the lot projected out on a dogleg onto the golf course and that people had been shooting right through the house site for over 10 years. The salesman had shown the lot early in the morning before the golfers were out, meticulously picking up all of the stray golf balls on the lot. A further complication was that the "Deed Restrictions" included large setbacks from the golf course and the road. That took care of three of our boundaries. The resultant building area was about the size of a postage stamp. Oh yes, the restrictions again. The house had to be a *minimum* of 2,000 square feet with 60 percent of that located on the first floor. Keep everything low and unobtrusive. After subtracting all of the setback areas, there was no place left for the house. Many angry phone calls started flowing back and forth. The lot was magnificent, the Shingletons still wanted it because of its delightful sense of privacy from other houses, golf course or no. Management offered to trade lots, but other lots which were still for sale were miserable. Finally, an agreement was reached and some of the setback restrictions were waived. Major fights were yet to come concerning our white roof to reflect the sun (forbidden, shows up too much) and our natural-weathered cypress siding (approved colors are grey green, green grey, beige, etc.).

The large skylight in the steeply sloping roof functions as a window from the second-floor level. It brightly lights the stairs and the second-floor hall as well as admitting light to the main hall downstairs. The opening on the landing allows view and light to the end of the living room.

View from the family room to the greenhouse. Part of wall is left out between family room and upstairs bedroom to increase feeling of space in both rooms. Communication and supervision of children are also improved. A very wide built-in desk provides lots of working space for the bedroom and also gives visual privacy to the bedroom. There is also plenty of room for a row of plants along the back edge of the desk. A simple can-type light fixture (Prescolite) provides up and down lighting.

Upstairs bedroom uses the space over the hall. Extra sleeping-storage space is provided by upper-level deck which is reached by a ladder. The rooftop sun deck is reached by the window at top center.

The two-level child's bedroom provides lots of space. The ladder to the upper-level loft (to the right of triangular window) is simply made with dowels drilled between two sideboards.

My reasons for going into all of this in detail are to show you what to watch for in buying a piece of property. Since this is a famous resort, these restrictions are widely copied by other "exclusive" developments. Since many don't want to spend a lot of money on sleazy lawyers, they simply copy deed restrictions already in existence. In many cases, the restrictions perform a service and keep out pop architecture, but read them carefully. For a "good" set of restrictions, see the Perlberg House, Number 24.

Management still had to approve the actual design for the house. By this time, so much arguing had taken place that they caved in on a design which they would otherwise certainly have rejected.

This still left the seemingly insurmountable problem of actual construction of the house itself. Since the Great Nixon Depression was already underway and architectural work had vanished in New York, I decided to put together a firm to build the house. Materials were yet another problem. Even though the depression had begun to wipe out the architects, the building industry was still rushing ahead full speed and shortages were rampant, particularly on the island with its multimillion-dollar construction boom. I was tied up with my job and couldn't leave New York for several months. We decided to prefab the house in New York and truck it to the island. I hired a young Norwegian cabinetmaker, Gunnar Reicheldt,* to help build the panels. The walls were prefabricated in 8 × 8-foot sections laminated together with an industrial epoxy.† Interior and exterior finishes were applied and doors and windows framed and hung. Wiring was installed inside the panels where necessary. The panels were constructed with cypress plywood as an

Master bedroom. Even though this room has only one outside window, the room is very bright due to borrowed light from the sleeping loft. Note the strip of glass at the upper right.

Bathrooms use space- and water-saving Adamsez fixtures from England. The water cistern is located behind the wall in space which would otherwise be wasted. The light fixture is enclosed in a shelf and casts light upward. A white Plexiglas shelf covers the fixture and diffuses the light.

*Gunnar is still in the cabinet business and can be reached at North Road, Tivoli, NY 12583.

† The epoxy can be gotten from Adhesive Engineering Company, 1411 Industrial Road, San Carlos, CA 94070.

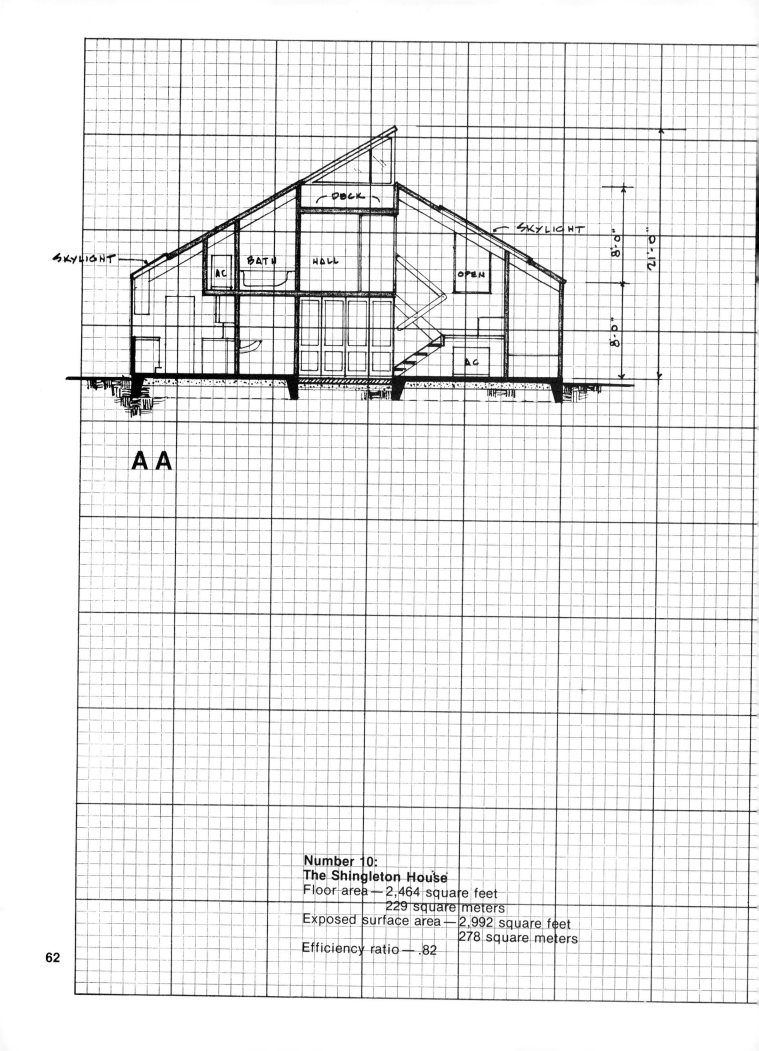

SKYLIGHT

SKYLIGHT

DECK

BATH

HALL

OPEN

AC

AC

8'-0"

8'-0"

21'-0"

AA

Number 10:
The Shingleton House
Floor area — 2,464 square feet
229 square meters
Exposed surface area — 2,992 square feet
278 square meters

Efficiency ratio — .82

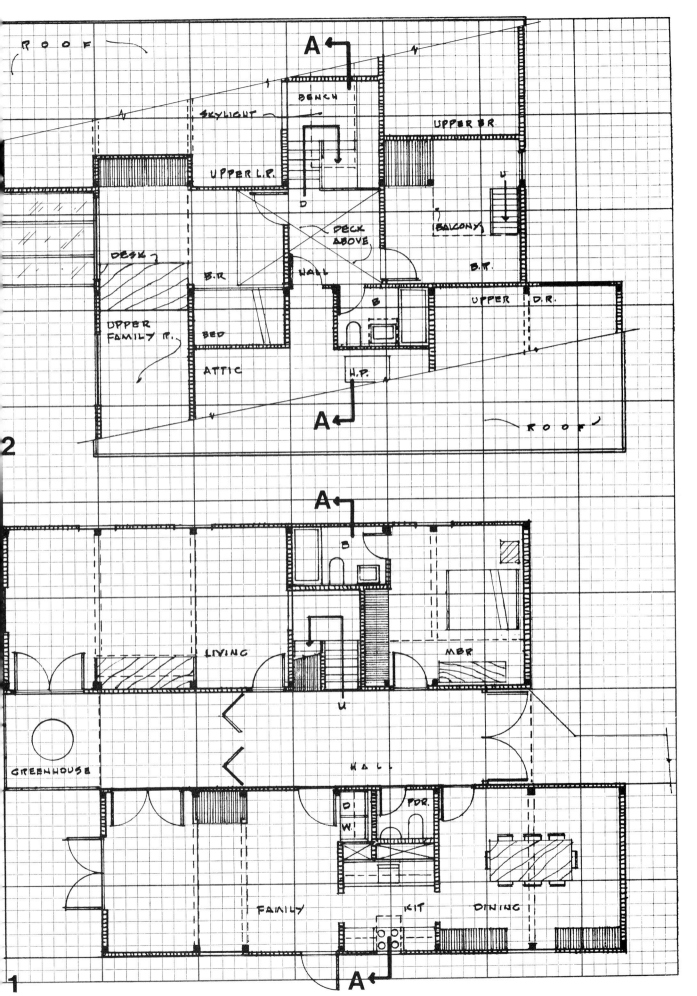

ROOF

A

BENCH

SKYLIGHT

UPPER B.R.

UPPER L.P.

U

D

DECK ABOVE

(BALCONY)

DESK

B.R.

HALL

B.T.

B

UPPER D.R.

UPPER FAMILY R.

BED

ATTIC

H.P.

A

ROOF

2

A

B

LIVING

MBR

U

GREENHOUSE

HALL

D
W

PDR.

FAMILY

KIT

DINING

A

1

exterior finish, polystyrene foam as an interior core, and more plywood as an interior finish. Book-matched oak was found at surplus and used for interior finish in some areas. This part of the operation went like clockwork. Panels were done on time and with *no* mistakes. All of them fitted together in the field perfectly.

Initial work in the field went equally well. Concrete floor slabs were poured and the panels set into place. Within two weeks we were installing the roof on a substantially completed house. The natives, some of whom had been waiting for several years for their houses, were astounded. The local contractors were not amused. Our meager sources of supply suddenly dried up. I had a large crew and little material for them to work with. What lumber was available was extremely high priced and of very poor quality. The water-saving plumbing fixtures had vanished on a freighter enroute from England. A trip to Charleston, South Carolina, resulted in the purchase of a truckload of antique English ballast brick for a terrace. Upon return after dark, the crew got the truck stuck attempting to unload it and were promptly arrested. Morale and workmanship suffered severely. Living expenses were among the highest in the world. Costs mounted and we began to run over the budget. Quality of finish work and painting declined to disasterous levels. I came down with an ear infection and an extreme case of depression. Most of the crew were dispatched to the North and a couple of local carpenters were hired to try to finish off details so that the Shingletons could move in.

The design of the house itself is quite unique. It is actually two houses with a brick "street" flowing between them, somewhat in the fashion of medieval houses where they built rooms right across the streets. In this case, the brick front walk becomes a brick hall when it enters the house and exits through a greenhouse. Each half of the house is heated and cooled by its own small heat pump so that temperature fluctuations due to different exposures can be easily handled. It also makes it possible to save a lot of electricity by only using the system for one half of the house if necessary.

The upper levels of this house contain the most unusual design features. The second floor occupies only the centermost portion of the house. The structure is only eight feet high at the eaves and the roofs slope upward so sharply that there is room for a couple of sleeping lofts for the grandchildren on the third level. These sleeping lofts open onto a secluded roof deck right in the center of the house. The deck is sort of a waterproofed sunken tub made possible by a synthetic rubber material called Hypalon.*

The house is designed for natural ventilation by means of the chimney effect. While many windows are fixed, certain critical ones are able to open. Air is taken in through many sets of French doors and exhausted out through doors to the deck at the very top of the house. Concrete slabs-on-grade provide a year-round tempering effect for the inside temperatures of the house.

---

*Hypalon is available from Gates Engineering, Wilmington, DE 19800.

Chapter 2

Small Houses and Studio-Livingspaces

Over one-half of the people in this country are systematically denied access to the housing market. Detached houses are invariably designed for the typical family with 2.6 children. Single people, couples who do not have or plan to have children, or professionals who want to combine a workspace with a living unit, all find that the housing industry has turned its back on them. Even if they find a small design which meets their needs, the bank, the building inspector, and contractors gang up to prevent them from constructing a structure which is suited to their living style. There are ways around these difficulties, but they are not easy. In this chapter, I show a number of good designs which use space judicially and are suitable for the small household or the person who wishes to work at home.

My own interest in small livingspaces was whetted by my good friend Elisha Mowry. Twenty-five years ago, in his usual thorough fashion, Mr. Mowry began to make preparations for his old age. These consisted of building a tiny apartment on the end of his huge summerhouse with a couple of bedrooms above for someone to look after him. The apartment is only 8 × 22 feet; it is a marvel of efficiency. I was amazed by the usefulness of this space and started thinking about planning small houses.

Getting the money is one of the most difficult snags in building a small house, or indeed even a normal-sized, energy-efficient house. Banks have rigid rules against loaning money for small houses or to single people. It may, therefore, be necessary to resort to subterfuge. One of the cleverest tactics is the good old American business technique of "bait and switch." Businesses play this game by advertising an attractive item which doesn't really exist and then switching to a more or less expensive item which they want to unload. This same game can be played with the bank. First, show them an "acceptable" house plan which you don't really want in order to get them to okay your credit. If you have really good credit, you may be able to get them to switch the loan to a house which you really want. Be sure to act excited about your "new" plans and make sure that this house will cost less than the original plans which you presented. A monthly heat cost savings figure will also help. Maybe you can save enough to be able to offer to pay the bank off in a shorter time period; this will cost you less money in interest and give them more confidence in your ability to pay.

Another tack is to apply for a trailer loan which you don't want either. These carry a higher interest rate as the bank considers a trailer a poor risk item. After you have the loan set up, you can "discover" a small house design which you can build for less than the trailer and ask the bank to apply the loan money to your small house. Since they are charging a higher rate, they may agree to provide the funds for a small house. Be sure that you point out to the bank that you are building a permanent house which will *appreciate* as opposed to a trailer which will *depreciate*. Also, plan to insulate well and point out this superiority to the bank.

If you build small and do it yourself, you may be able to combat both the banks and contractors at once. If you only need a few thousand dollars, you may be able to secure a personal loan instead of a mortgage. If you are having trouble with bank approval of doing work yourself, try to find a small contractor to do the foundation or the shell. This may give the bank confidence that you can finish the job yourself. Most families could save a great deal of money if they went on a strict austerity budget for a year or two. Pretend that some disaster has befallen and that you have to make do with as little as possible. Don't buy anything new unless it is an absolute necessity. If you analyze your budget carefully, you may be surprised to see how many of the things you thought were necessities you can actually do without. Most people in this world live on a tiny fraction of our income. Many live very comfortably for much less.

Materials for any of the houses in this chapter can be purchased for under $5,000, very well under in the case of the three smallest designs. If some contractor wants $15,000 or $20,000 for one of these small houses, you will know you are getting taken and have one more reason to do the work yourself. I've observed from bitter past experience that contractors tend to want a fixed amount of profit per house. Therefore, they are likely to overcharge considerably for a small house so that they can make their usual dollar profit per unit. To be fair, many of the administrative and organizational costs are approximately the same, regardless of the size of the house. Also, building any house is fraught with risk because of the disorganized nature of our building industry. More arguments for getting in there and doing the work yourself.

Codes are another problem, but usually these are a bit easier to deal with. It is probable that the imaginative sort of person who wants a small house will not be likely to build it in an urban area with restrictive codes. The states of California, Oregon, and Massachusetts (particularly the latter) have extremely repressive codes so that you would want to think twice about settling in these states. Vigorous protest movements have been set up, and particularly in California, progress is being made. Check the applicable codes very carefully before committing yourself to the purchase of a piece of property. See my chapter on "Problems" in *Low-Cost, Energy-Efficient Shelter* for a more detailed approach to codes and building inspectors.

This is my own. It has a curious history. Shortly after I met Mr. Mowry, I was asked by a modular home company to design a small modular vacation house which they could sell for around $5,000. I designed an 11 × 20-foot module which was one-and-one-half stories high. In order to transport the unit over the road, the roof had to fold down. Folded, the roof projected one foot, making the standard 12-foot width which can be transported without a special permit. This accounts for the unusual 11-foot width. The modular home company was one of the many victims of the recent depression, so the unit never went into production.

One of my clients built a house out on a remote hilltop and I asked permission to build a small storage shed for some of my belongings as I was spending much of my time traveling around the country and had rented my apartment to friends. I decided to do a research project and try out several experimental ideas, the central theme of which was to build in the least expensive manner possible. Shortly after getting the basic structure up, I was in a disabling automobile accident which changed the nature of the house from an interesting research project to dire necessity to provide myself with as low-cost a housing unit as possible. I was faced with the possibility of being disabled for life with little or no income, so every aspect of the house had to be studied from both a first cost and maintenance standpoint to provide the most for the least.

Since I had already bought the materials for the shell of the house, there was no chance to save there by recycling old materials. Anyhow, I wasn't in any shape to travel to find them or transport them. For this reason, most of the materials in the house were bought new. Some exceptions were the used brick for the floor and some of the doors and windows.

Almost every aspect of the house is innovative in one way or another. The basic structure consists of six 4 × 4 roughsawn pine posts embedded in the ground on 10-foot centers. This creates a building which is 10 × 20 feet overall. The posts as well as the sill members were soaked in creosote before I installed them. There is nothing which could be described as a foundation. There is perimeter insulation which is simply 2 × 8-foot sheets of Styrofoam embedded in the ground under the sill member. The floor itself is used brick set directly on the ground. The sod was first removed and the ground was raked level before installing the brick. Three people with no experience installed the whole floor in about three hours. Later, I swept sand into the cracks between the brick. I did not install a vapor barrier as I have many plants and I

Number 11: The Wade House

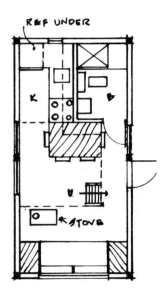

Plan of my house in its original vacation house layout.

Picture of interior taken from the built-in couch. Sauna-bathroom is at lower right. Sleeping loft is above the kitchen area. My study is above photographer's head.

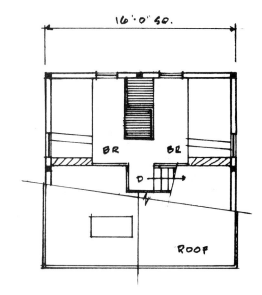

wanted the water to be able to soak into the floor. The brick floor is also an ideal way to introduce moisture into the air in winter: I simply spray the floor with water and the sun from the solar greenhouse evaporates the water into the air. I do not recommend this type of floor for any place other than a well-drained high spot. Otherwise, you might have to bail out the ship.

The 1-inch roughsawn pine siding serves both as siding and structural bracing for the posts. The siding is placed on a 45° diagonal to provide this bracing. In this way, I can eliminate sheathing or extra bracing as well as give an interesting texture to the outside of the house. Cracks between the boards are covered with 1 × 2 battens.

The north side of my house faces a dramatic view of distant mountains. It would have been nice to have many windows facing this view. Instead, I constructed a large insulated flap which is also a door to a small second-floor deck which overlooks the view. The front door also opens out to this view on the first floor. In the summer, I can open both doors and have a full view of the mountains on both floors. I did relent and put in one window upstairs and one downstairs which face north. In the winter, I enter through the solar greenhouse. In this way, the greenhouse serves as an air lock and I can also store firewood in it. The windows are covered with insulating panels as described in chapter 7.

The solar greenhouse is a simple lean-to structure which enables me to keep the house warm with a minimum of fossil fuel. The angle is slightly off (it should be due south but is really southeast) and the greenhouse doesn't work as well as it should during late December and early January. Even in extremely cold weather such as this past winter (1976/77), the greenhouse generates enough heat to keep the house quite warm if the weather is calm and sunny. An antique woodstove provides the necessary backup. For occasional extended trips or overnight visits, I leave one gas burner turned low, providing enough heat combined with the daytime sun to keep pipes and plants from freezing even in severe weather, which is quite common here in New York.

The original kitchen design showed a small apartment-sized range and refrigerator. Of course, I came across a magnificent full-sized Glenwood range and a built-in stainless steel refrigerator. The cost of both was only $40. The range worked well; the refrigerator didn't. But how on earth could I fit them into the tiny kitchen? I solved the problem by recessing the refrigerator into the outside wall. In the winter, the outside temperature keeps food cold and in the summer, I use the freezer section which is located on the bottom as an ice chest. The mechanism has since been rebuilt, so I just unplug it in the winter and save electricity. The range is so efficient that one 20-pound tank of bottled gas usually lasts two months.

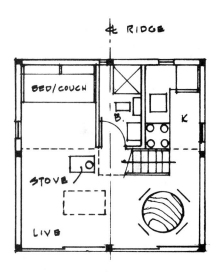

A larger variation of my simple, basic house. This one has a gable roof.

Water and electricity for my house are supplied from the client's house which is about 250 feet away. Both services were buried underground. The electricity consists of one 20-amp. circuit, fused at 15 amp. on my end. Despite this very small service, I have not blown a fuse in two years. I will admit that I am not addicted to gadgets, but I do have a hi-fi set, electric typewriter, toaster, iron, waffle iron, and quite adequate lighting. So much for the "required" 100-amp. service.

The plumbing system is one of my favorite features of the house. I was inspired by a system described in Ken Kern's book, *The Owner-Built Home* (1972).* In it he describes a squat-type toilet combined with a shower. I had originally planned to install a small septic system to handle the greywater and to use an outhouse. Part of the reason for this was that I wanted the shower room to double as a sauna. I had acquired a tiny cast-iron ship's galley stove which was ideal for heating the sauna. I was in constant pain from the operation, and the heat from the sauna was very necessary to keep it under control. I was buying piping to install a simple drain for a back-to-back shower and kitchen sink when I spied an unusual fitting. It was a 3-inch-diameter, 90° el with a 1½-inch inlet right in the middle of the bend. I picked it up and wondered

The north side of the house is shown with everything opened to enjoy the distant view of the mountains. Front door is lower right. Insulating door is upper left. Both are open.

*Available from Charles Scribner's Sons, 597 Fifth Avenue, New York, NY 10017, or from the author at Box 550, Oakhurst, CA 93644.

Exterior of house with north doors open. Diagonal siding serves double duty as bracing for frame.

what it might be good for. Suddenly, I had an inspiration. If I connected the el to a trap and the 1½-inch inlet to the kitchen sink, I could make one trap serve the shower, toilet, and kitchen sink. Furthermore, the side inlet makes it possible to flush the toilet by filling the kitchen sink. The sink itself is a small, black cast-iron bar sink ($8 at salvage) which holds only about three gallons of water. Since the sink is three feet up and the velocity is high it only takes about two gallons to flush the toilet. The shower is used to rinse the toilet and has an old-fashioned low-velocity head which spreads the water in a wide circle like a gentle rain. There are many advantages to the system. First, and most important to me, I saved enough space to include the sauna heater in the bathroom and have the room double as a sauna. Second, the system uses very little water; eight gallons per day per person. And finally, it is not only very low cost (less than $100), but the only trap is buried so it is virtually freezeproof. Those people who have come home to a china toilet lying in pieces on the floor will appreciate the latter feature.

Hot water is provided by a small electric water heater salvaged from the dump. It was a very high-quality marine unit which needed a new cord and new piping fittings. I rarely use the electric element as the tank is hooked up to a coil inserted in my stovepipe. In this fashion, I recycle much of the heat which would otherwise be wasted up the chimney by my antique stove. I placed the damper high up the chimney so that there is plenty of heat in the stovepipe to warm the water coil.

Living in the house for two years has had its ups and downs. Insect life, particularly wasps and spiders, are attracted to the roughsawn wood. The spiders love the snug recesses in the roof. A squadron of little Charlottes is descending around me as I write. Construction is hap-

A small walkway bridges the two balconies. My desk is at the upper left.

Number 11:
The Wade House
Floor area — 336 square feet
31 square meters
Exposed surface area — 880 square feet
77 square meters
Efficiency ratio — .34

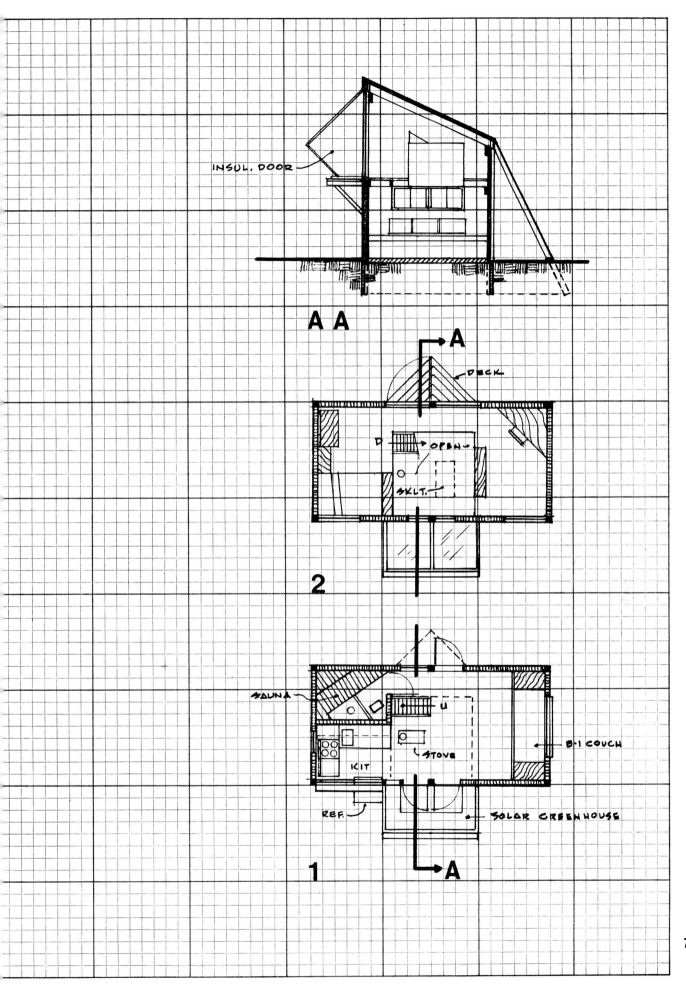

INSUL. DOOR

A A

DECK

D →OPEN↙

SKLT.

2

SAUNA

U

B-1 COUCH

STOVE

KIT

REF.

SOLAR GREENHOUSE

1

73

hazard enough so that the house loses heat rapidly in very cold, windy weather. This is of course compensated for by the marvelous solar greenhouse. The total cost of the greenhouse was $43 for three roughcut 2 × 4s 10 feet long, two used storm windows, and 100 square feet of 20-mil clear vinyl plastic. The latter item is very difficult to find since the oil crisis. I just open the church doors and the sun streams in and warms both the brick floor and the inside surfaces of the massive doors. When the sun goes down I close these doors and the brick and doors return their stored heat to the inside of the house. I have been quite comfortable during a winter of misery for many, and amazingly, I have had no extra costs due to the very cold weather.

"Okay. The sun warms you in the winter, you'll burn up in that place in the summer." Not so. In fact, it's the most comfortable place I've ever been in the summer. The greenhouse is shaded by trees and wisteria and morning glory vines. There are numerous openings which are designed to circulate the night air properly, and windows right over the beds provide perfect cooling.

Yes, there are drawbacks. There isn't space for a dining table for a dinner party. (The original plan on page 69 does have such space but I put the woodstove there so I could connect it to the one in the sauna and have only one flue.) The woodstove and the brick floor create a mess in winter. Wood chips, bark, ashes, etc. work their way between the brick and ashes and dust gets on everything, including the numerous cobwebs.

But again, the house cost just $1,180 including $190 to hire an excavator to dig the trench to the adjoining house. Operating expenses for the

Built-in couch has storage under it. Note how the windows swing up against the ceiling to provide a full opening. An extra set of matching sash is installed in the winter for double-glazing.

The doors salvaged from an old church now
demolished lead to the solar greenhouse.

past year (electricity and propane for the stove) were about $160. In this
way, my expenses are reduced to a bare minimum and I can afford to
be generous with my time in advising others.

I was asked to design a slightly larger "basic living unit" to be built on a
totally remote mountaintop in Vermont. This house has 480 square feet
on two levels as opposed to mine which has only 336. Both areas ex-
clude the optional solar greenhouse from the total.

Number 12: The Howard House

House Number 12 belongs to a small-house genius, architect David Howard. We have seen his work before; Nick Page's large house used one of David's famous braced-oak frames. For himself, David designed a tiny saltbox-shaped house which contains an amazing amount of useful space for its small overall size—11 × 24 feet for a total of 528 square feet exclusive of basement. The first floor is one wide-open space combining living, dining, and kitchen functions. It includes a front door to a large south-facing sun deck, and a back door to a north-facing porch. The roof sweeps down over the porch to make the saltbox shape and provide copious wood storage.

The stove is one of the great Defiants which will be described in detail in chapter 9. It used one-third as much wood this very cold winter as its predecessor, an Ashley, and it heated the house more evenly.

The entire house makes use of recycled materials where possible. The total cost including septic system, well, and pump was $3,800. All of the window sash and the skylight were compliments of the town dump. The basement was an existing cellar for an old house. Since the heat source is on the first floor, the cellar is used as a root cellar for food storage, but also houses a washer and dryer, the cat, and some of Amy's toys.

The tiny Howard house sits on old stone foundation and has windows which were recycled from the dump. Enough money was saved by recycling to have an elegant cedar-shake exterior.

An extension of the roof creates saltbox shape, providing covered wood storage and a screened porch.

Living-dining and kitchen areas flow together into one efficient space, but the L-shaped kitchen doesn't intrude upon living area. I would improve storage by providing open shelves at side of refrigerator.

David and Amy in "Amy's house" which appeared mysteriously Christmas morning.

Lift-up flap at top of picture saves space from the basement stairway.

David uses materials which are quite unusual these days. The roof is V-ribbed galvanized iron painted a warm grey. The windows were all installed in new frames painted teal blue before installation (this is a good idea as it saves a lot of masking later and makes for a very professional-looking job). The exterior walls are sided with cedar shakes. The interior walls are natural grey plaster. Floors and ceilings are exposed wood structure. I remarked on the handsome wide-plank floor. "Oh that," said David. "those are just #2 pine shelving boards from Grossmans' Lumber." They are installed with cut nails to keep them from warping and certainly look like a very expensive floor. The built-in couch occupies a small protrusion that currently has a nice translucent fiberglass roof. Insulating glass is planned as an eventual

A built-in bed saves space in Amy's tiny bedroom.

A built-in couch at right saves space in the living room. A translucent roof makes it cheery and bright.

replacement. The woodstove is set immediately in front of the couch, making this a snug corner in which to curl up.

David is an avid do-it-yourself fan and he and his wife did most of the construction themselves. I asked Pamela what she did. "I was pregnant at the time and did very little, just the plastering, trim, painting, and kitchen cabinets." David later mentioned that she also installed most of the cedar shakes.

The house abounds in nice details. The front door is a Dutch door with solid walnut hardware.* The stairs to the basement are hidden by a trapdoor which folds up neatly against the bottom of the stairs to the second floor so that the visual flow of space on the first floor is not interrupted. Lighting has been planned so that all lights are installed where they are actually needed instead of just outlets scattered at random as required by electric codes.

This house is an excellent example of how comfortable a small house can really be. A dinner party at the handmade dining table showed off the small house on a cold night. Every piece of furniture in the house is planned so that it is used to maximum advantage. The dining table can double as a kitchen workspace. The kitchen is efficiently arranged across one end of the main livingspace and doesn't intrude upon the sweeping spacious feeling of the room.

*Available from Connecticut River Valley Boat Works, Bellows Falls, VT 05101.

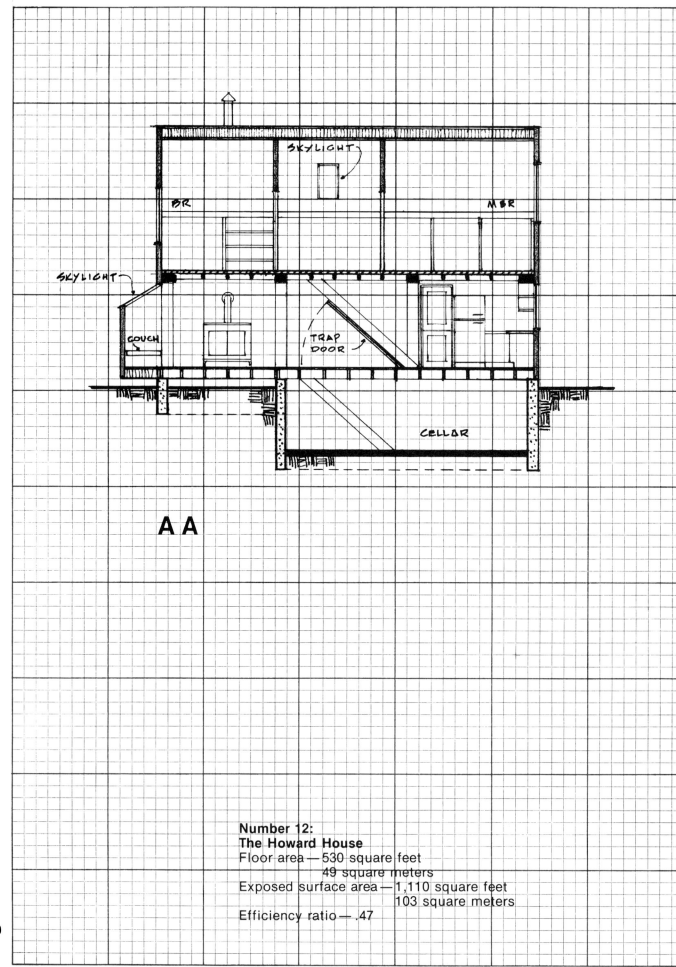

SKYLIGHT

BR

MBR

SKYLIGHT

COUCH

TRAP DOOR

CELLAR

A A

Number 12:
The Howard House
Floor area — 530 square feet
49 square meters
Exposed surface area — 1,110 square feet
103 square meters

Efficiency ratio — .47

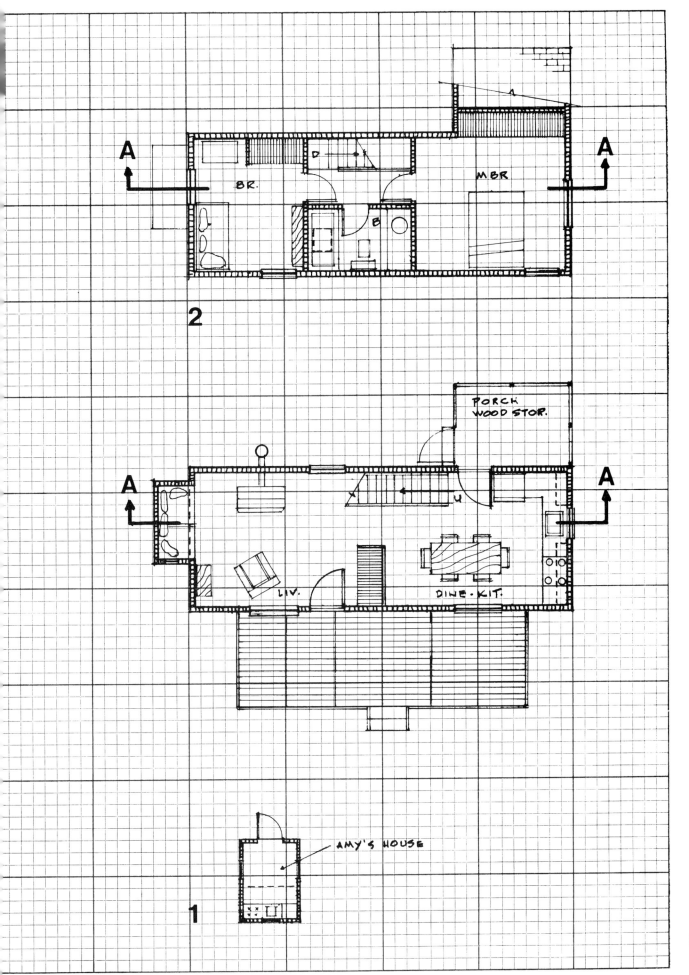

BR.

D

MBR

B

2

PORCH
WOOD STOR.

LIV.

DINE·KIT.

A

A

AMY'S HOUSE

1

Number 13: The Mackey House

House Number 13 belongs to Michael and Susan Mackey of Tinmouth, Vermont. It is a small saltbox containing 896 square feet. Neither of the Mackeys had had any previous construction experience, yet they were able to complete their house in time for Thanksgiving dinner by starting in mid-August. The thing which made all of this possible was the tremendous enthusiasm of David Howard. He transmits this feeling to all around him. Timid sorts who have had no construction experience suddenly gain courage and decide that they can do it too. Another major factor in gaining this confidence is his frame—an elegant, roughsawn, oak masterpiece. It totally dominates the interior of the house; if there are any imperfections, they will hardly show. David furnishes his clients with clear step-by-step instructions for each phase of the job. There were only three phone calls from the Mackeys after the frame was erected by David and his crew on the Mackey's foundation.

A small dormer provides headroom for the front door of the Mackey's compact saltbox house.

David shows Michael and Susan some of the changes which have taken place since he built their house. The Mackeys were his first clients to build their own.

Traditional saltbox shape presents a low sloping roof to the north winds and a high wall to the south. Michael was so encouraged by his house construction that he added a saltbox-shaped garage (foreground) that also provides covered storage for firewood.

The Riteway stove heats the whole house comfortably, but Susan plans to replace it with a wood cookstove so that the same fire will warm their house and cook the food. The Riteway will be moved to the basement as a backup heat source.

One unique feature of David's houses is that most of them are plastered, almost always by the owners. The walls of the frame are wrapped with chicken wire which is covered on the outside with 3½ inches of Styrofoam. The plaster is applied to the inside of the Styrofoam between the oak framing members. The difficult plastering jobs of corners and ceilings are eliminated since all ceilings are of wood construction and all corners contain posts. The plastering takes a great deal of time, but costs virtually nothing. You also save the cost of paint as the natural grey color of the plaster harmonizes nicely with the natural oak frames. Since it requires much time and patience and no special skills in using power tools, the person with the least building experience usually elects to tackle the project. The step-by-step directions have guided all but one of David's clients to success. That one got a bad batch of plaster and forgot to test it. (David's directions also tell how to check the plaster.)

The Mackeys did have a few problems. The plumbing was installed in such a mess that the ceiling had to be dropped to cover it. The mason blithely ignored instructions to build a Rumsford fireplace and built a heat-waster, and finally the roofer put on a roof which promptly blew off. "Funny thing," muses Michael, "the only things we didn't do were the only things which got screwed up." Think about that one awhile.

The Mackeys heat their house entirely with a Riteway woodstove. To their amazement the bank approved of the wood heat without blinking. (The bank also approved of their building the house themselves with no previous experience.) Susan and Michael are replacing the Riteway with a wood cookstove and plan to move the Riteway to the basement as backup heating.

The Mackeys had a good deal of help from friends, most of whom were assigned some small project such as a staircase or a cabinet. They have gained so much confidence that they went ahead and built a large sun deck and a small saltbox garage which matches the house nicely. Michael says, "If we could do it, anyone can."

A house similar to the Mackey's under construction. Styrofoam planks and chicken wire are being placed over the oak frame.

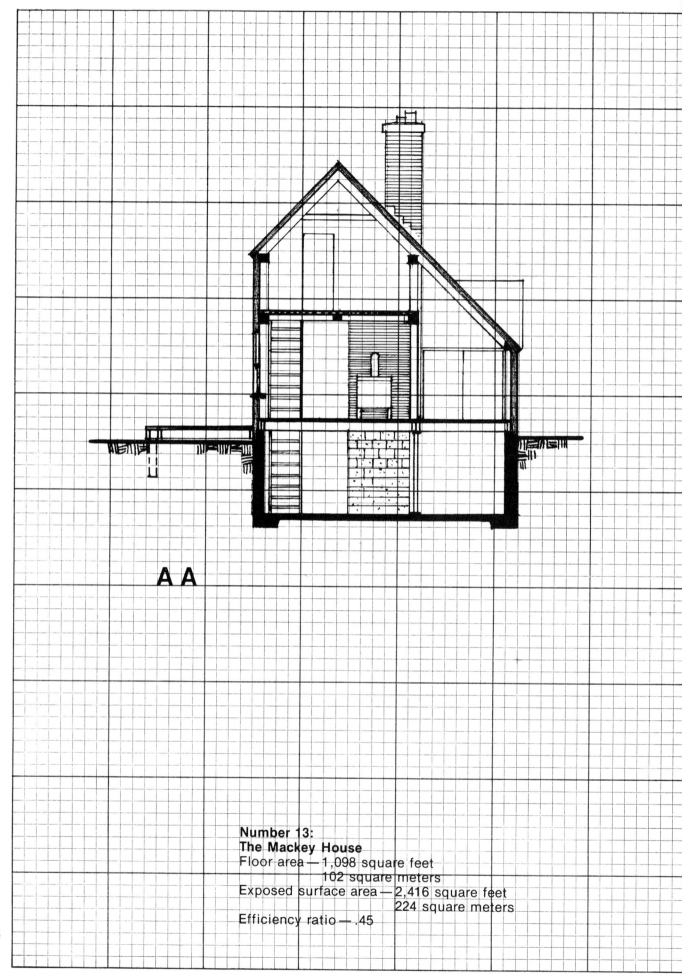

A A

Number 13:
The Mackey House
Floor area — 1,098 square feet
                102 square meters
Exposed surface area — 2,416 square feet
                        224 square meters
Efficiency ratio — .45

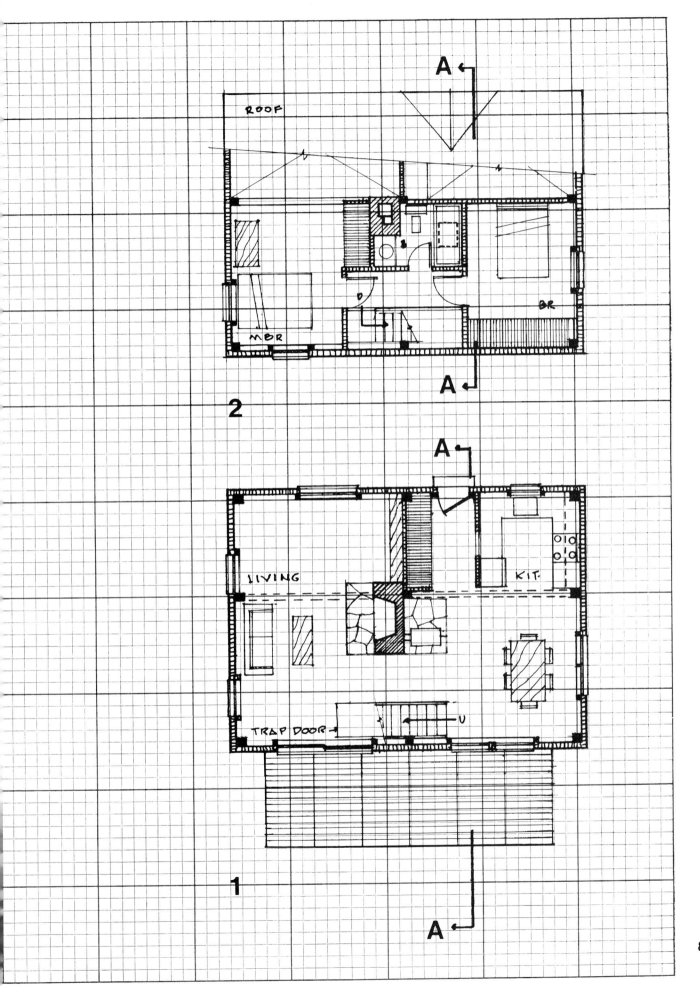

ROOF

A

A

MBR

BR

2

A

LIVING

KIT.

TRAP DOOR

U

1

A

Number 14: The Steinberg House

This one, which is actually two tiny houses, is a custom design, again by David Howard, but using conventional 2 × 4 frame construction. That's about the only thing which is conventional about this house, though.

The house is particularly unusual in that it provides completely separate livingspaces for the parents and children. The parents' house is an 8 × 12-foot rectangle two stories high while the children's house is 8 × 8 feet and three stories high. The house actually has four different

These guest houses make great expansion space. Consider building one of these for expansion, rather than adding on to an existing space.

levels. The two small houses face each other across a small platform and make a striking complex. This was designed as a guest house, but could be used equally well as a starter house for a couple or a summerhouse if one must have one. The total cost was less than $3,000. In this case, Mr. Howard's firm prefabricated the tiny units and trucked them to the site.

This project provides yet another different approach to obtaining a livingspace for minimal cost. Since these units are both small enough to be transported by truck, you could build them in your backyard or a large shed and then transport them to a building site. Let's say that you are planning to build your own larger house. If you were to build one or the other of these tiny units (depending upon size of family), you could truck it to the site and use it as livingspace while you construct the main house, and still have the extra building for use as a study, guest space, or children's bunkhouse. Materials for either of these little houses were about $500.

The skylight over built-in couch provides pleasant natural daylight to the whole room.

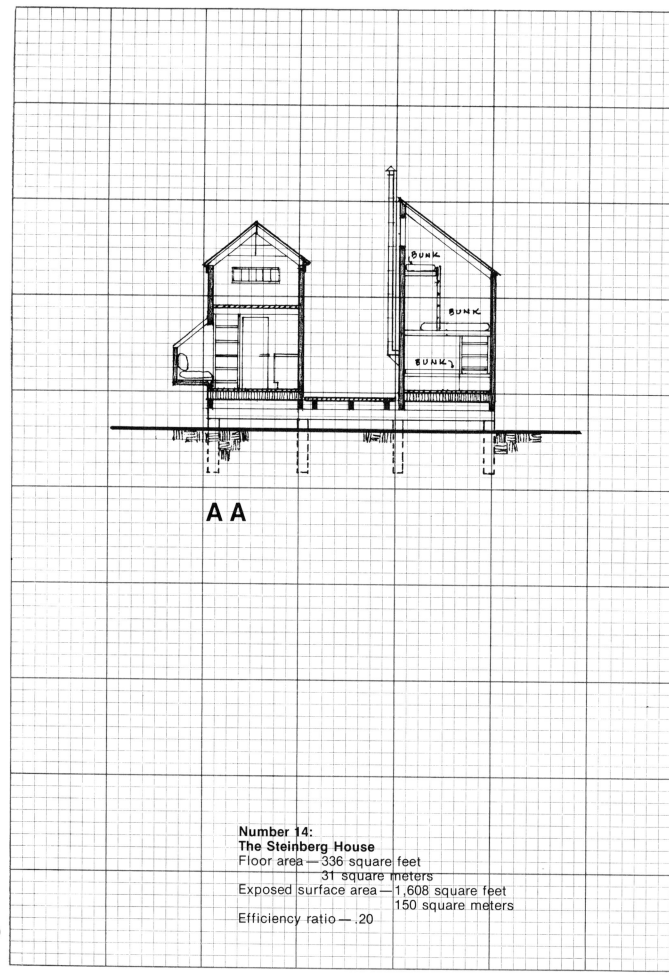

A A

Number 14:
The Steinberg House
Floor area — 336 square feet
  31 square meters
Exposed surface area — 1,608 square feet
  150 square meters
Efficiency ratio — .20

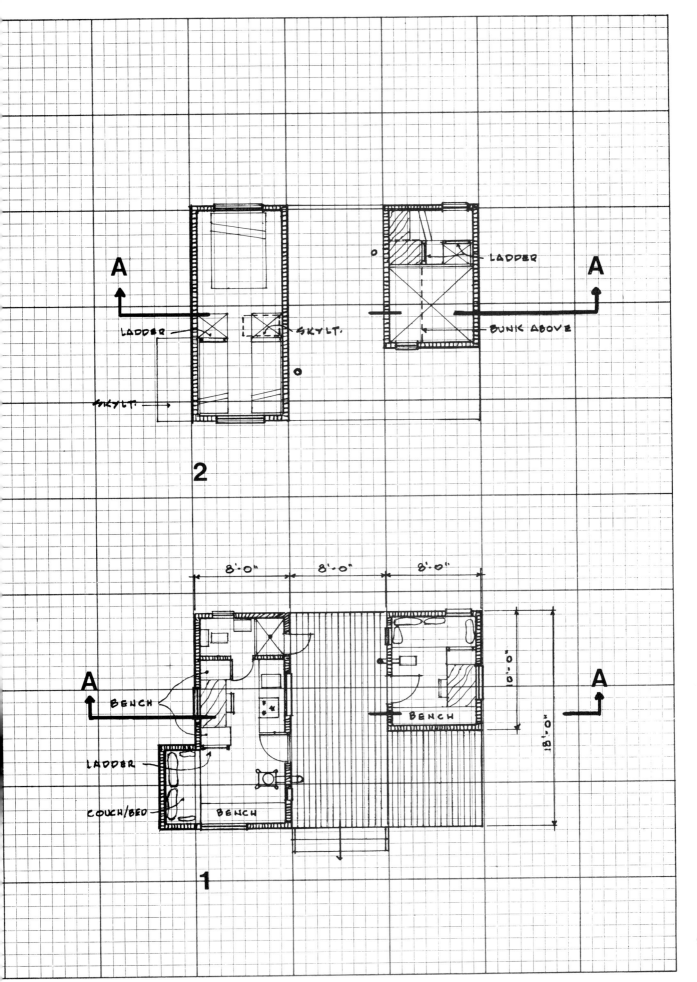

2

A
LADDER
SKYLT.
SKYLT.

LADDER
BUNK ABOVE
A

8'-0"   8'-0"   8'-0"

A
BENCH

A

LADDER

COUCH/BED
BENCH
BENCH

10'-0"
18'-0"

1

Number 15: The Simon Studio

This, the first of the combined studio-livingspaces, was built on a remote mountaintop in the middle of the Catskill Mountains. The design of this building was predicated by its intended use as a rehearsal and recording space for a musician. His acoustical engineer wanted a curved roof structure for special sound effects. (I had always heard that curves were a disaster, but that's what he wanted.) I was called in as structural consultant to help design the curved beams to support the roof. Since I had just designed the contractor's own house, we were well acquainted. This dwelling actually consists of three separate but interconnected buildings which step up a steep hillside. The three units are a compact living unit (which could be built all by itself), a large sound studio, and a control and equipment storage space which was added later.

The curved roofs of the studio and livingspace presented real construction problems. The obvious solution was to buy laminated timbers. A quick check with several suppliers brought us back down to earth. Twelve weeks to six months were typical delivery dates and the prices were so high that we couldn't afford them anyway. Back to the drawing

Curved roof shapes step gracefully down a hillside. Studio is in foreground; living quarters at rear.

board. "Why not make our own?" Why not. Plywood box beams were very common in the construction field; we would simply build curved ones.

I called the engineering department of a large plywood company and asked a few questions. They felt that our project was quite feasible but suggested that we use commercial-grade adhesives instead of normal hardware store glue. They recommended contacting Adhesive Engineering Company, 1411 Industrial Road, San Carlos, CA 94070, a company which makes an incredible variety of epoxy-type adhesives which do everything from glue airplanes together to repair concrete bridges. Their brochure illustrates unbelievable applications. The before and after picture of a concrete bridge which actually broke in two and was propped up and glued back together with epoxy will boggle the mind (not that I would want to drive on it). Adhesive Engineering had just the product for us—an adhesive called #1080 Concresive—which can be obtained from the aforementioned address. It cost about $30 a gallon, but was well worth it.

I have since made extensive use of this clear epoxy for assembling doors, windows, cabinetwork and the like. Once, a newly constructed door blew off a truck, smashing several members. We simply injected the epoxy into the cracks, clamped the door and sanded off the excess. The repair was undetectable.

We made up a simple jig and bent the top and bottom members of the beams into a curve and then applied ¾-inch plywood side members adding a final curved trim piece to cover the edges of the plywood. These beams are very light and strong. Full details for fabricating structural

Living quarters perch on a small concrete-block utility core which houses an oil-fired hot water boiler.

Giant "bubble" inflated window forms link between living quarters and studio proper. All windows are custom-made with 20-mil water-clear vinyl, inflated after installation to provide superior insulation.

Number 15:
The Simon Studio
Floor area — 896 square feet
　　　　　83 square meters
Exposed surface area — 2,102 square feet
　　　　　　　　199 square meters
Efficiency ratio — .41

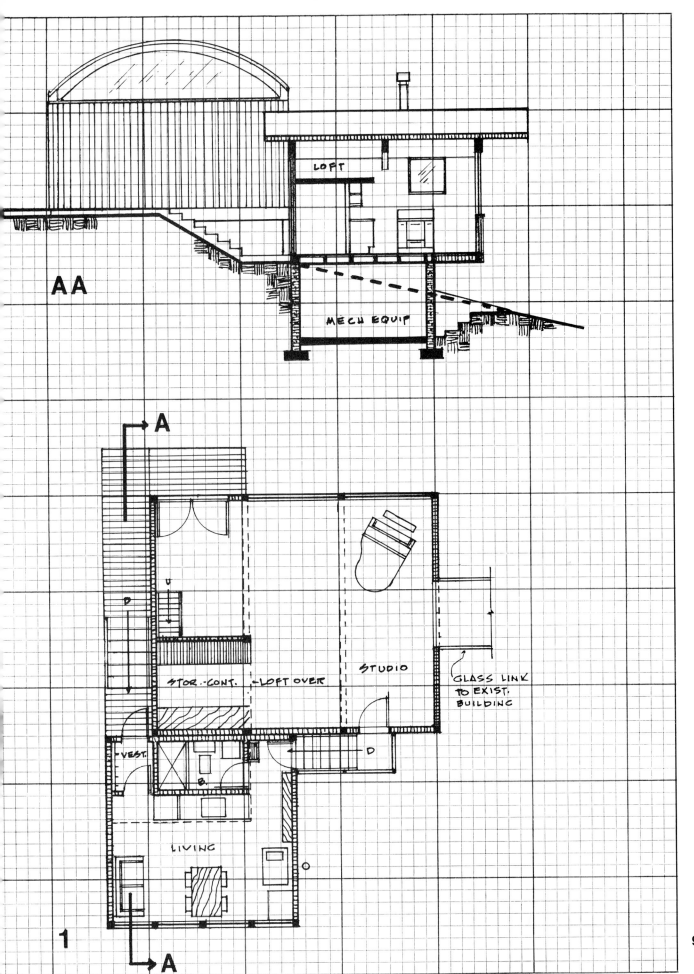

AA

LOFT

MECH EQUIP

A

STUDIO

GLASS LINK
TO EXIST.
BUILDING

STOR.·CONT. ·LOFT OVER

·VEST.

D

B.

D

LIVING

1

A

95

members of plywood may be obtained from the American Plywood Association in Chicago. I mention this incident because there may be cases when you need a large structural member and cannot get a roughsawn member large or long enough. Also, solid beams can be very heavy and require expensive machinery to set into place. For another type of structural beam, using plywood and glue, see House Number 29: The Pergola House.

As you can see from the pictures, the windows are highly unusual. These windows were all fabricated at the jobsite from 20-mil clear vinyl. The edges are heat sealed, a valve is inserted, and the units are stapled into place on the window frames. Then they are inflated. These windows provide superior insulating qualities and of course give almost complete freedom as to size and shape. Some people have questioned the durability of these units. Previous installations have been functioning for as long as 10 years and still seem to be in good shape. My own solar greenhouse is glazed with this material (but only in single thickness). The material is very tough but somewhat stretchable. For this reason, it is sold only as full rolls 54 inches wide by 100 feet long. Cut pieces must be installed as the stuff neither rolls nor folds well. It is water-clear, makes excellent storm windows, and it can even be double-layered and not lose much image transmission. Since quite a bit of the material comes in a roll, you may have to get together with some friends to share one roll. Make sure that you get *clear* vinyl—many supply houses will not have it and will try to switch you to something inferior. I would suggest checking the Yellow Pages under Plastics in the nearest large city. I got my vinyl from Almac Plastics, Long Island City, NY 11100.

The siding on this building is cypress plywood left to weather naturally. This material is quick and easy to install and makes a nice finish. It is excellent for bracing post and beam structures. Construction adhesive was used on the surfaces of all posts and studs to provide better adhesion. While most people would not want to build this studio just as it is, I have included it to illustrate a number of unusual materials which may have application on other houses. The designer and contractor, Bill Bettridge, is well versed in building small post and beam structures and is a meticulous workman.

Number 16: The Rice Studio This one was designed as a combination sculpture studio and living-space by Mr. Dustin Rice, a former teacher at Columbia University. Dustin is a born scavenger and spent much of his lifetime dragging home incredible pieces of buildings. Virtually everything in his studio is recycled. Windows came from an old church; siding and old beams from a building which had fallen down. Bits and pieces of stone carving are inserted in new stone walls. Old dark beams make an exposed-beam ceiling.

The building itself is two stories high and is dug into a north slope. This is a bad choice for siting a building, but that is how the property sloped, so that's where the building was built. The situation was remedied somewhat by installing two large south-facing skylights on the front of the building. The back opens out onto a field. Since much of the building is buried, it loses little heat to the outside air and the skylights let in a great deal of heat from the sun both in summer and winter. Insulating flaps are a must for such large skylights. These skylights also leak despite repeated attempts at sealing them because they were installed on a very low-pitch roof with high curbs where water is bound to back up under almost any flashing. This is a hard lesson. Low-pitch roofs drain poorly and are subject to leakage, particularly if covered with asphalt shingles. If you have a low-pitch roof, use double-coverage roofing which is fully sealed down. Its application is fully described in chapter 8 of *Low-Cost, Energy-Efficient Shelter*.

Northeast view of studio. Virtually every item in the building was recycled. The stained-glass windows were actually being thrown away when Rice rescued them.

The studio is divided into a large workspace downstairs with the livingspace located in a half-floor on the second level. This permits both levels to partake of a dramatic two-story space. The livingspace on the second level is separated from the main workspace by handmade sliding glass doors.

Giant south-facing skylights compensate for the north-facing slope. Fireplace and woodstove provide heat.

A dining alcove is nestled under one of the nicest windows I have ever seen.

Running water has not been installed, so an aqua-privy is used instead. Rainwater is collected from the roof for washing and a drainage system in the building connects with the tank under the aqua-privy. Heat is supplied by a Riteway woodstove with electric backup.

Dustin has a thorough knowledge of the use of tools, but no proper background in construction. In certain areas such as weatherproofing and insulation the building is lacking, but in the balance it is very well designed.

Second-floor living quarters are separated from the main studio by owner-built sliding-glass doors.

One of the many "pieces" of Dustin's collection was set over the mantle. Stove was recycled as were most of the materials in the building.

Dustin at work.

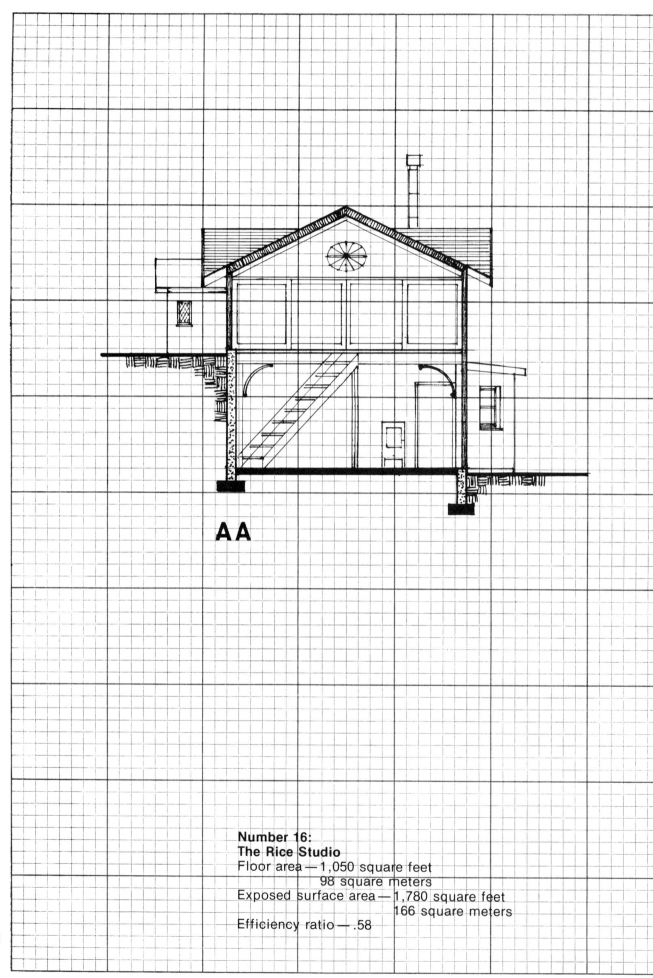

A A

Number 16:
The Rice Studio
Floor area — 1,050 square feet
98 square meters
Exposed surface area — 1,780 square feet
166 square meters

Efficiency ratio — .58

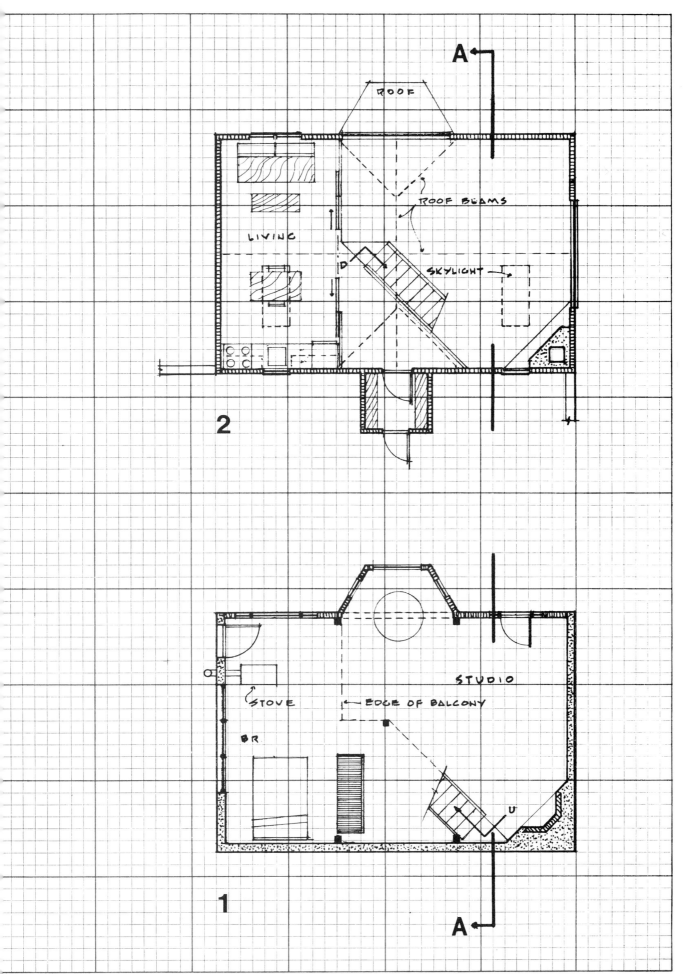

Number 17: The Nedds Studio

Patrica Nedds' building is another combined studio/livingspace. I designed it as a replacement for Dustin Rice's studio which was sold. Unfortunately, due to local zoning regulations, the original studio could not be separated from a conglomeration of other buildings which had become burdensome to the Rices. The new building was designed to fit an exact set of circumstances. Dustin had a casting foundry in Spain where he spent winters. The studio was therefore designed for summer use only with no insulation. Furthermore, since it was to be a low-budget building, an exposed post and beam frame was used with solid exterior walls; just plywood, building paper, and roughsawn siding. Later, I was to regret this cost-saving construction method.

Again, the building is dug into a north slope instead of the ideal south-facing one. In this case, we resorted to numerous skylights and light wells to push the south light down to the lower level of the studio. One skylight is located directly over a floor-level access hatch so that the skylight gives natural daylight to two levels at once. Another technique was to use an insulating flap on the one south window in the lower level to act as a reflector to bounce light into the workspace. In this case, the flap is hinged at the bottom and swings out to the desired angle to reflect the sun into the room.

Main exhibit space opens to outdoors.

Trish at work at her printing press.

This studio was built while I was waiting for a court decision on the Gummere house in Massachusetts. The crew was already disheartened from the nasty experience of being stopped right after we really got going on the other house. More discouragement lay ahead: rain. Weeks of it. The rains would occasionally stop for a day or two, but never long enough for the soft clay bank to dry up sufficiently for the excavator to dig out the site. Finally, I dismissed most of the crew and sat back to await more favorable weather conditions. We had a very tight budget ($15,000) with which to try to build 1,600 square feet of studio space and we couldn't pay a crew who was unable to work. I figured I could pick up some workers from the nearby college which was due to close for the summer in a few weeks. Anyhow, I desperately needed the time to finish designing the building which, since it was somewhat spur-of-the-moment, had never been fully designed. Fortunately, the rain stopped suddenly and then we were faced with hot, dry weather for the rest of the summer.

The excavator was impatient for work and moved his machine into the sticky goo almost immediately. Indeed, the expected parade of students did show up asking for jobs. A few had even used a hammer. Since much of the building was underground and in a treacherous clay bank, it was necessary to build a massive reinforced concrete retaining wall. Many hours of carpentry work was required to construct the forms. A lot of expensive plywood was also used, but we were able to reuse it for wall sheathing and roof deck.

The concrete floor slab was one of those areas where my inexperience caught up to me. The concrete truck arrived several hours late one very hot afternoon. The driver had forgotten to bring his extension chutes (possibly because one of the college kids had left him a note not to forget the "shoots"). When the extension chutes did arrive, they were too short to reach the outer edges of the slab and the concrete had to be moved around by hand. One of the students waded in in his sneakers and promptly lost them. But, the major mistake was mine in trying to make one big pour for the whole floor. It would have been much better to pour it in two square sections with a joint in the middle.

Unfortunately, I had designed the building three bays long, not four, so there was no convenient place to stop the pour. The warm dry air caused the concrete to set up so quickly that screeding it level was very difficult. The results bore a resemblance to the surface of the moon.

Although the floor was a visual disaster, it was structurally quite solid. We wet it down thoroughly and covered it with straw. We were very lucky that the next two days were cloudy with intermittent gentle rain; ideal conditions for curing concrete. Concrete is a very delicate material, it must not get too hot or too cold, too wet or too dry. Many people are tempted to add water to the concrete mix to get it to spread more easily; this weakens the concrete. It should not be allowed to dry out for three to five days and it should be protected from freezing in cold weather for the same period of time. Do not let anyone talk you into adding calcium chloride or other adulterants to the concrete to lower its freezing point. Cover it and add heat; or better still arrange your schedule so that you don't pour concrete in freezing weather.

We still had to contend with the messy slab surface. After various quarry tiles and the like were rejected as being too expensive, we decided to apply a concrete topping. This required much hand labor and a good bit of expensive concrete bonding agent. If you ever have to attach new concrete to old, use a bonding agent. These are chemical compounds which make the new material adhere to the old. All dirt must be thoroughly removed with a wire brush before beginning work.

Next, I set my apprentices to work building concrete block walls for the above-grade walls of the lower level. This was a good example of the blind leading the blind. Fortunately, I did have a mason friend who was cajoled into coming up for a weekend teaching session. Somehow, with four different masons working, the walls came out remarkably plumb and true. Lots of excess mortar did have to be cleaned off the block and certainly it's not the most handsome job ever. But it's not in a prime visual area of the building and several people did learn how to lay up block.

The framing was a different matter. It was simple, easy-to-understand post and beam in which all of the structure remained as finish surfaces. Everyone had had some experience at carpentry work and I jumped in and helped directly. This phase of construction literally flew. Not only that, but unlike some of the earlier work, the crew did a fine job. We were cheered on by the Watergate hearings blaring out of a speaker from the house next door. Mr. Dean, of course, stopped the show completely.

Just as we were starting finish work, disaster struck. Mr. Rice suffered a stroke leaving him paralyzed. His wife still wanted the work completed, but now the building was to be put up for sale. Somehow, no one had any enthusiasm for finishing the job. Work dragged on interminably. Students went back to school and I worked at the building sporadically. All of the money in the budget had been consumed. Somehow, it got finished enough to be able to put it up for sale with the idea that whoever bought it would finish it off to suit his or her own purposes, but

Trish's bedroom faces a small private deck.

since it had been designed especially for Dustin, prospects for a quick sale were very dim. Vandals broke into the studio and stole Dustin's prize bronzes and wood sculptures, further discouraging us all.

Realtors showed the studio to no avail. No one really had a need for the space. The realtors were elderly and I'm sure had no sympathy of their own for the space. Then, along came Trish, who fell in love at first sight. Better still, the studio was perfectly suited to her purposes—well almost. It just needed to be winterized and have running water and a few thousand other things. But she was game and took the plunge and persuaded friends to help buy the place. The house would have to be rented to pay the mortgage, so the studio was fixed up to serve as a livingspace as well.

Trish is a printer, and the large basement workshop is ideal for her presses. Dustin's trapdoor in the floor, designed to help in hoisting heavy bronzes, was used to set the presses. The tool storage room with its massive vault door became the ideal darkroom. The tiny upstairs spare room, originally intended as a guest space, became Trish's bedroom. The upstairs garage space has become a combined living room/gallery, the heavy decking refinished to glowing beauty, all of the abuse, grease, oil, and other seeming disasters giving it a slight antique character.

I saved quite a lot on materials for the building by buying in bulk. Since this studio had been planned for construction as soon as we finished the Gummere house, I bought materials for both jobs together when I could. One example is the 3-inch laminated floor decking. It is used for the heavy-duty floor deck in the studio and for the exterior walls in the Gummere house. The material had been special ordered by one of the local lumberyards and they were stuck with it and unloaded it very cheaply. The material is very nice and will easily span 8 feet for a floor. On the Gummere house, we used it for walls to span between posts spaced 10 feet on center. The actual span was much greater as we were installing the decking on the diagonal.

A client of mine in South Carolina wanted to use this decking for a floor, but couldn't wait 10 weeks for delivery. Since he had lots of free help, they proceeded to make the decking. It's really quite easy. The decking is made very simply from three pieces of ¾-inch-thick pine with the center board offset by about ¾-inch, thereby making a tongue on one side and a groove on the other. The center board is similarly offset end to end, making a considerable saving in that the boards can be joined together anywhere instead of right over a support. This is called "end matching." You can get 2 × 6 solid decking made that way also. If you install decking this way, make sure that you stagger the joints as you will dangerously weaken the floor if they are constantly close to the same spot. Laminating the boards together makes the resulting plank much stronger than a solid plank of the same dimensions.

Both the studio and the Gummere house have standing-seam terne roofs. I bought all of the materials for both jobs at once and had them formed in a sheet-metal shop into "pans" to be installed on the roofs. One of the college kids was considerably less experienced than the others and was constantly getting kicked around. I gave him the project of doing the roof. He could work his own hours and not have to be congenial with anyone. For the first time, he really got down to work. This was his project and he took pride in it. Also, he wanted to do it in a hurry to show off to the others. This is the kind of time-consuming, but very satisfying project which can be undertaken by someone without other construction skills. Some people just can't seem to get the hang of carpentry work, no matter how hard they try. There are entirely too many jobs to be done in building a house to worry about such limitations. If you are in a joint venture with several people, find the things you do best and try to get to do them. Get busy and learn or otherwise you will be relegated to the bottom of the totem pole as go-fer or nail puller.

Insulation of the upper level posed quite a problem for all of us. Much of the charm of the building lay in its exposed structure. This same exposed structure did not lend itself at all easily to the installation of usual insulation materials. The easy, cheap solution would be to furr everything out and install acres of Sheetrock. Fortunately, Trish didn't buy that. Styrofoam boards were installed in all of the paneled spaces

Deck from the south.

of the roof and covered with Sheetrock. Trish and Susan Quasha, a neighbor, worked many nights all night to get it finished. I had no idea they were saving the original ceiling and was dumbfounded when I walked in. The sidewalls were insulated with fiberglass, but trim boards were put up to match the original framing pattern. Someone without such good taste could have easily ruined the building, but as it is, the results are spectacular. The only area in which the insulation fails is in the windows. These are of large, odd shape and were originally single-glazed with 20-mil water-clear vinyl. Unfortunately, this material can now be gotten only on special order with a wait of several months. An inferior plastic was used as an extra layer of covering for the window areas.

The original heating system for the building wouldn't do for a living-space; it was a noisy portable heater and although vented to a chimney, it did not make the place habitable. Warm, yes; expensive, yes; habitable, no. It was sold separately from the property. A combination coal-wood-oil, forced-air furnace has been installed as a permanent heating system. The young man who was hired to do the ductwork was a little overawed by the task and called in his union plumber uncle. Uncle did quite a job. He measured up the whole place, figured how to put in acres of ductwork (effectively ruining all the exposed structure which had been so carefully preserved), and came up with the staggering estimate of $1,900—just for the ductwork! So much for union plumbers. Anyway, I sat down with the furnace supplier and we worked out a nice simple duct system which cost less than $300. This one was simple enough for Trish and her friends to install themselves. Once you have started doing something yourself, you should stick to it as the pros will want to make up for their lost wages all at once.

Trish has had one final hassle which deserves attention. The Rices originally had the building insured with a reasonable local agent. Plans were submitted and all was approved. When Trish took over the building, she got a new insurance company and the fun began. Since security had become a major problem due to theft of the sculptures, doors

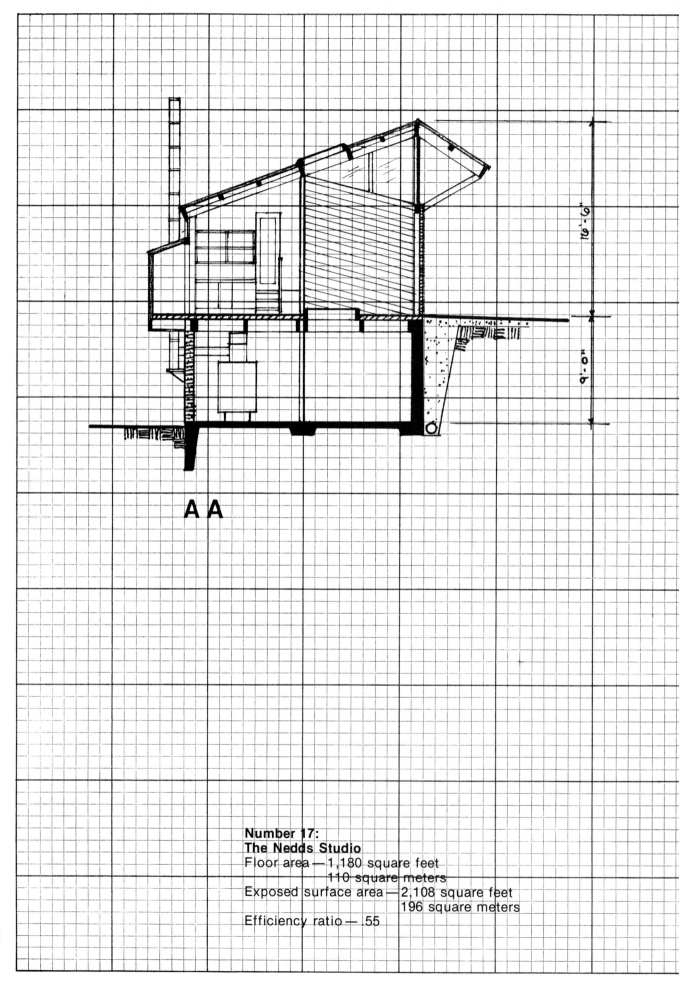

A A

Number 17:
The Nedds Studio
Floor area—1,180 square feet
110 square meters
Exposed surface area—2,108 square feet
196 square meters

Efficiency ratio—.55

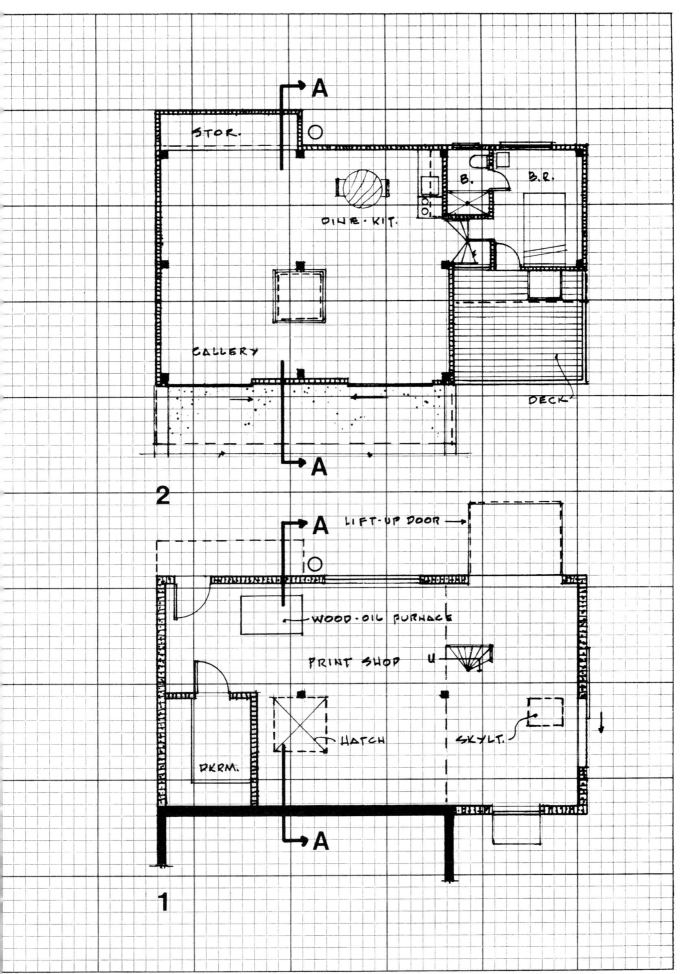

STOR.

A

B. B.R.

DINE · KIT.

GALLERY

DECK

A

2

A LIFT-UP DOOR →

WOOD · OIL FURNACE

PRINT SHOP U

HATCH SKYLT.

DKRM.

A

1

111

Southeast view of the studio. Much of the building is hidden by the bank.

had been set up with bars and other protective devices. The insurance company seemed to think that they were insuring a commercial building. Exits must be kept clear; doors must swing out. These people were too dumb to notice that the building is built into a hillside and opens to grade on both levels. There are several exits on each level. Of course, there was no building code, so the insurance guys felt free to make up their own on the spur of the moment. Don't think that just because you are out in the country where there is no code you are home free. I know of some people who bought a tract of land jointly for several families and then set money aside for investment to cover any fire losses. Sort of their own insurance company. If you are clever, you can get around any of these people, but it can take lots of time and effort. In Trish's case the easy solution was to dump the recalcitrant insurance company and reinsure with a more reasonable one.

Chapter 3

South-Facing
Hillside Houses

I find these houses the most exciting in the book. They absorb heat from the sun just by their mode of construction. They are ideal use for steep south-facing slopes which are usually passed over by developers and hence can usually be bought cheaply.

The earth remains at a constant temperature several feet down year-round—52°F. in most areas of this country. By taking advantage of this moderate temperature, we can achieve warmer winter temperatures and cooler summer ones with little or no expenditure of energy; the earth will do it for us. There does have to be some insulation, or the ground will act as a heat sink and will try to bring the inside of the house down to 52°F., a temperature most of us find uncomfortable. The easy way to take advantage of this principle is to find a steep south-facing slope and bury the north wall in the slope. In this way, the south elevation can absorb the sun's rays while the north face is protected against heat loss. The site should be terraced so that the east and west walls are substantially buried also. Unlike some of the other designs in this book, a long narrow house usually works best for this application. Basic construction costs do have to be increased to allow for masonry retaining walls, waterproofing, and drainage. However, with this type of construction you are increasing the masonry mass within the structure and providing an ideal place to store the sun's heat. Insulation installed on the outside of these walls makes them available for storage of heat or cold (depending upon the season). They will stabilize the inside temperatures, making the house warmer at night in winter and cooler in the daytime in summer.

This approach requires careful consideration of structure and waterproofing. The plans for the south-facing houses shown here have taken these matters into account.

113

Number 18: The Householder House

This was my first effort at post and beam construction. It is set on a dramatic south-facing hillside near Pittsburgh. In this case the site dictated the design solution. Because this lot was so steep and inaccessible, it had been passed over by many people. The Householders fell in love with the strangely shaped lot and came to me for advice. Would it be possible to build a house for a large family (four children) on this lot and still stay within both the setback lines and their budget? They were particularly concerned that the house would not disturb the natural beauty of their site. Naively I said it would be easy. Then came the fun. In order to get the required 2,000 square feet of space, it was necessary to bury one level of the house and step a second level up the hillside. A third level cantilevers out over the first level. Because the lot tapers as it goes up the hillside, the second level had to be shorter than the others.

The derivation of this design is of interest. I was confronted with a very tight budget of $12.50 per square foot which even 20 years ago was rock-bottom for a custom-built house. My first discussions with the contractor indicated that he could build a custom house for $18 per square foot *with basement*. I thought about this for awhile. Why not

View from the southeast shows how
house steps down the slope.

open the basement out to grade with a glass wall and make it part of the livingspace? It shouldn't cost too much more than an unfinished basement. When I got the lot survey and discovered how small the actual building area was, I modified the scheme to step up the hillside.

Master bedroom and covered balcony overhang front entrance to form carport. Entrance walk of dark slate is between cars.

Since the others in the office had warned direly of the consequences of using the basement as livingspace (damp, dark, cold, etc.) I took extra care in the detailing of the waterproofing. The floor slab and the foundation were poured in one integral unit so that the edge of the slab was flush with the wall to make the waterproofing absolutely foolproof. A good perimeter drain was installed with a coarse gravel used to fill in the excavation so that surface water would drain into the pipe instead of building up pressure against the wall of the house. Reinforcing rods were left sticking up out of the slab to tie the concrete-block wall to the slab. The cores of the block were then filled with concrete reinforced with more rods. This monolithic slab-footing combination actually costs less than separate footings, basement wall, and floor slab; since it is all poured in one operation, it also speeds construction.

Next, I turned my attention to the basic structure of the house. I had always been fascinated by post and beam framing, but I was told it was too expensive because of the expensive joinery requiring much hand labor. Also, mechanical work was expensive and difficult to conceal. Nina and Sam, the Householders, wanted to have a flat roof. While I am not fond of flat roofs, I decided to make this one interesting. I devised a simple system of using standard framing lumber to make up hollow beams, thus solving the cost and mechanical problems all at once. Low-cost, framing-grade lumber was used exposed wherever possible in the house. A coat of stain provided the finish. Sam and Nina were both concerned that the house be as maintenance-free as possible. With this in mind, we ordered cypress for the entire exterior. All exterior woodwork, including custom-made windows, were made of cypress, left to weather naturally. I designed a simple repetitive awning window which we had made up at the local millwork shop. I had intended them to be top-hinged with ordinary butt hinges, but when I got to the job after they were installed, Chuck Liston, the builder, had a surprise for me. He had found awning hardware which let the window drop down at the top as it was pushed out. This gives superior ventilation and the windows can be pushed far enough so that they can be washed from the inside.*

If the house was to be built for such a low cost, we had to do something about plumbing costs. I was still faced with fitting the piping into the post and beam frame. The solution was to place all of the plumbing around a common piping chase which adjoined the utility room. Costs were reduced dramatically, and we did not have to try to cut through any beams. Mr. Hibbs, one of the few good mechanical engineers in this world, rose to the challenge in fitting the boiler, water heater, pumps,

West side of house faces street. Wide overhang shuts out afternoon sun.

*The hinges are available from Blaine Hardware Company, Hagerstown, MD 21740. (This company also stocks hardware parts for virtually every door and window ever made.)

tanks, controls, etc. into a tiny 3 × 4-foot space. Years later I was told by a world-famous New York City mechanical consulting firm that this was "impossible." I have found that "the impossible" usually just takes skill and imagination.

The final bid for the house, complete with multizoned hot-water heat, plaster walls, four bedrooms, and 3½ baths was just $500 over the Householder's $25,000 budget. Quite a feat. I had worked very hard to convince the winning contractor that the system would save money. He believed me. The only other bid on the house was for $43,000. Not only

South face of house is virtually all glass. Bracing for wall is provided by solid wall area under kitchen windows.

that, the contractor made a nice profit on the house, primarily due to superior workmen. I visited the job at noon on a Wednesday to inspect the finished floor slabs. Chuck and a helper were just starting to build the frame. Sam, Nina, and I came back Saturday when we wouldn't disturb the work to discuss kitchen layout. To our amazement, we found the house under roof. Typical union carpenters would have barely gotten the first floor framed.

Construction sped along nicely, getting done in almost record time. The only real holdups were the plastering and kitchen cabinets. A local cabinetmaker constructed all of the cabinets of solid walnut—such craftsmanship takes time.

Now enters the villain of the piece; the *bank*. Money for construction was provided without a hitch by a local bank. Since Sam was an executive for the United Mineworkers' Hospital system, they didn't even ask to see the plans. The final mortgage was taken over by an insurance company from North Carolina. The inspector nearly had heart failure and wrote a scathing letter rejecting the house for a mortgage. It seems

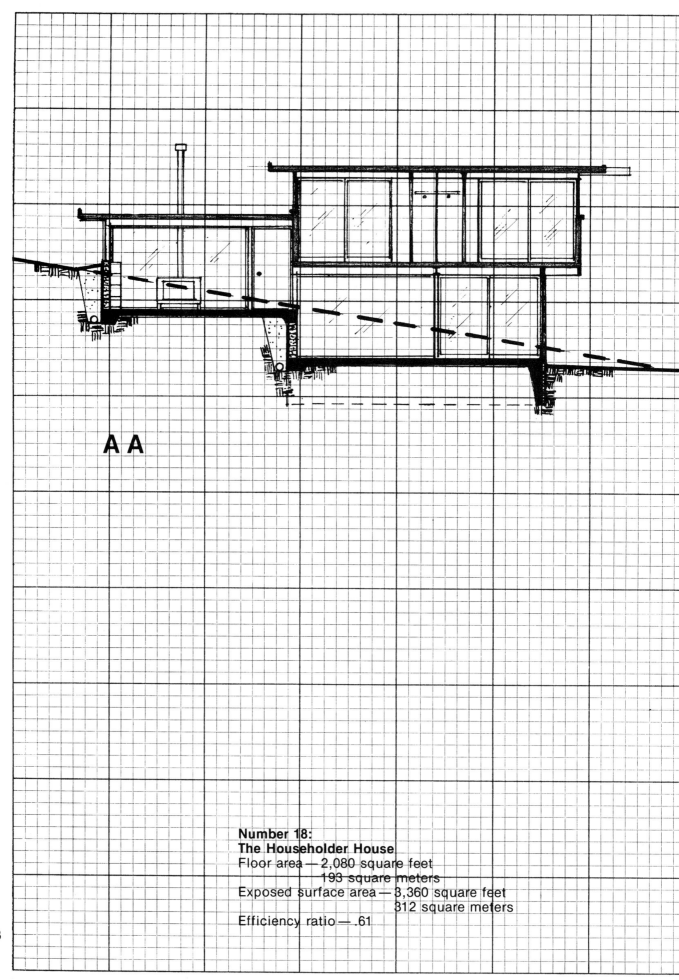

A A

Number 18:
The Householder House
Floor area — 2,080 square feet
193 square meters
Exposed surface area — 3,360 square feet
312 square meters
Efficiency ratio — .61

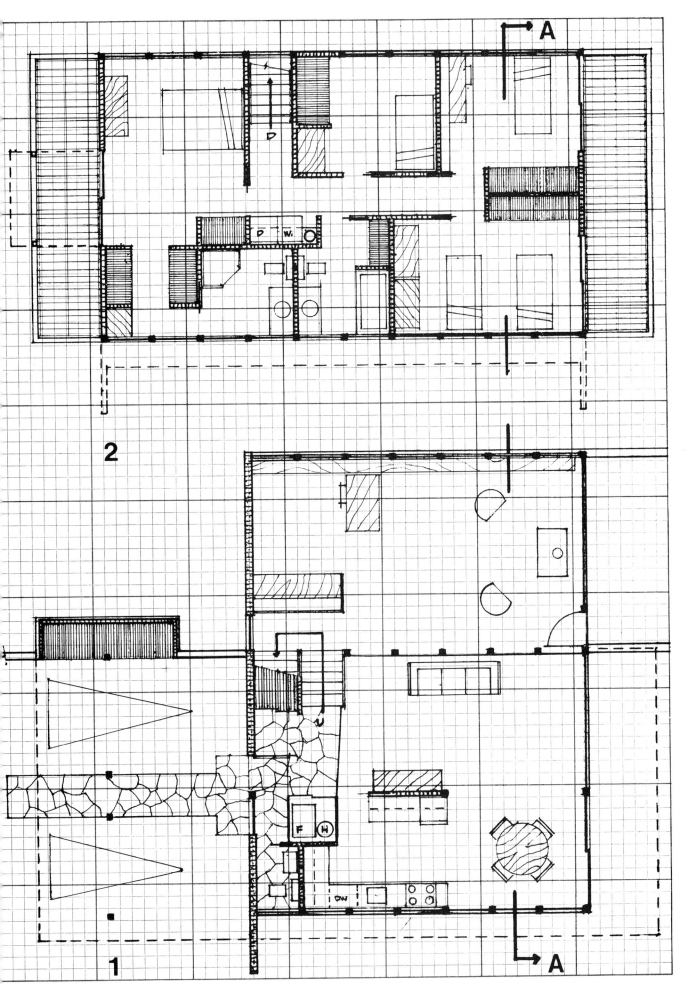

A

2

1

119

that the house was unfinished. We hadn't painted the cypress siding or the white plaster walls. Furthermore, there were no finished floors, just bare concrete. I wrote a much more scathing letter to the president of the insurance company suggesting that he hire competent inspectors. I enclosed copies of pertinent sections of the specifications showing that we had gotten what the contractor bid upon. We finally agreed to carpet the living room, and the insurance company grudgingly gave in and accepted the mortgage.

This house is extremely easy to heat and cool, somewhat to everyone's surprise since I did not intend it to have any special qualities. The flat roof is well insulated and holds great quantities of snow in the winter. We also made provisions to flood it in summer, but the house stays so cool that this hasn't been necessary. Since we couldn't afford insulating glass for the custom-sized windows, insulated drapes were made for all of the large glass areas. In the winter, sun streams through the south-facing glass areas and warms the interior masonry surfaces. At night this heat is radiated back to the inside of the house. In summer, overhangs and a large wisteria vine shades the full-length glass. Heating bills are still very low for the house, but the Householders are installing some solar collectors on the roof to provide hot water and thereby cut down on the gas usage.

How has the house held up after 20 years? Very, very well. There has been one roof leak. The kitchen range top was replaced; another cabinet was added. Original paint and stain are still very much intact. Most of the plaster walls have now been painted. The natural-colored pegboard storage walls are still there. A few of the cork tiles are coming up in the family room. No leaks through those underground walls. At least not yet.

Number 19: The Hess House

House Number 19 belongs to Terese Hess. Actually her husband Karl lives there too, but since Karl is a tax resister and can't legally own anything, it's Terese's house. The house is buried in a West Virginia hillside near Martinsburg. The trip to the Hess house brings back many memories. My very first project upon graduation from school was a control tower for the Air Force—at Martinsburg. One wrong turn on the way to the Hesses' had me at the air base staring at my control tower. Since our firm didn't have supervision of the construction phase, I had never seen the actual tower; but I did remember the design well. It was quite startling to have it appear on the horizon as a ghost from the past.

Karl said, "We bought your other book, but we violated everything in it." Not quite, but the house is exceptionally interesting for both its good and bad points. Actually, there is only one really serious mistake—no plans. The Hesses just designed it as they went along. Considering this, they have done a remarkable job. The house is big, too big. It wastes space. But since they built it themselves, they could afford to waste some space.

Large sliding-glass doors (bought at salvage) and a continuous clerestory made of Andersen basement vents comprise the south-facing glass area for this partially buried house. The clerestory lights the rear of the house.

From the north all that is visible is the top of the roof.

The only other quarrel which I have with the Hess house is the plumbing. Again, the lack of proper plans meant that there was uncertainty in the placement of underfloor drainage piping. Karl says, "We just put in a lot of drainage connections and figured we'd work out the fixture layout later." What this meant was a huge bathroom and a small kitchen to allow them to put the fixtures where the pipes were. Since the kitchen faces south, it should have been bigger and the bathroom should have been smaller.

Most of the major expenses for the Hesses were involved in site preparation and utilities. They had to build a road, set poles for a power line, drill a well, and install a septic system. The only code requirements were for the well and septic system which had to meet county health department requirements. Almost half of the $12,000 construction costs went for basic preparation before the house itself was even started.

The way the Hesses arrived at the large-size house may be instructive for others. They had decided to use post and beam construction set on a 10 × 10-foot grid. After the initial layout, Karl parked the truck in the middle of the excavation and Terese was immediately concerned that the house was much too small. So, they made it 10 feet longer. This concern about size is quite common. There is something very difficult to visualize about a stakeout for a house if it is set in an open field. Even when the house is in the rough framing stages, the views directly through the outside walls make the house itself seem much smaller than it actually is. I have had many arguments over the years with clients who insisted that the house "doesn't look nearly big enough." If you are in doubt, go look at a finished room which is the same size as the space which you contemplate. Remember that most of the designs in this book are arranged in such a way that spaces flow into one another, making them look much larger than they really are.

Another way in which the Hess house wastes space is by not using the upper areas of the house. They are just sweeping spaces up under the roof. Very dramatic, but not functional.

In order to save as much money as possible, Karl went shopping for salvage materials and items which were on sale. The front of the south-facing house is solid sliding glass doors which would have cost a bundle if bought at market price. The doors were made by a company no longer in business and the hardware packages had been lost, so they were for sale very cheap, less than half the cost of the glass alone. The Andersen basement vents were of a discontinued size and were on sale at auction at a trifle for the whole lot. Karl said, "I didn't have any idea where we would use them, but I figured we'd work them in somehow." They work in very nicely as a continuous strip of ventilation right at the ridge, or where the ridge would be if the windows weren't there. The corrugated aluminum roofing was dented, just one of the charming attributes of aluminum. Anyhow, corrugated aluminum is very easy for the beginner to install, it was quite cheap, and the dents hardly show.

Karl Hess—designer and builder; but not owner.

A large stack of 2 × 3-foot prefinished white Masonite panels bought at salvage suggested a novel ceiling treatment. Instead of just applying standard Sheetrock to the bottom of the joists, the Masonite is fitted up between the joists leaving about one inch of the bottom of the joist exposed. This makes it very easy for one person to do the installation work, and, since the Masonite is prefinished, there is no painting or spackling to do way up in the air. A very clever innovation on Karl's part.

The finished floor is just polished concrete with a few nice rugs. All of the concrete near the windows where the sun will strike it is left bare to absorb heat. One of the few difficulties which the Hesses had came with the finishing of the concrete. A power trowel was rented for the finish work. In order to get a really good finish on concrete, one of these is almost absolutely necessary. Anyhow, when they were finished using the beast (which looks like a giant fan with a gasoline motor atop it, somewhat like a three-foot-diameter power lawn mower with fan blades instead of cutter bars) the thing somehow restarted itself. The results were devastating. It started digging a hole in the new concrete slab. The upper part of the machine was spinning around dangerously. A not-too-bright carpenter threw a hammer at the whirling machine, which shat-

The heat from the sun warms the concrete floor on a cold winter day.

An excellent example of an unsafe stovepipe installation. Long horizontal runs of stovepipe can build up with very, very dangerous concentrations of creosote particularly with the "airtight" stoves currently in vogue. Even if they say they are going to take down and clean the pipes regularly, all people tend to forget or be a bit too lazy. It only takes one fire to lose a house.

tered the hammer. Finally Karl picked up a 6 × 6 and cold cocked the beast.

The other mishap occurred with the submersible pump. As with everything else, Karl and Terese installed it themselves. Somehow, the instructions were misplaced and the pump wiring was hooked up by guesswork, burning out the motor. It is one thing to burn out a motor sitting on top of the ground and quite another to burn out one which is 200 feet down a well. Actually, installing a submersible pump is quite easy and doesn't require much, if any, skill—just read the directions. This particular pump was a Sears and Roebuck product and they come with very clear directions for the do-it-yourselfer. Karl says they are now experts at taking the pump out and putting it back, so if it ever has difficulties again, they know just what to do. That is another nice aspect of doing things yourself. The Hesses now know exactly how the pump should be wired and they will not need to pay a plumber an exorbitant price should the pump ever need service.

Supplemental heating is provided by two woodstoves. The morning Neal and I visited was cold and sunny. It was just before noon; the

Although this picture was taken while the Hess house was still under construction, it gives one a good idea of the spaciousness of the downstairs. It was taken in the kitchen, looking toward the living area.

Number 19:
The Hess House
Floor area — 1,800 square feet
167 square meters
Exposed surface area — 2,950 square feet
277 square meters

Efficiency ratio — .61

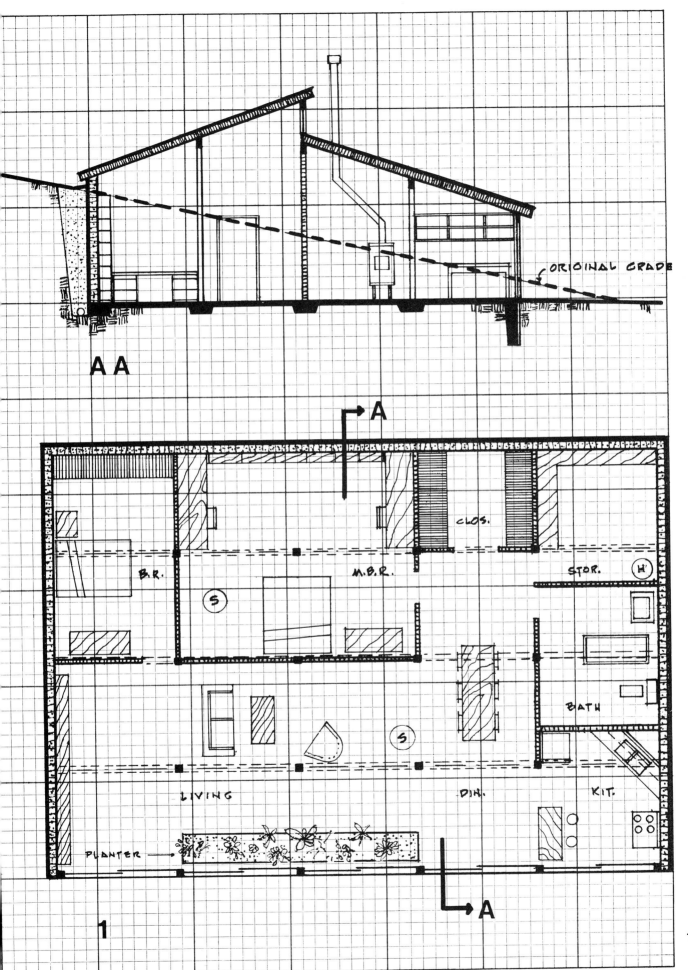

ORIGINAL GRADE

AA

A

CLOS.

B.R.   M.B.R.   STOR.   H

S

S

BATH

LIVING   DIN.   KIT.

PLANTER

A

1

stoves were cold and the house was warm. The stoves are old ones, not the least bit airtight. Karl installed long stovepipes to get the most heat out of the inefficient units. The sun was doing a fine job the morning we were there even though there were still gaps in the sidewalls where you could see right outside. Only a small portion of the roof had been insulated.

The house is designed so that the back wall is completely buried and the two end walls approximately half-buried. Karl worries that some night some drunk might drive right up onto their roof. If you look at the picture, this seems entirely possible.

Karl had quite a time with the plumbing. Despite the fact that he works with metals as a living (he's a welder), he "discovered" plastic piping. He has used it for both supply and waste systems. This is an ideal material for a beginner. You just cut the stuff to size, put glue on it, and push it together. Nothing to it, except if you make a mistake, you have to cut out the offending area and discard it. Also, many building codes prohibit the use of plastic piping for supply lines. This is because it is brittle and bursts easily, particularly in cold weather. Copper pipes will usually stand a light freeze while plastic pipes will freeze and burst totally and disasterously. If you use plastic, make sure it is easy to drain. If you are in a southern climate or are using plastic pipe in a summerhouse, I would have complete confidence in its ability to hold up.

All in all, this house is a masterpiece. When you consider that these people designed and built their own house completely from scratch, the feat is monumental. If the results had been just a mediocre house it wouldn't be too impressive. It makes one wonder a bit about those architects with years of training who are still out there designing sterile white glassy boxes.

Number 20: The Dowling — Miller House

This one is for Colette Dowling and Lowell Miller. They are both writers and require quiet and privacy; moreover, Colette has three teenage children. As soon as I started talking about compact and efficient houses, I started getting negative looks from Colette and Lowell. Colette said, "I couldn't stand a house like that; I have to be able to get away and concentrate." We talked a bit more. I suggested that building into a south-facing hillside was a good idea. Since property costs in our area are astronomical, I suggested that they try to find a steep south-facing slope which builders had passed up. Just maybe they could get it for very little money. Their budget for construction was very tight for the size house they wanted. As soon as I started talking about the advantages of building into a slope, Lowell brightened up. When he was in college he had built his own underground house. Of course he hadn't gotten a building permit (it wouldn't have been granted anyway). The "authorities" didn't discover this transgression until long after Lowell had moved. Lowell had built well. The roof was constructed of massive timbers with a ferrocement deck. The house was virtually indestructible as the town officials, who wanted to make sure that no one else ever

The extensive south-facing glass takes full advantage of the strongest rays of the sun. Note the double-decker children's rooms on the ground floor.

used the house, soon found. First, they tried smashing it with a bull-dozer. Nothing. Then they filled it full of debris and set it on fire. The massive green timbers and cement roof weren't about to burn. Finally, they gave up in disgust. One of those rare triumphs of good over fools.

I returned home to work on plans for a hillside house located on a hypothetical south-facing slope. Since privacy was a major factor for both Colette and Lowell, I divided the house into three zones. A parents' suite, a children's suite, and a common living area. In order to insure complete quiet, I put the adults' room off in a wing by itself with a bathroom and closets to separate it from the main living quarters. I also made sure to put in two doors between the spaces. Most people don't realize how much sound leaks through a thin residential door. The children's quarters were placed downstairs and are accessible through the front vestibule without entering the main part of the house. The children's suite consists of a large central room with a fireplace, three small separate rooms, and a bath. The three children's rooms are actually much larger than they appear on the plan. Since the hillside was to be very steep I stepped the children's rooms down so that they have 11-foot ceilings. This way, each room can have a sleeping loft. The children were not enchanted. "It's just like three identical cells" was a typical comment. Back to the drawing board. While keeping the same basic layout, each room was given its own identity. One room gets its own outside exit, the second gets a bay window, and the third an extra large loft and a special window in the loft.

Special attention was given to soundproofing the floor structure between the children's level and the main floor area above. An extra layer of insulation and a Sheetrock ceiling suspended on special acoustic slips were added to insure the least possible sound transmission. Stairways are very bad sound transmitters. This one is fully enclosed top and bottom. The stairway is also carpeted to further deaden the impact noise. Carpeting is usually waste of money. One exception is in halls, stairs, and general circulation spaces which open off of the center of a house. These spaces transmit sound very badly. Once I even carpeted a hall ceiling with some leftover carpet to cut down on sound transmission. The hall had a brick floor so we didn't want to cover that. Always buy undyed wool if you want a carpet to last forever.

After many months of hunting down south-facing slopes, a wonderful coincidence occurred. Howard and Kay Blume (see their house in chapter 11) received an unexpected gift when buying their old house. The previous owner had neglected to file proper documents to subdivide their house lot from the beautiful south-facing slope on the other side of the hill. But he had taken their money for the property. Legally, it was just his tough luck; his lawyer had goofed (mistakes by lawyers are frequent occurrences in my experience). Anyhow, the Blumes now own this beautiful site and are in the process of selling it to Colette and Lowell. Since it takes many months to subdivide property in New York, we are all sitting around staring at the model and concocting various schemes for actually getting to the house. Access is the one hitch. Other than that, the site is glorious—very secluded, with no visible neighbors, yet right in the middle of town with water, sewer, etc.

View from the east. The north wall is almost completely buried for two floors, leaving only a small strip of windows above grade.

A very steep road does lead up the cliff to the house site. Lowell figures that their four-wheel-drive Subaru will make it up easily; but what do they do about delivery trucks and guests with more plebian cars? Various schemes for putting in elaborate switchbacks (which would ruin much landscape) have been proposed. The electrician, an elevator mechanic back in the days before the Depression, has suggested a recycled freight elevator right up the side of the cliff. You park at the bottom and ride up the elevator. The kids will love it. The solution which is probably the most likely is something of a combination of the other suggestions. It is called an incline. Used rails would be set in the driveway and a motorized cable device used to pull the car or truck up the driveway. This would obviously be prohibitively expensive if bought new, but I have a former client who had stored all the necessary materials for a project which he never executed.

Colette and Lowell are both the type who like to work with their hands and get involved. However, they are very busy earning their living writing. Unlike an eight-to-five job, this can take every spare minute. Even so, they both plan to work on selected parts of the house. Colette shares my affection for standing-seam roofs and plans to do her own roof. Lowell loves masonry work. Since the retaining walls are a part of the main shell, it would hold up the contractor if he did that part of the work. Instead, he is going to build the chimney. Lots of hard work, but that way he can get a good Rumsford fireplace which produces heat efficiently, without endless fights with an unwilling mason.

The heating system for this house is basically wood. The Rumsford-type fireplace is located in the basement. On the first floor, we are planning to put a Defiant woodstove in the main living area. One main reason for selecting the Defiant is that the family all likes to have an open fire. The doors on the Defiant open so it can be used as an efficient airtight stove during the daytime and opened up into a cheery open fire in the evening. Closed again, it will provide heat through the night. An 80-gallon, gas hot-water heater is connected to a small loop of baseboard radiation which warms the two bathrooms and the remote master bedroom. Lowell plans to build some solar collectors on the roof which will eventually be connected to the water heater to cut the gas consumption.

Rising costs precluded the use of a standard brick chimney. The contractor, Charles Sims, devised a very novel concrete chimney. He is also a sculptor who works in concrete. The chimney is simple and economical. Standard 8-inch diameter stovepipe is used as a core for the chimney. Fiberboard forms 18 inches in diameter, which are normally used to cast concrete columns for large buildings, were tied in place to make a form for the outside of the two chimneys. Then concrete was poured between the steel liner and the fiberboard form. The results are a sturdy, permanent masonry chimney for about the same cost as the awful, flimsy prefabricated metal jobs.

The last feature of this house is highly unusual, Colette and Lowell need to have entirely private office spaces where they can get away to write. They both plan to build little studio spaces eight foot square with a desk

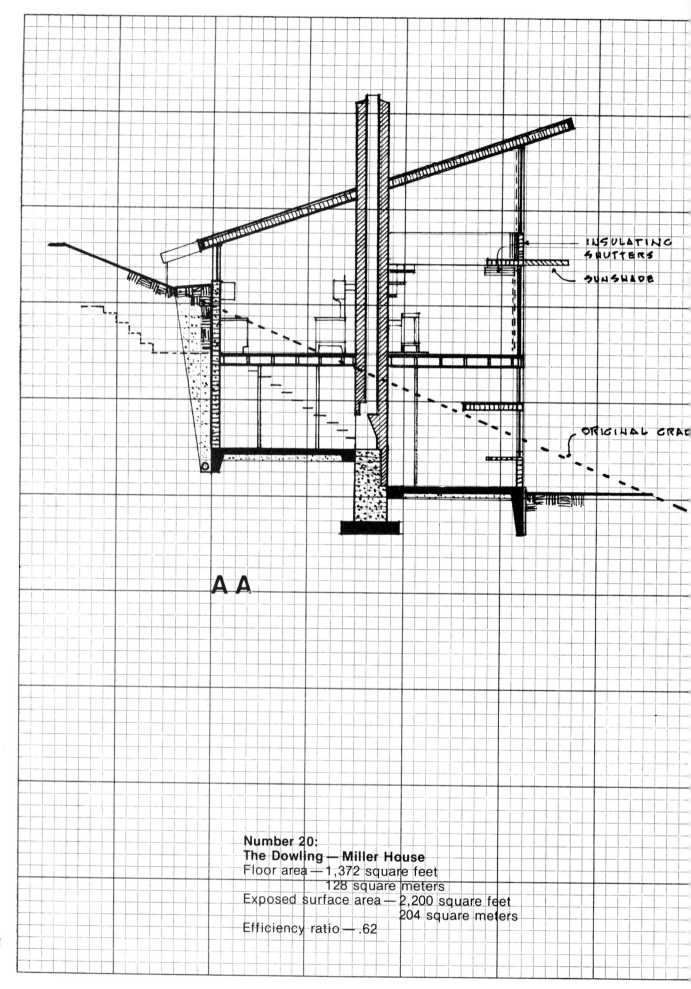

INSULATING
SHUTTERS

SUNSHADE

ORIGINAL GRAD

A A

Number 20:
The Dowling — Miller House
Floor area — 1,372 square feet
128 square meters
Exposed surface area — 2,200 square feet
204 square meters
Efficiency ratio — .62

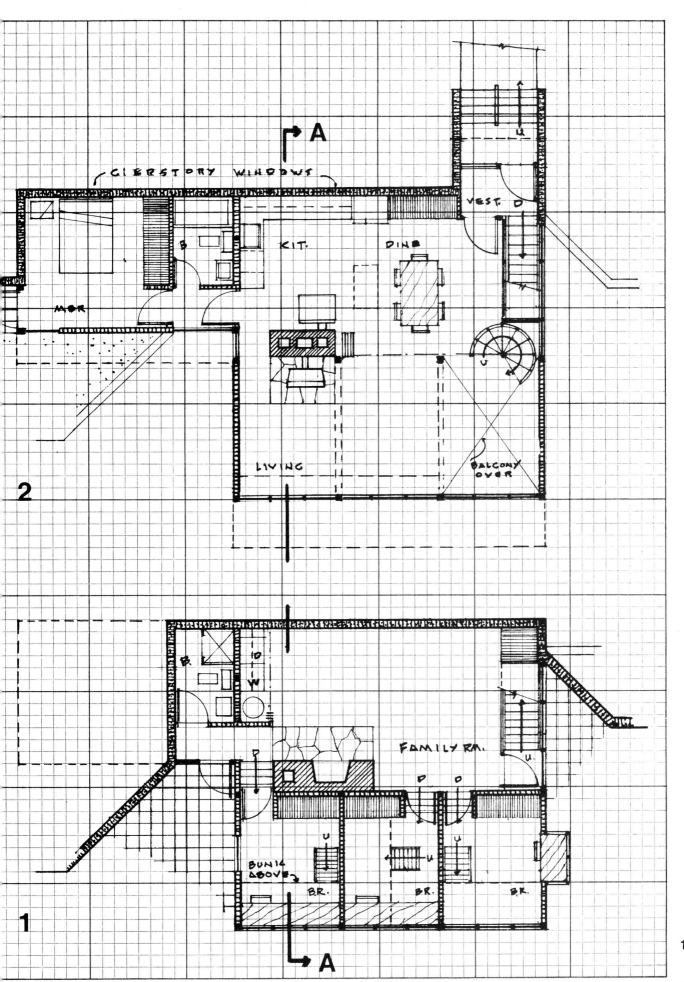

CLERSTORY WINDOWS

A

MBR

KIT.

DINE

VEST. D

B

LIVING

BALCONY OVER

2

FAMILY RM.

BUNK ABOVE

BR.

BR.

BR.

1

A

and a loft bed above set off in the woods well away from the main house. In this way, they can double as guest houses. Heat will be supplied by a small galley stove. Electricity will be run over from the main house. They plan to build one of these right away so that they can have a place to stay to work on their main house.

Number 21: The Sturgis House

This house belongs to a rugged individualist and inventor, Paul Sturgis. Paul's house uses solar energy in a bit different way—as wood heat. These days, wood heat is not the least bit unusual, and even efficient Scandinavian stoves are becoming commonplace. In the case of Paul's house, the wood heat *is* different. Very different. Paul is an engineer who has spent his life developing unusual solutions to heating and cooling problems and in this case, he has developed a method that extracts virtually all the usable heat out of the wood, thereby using very little wood. He does this with a fireplace which has a glass front so that the fire can be enjoyed. The system employs some very tricky engineering so that the wood is burned at extremely high temperatures. It is almost completely consumed and leaves little ash or creosote deposits.

Paul starts a very hot fire and gets a good draft going, then closes a bypass damper which reroutes the heat-laden exhaust downward through a multi-tube heat exchanger. The heat exchanger transfers the heat to the room air and then the exhaust is ducted back into the chimney. This is an efficient heating device, unlike the many rudimentary flue heat exchangers on the market which, when used with inefficient heating devices, clog with creosote, rendering them useless.

The house is designed to store heat, and one or two fires will heat the house on a moderate winter day with some temperature variation: Paul builds several small fires and lets them die out rather than keeping one going all of the time.

I find a few objections to this system. First, it may be inconvenient to build several small fires and a backup system may use considerable quantities of fuel. This would be particularly true if both members of the family worked all day and got home late in the evening. The second worry I have is the effect of all that intense heat on the system. In fact, Paul's firebox got so hot during his first experiment that he set the wall behind it on fire. Increasing the firebox by four inches of masonry corrected the problem (the mason had skimped on the back wall and no one had caught the error). The high heat burns up all of the corrosive gasses usually associated with wood burning, but I still would worry about deterioration of the metalwork after a few years. The exchanger itself is quite heavily constructed; the diagram shows how it would work if installed in a house with a basement.

House perches on a solid rock ledge which makes a conventional septic system impossible.

As a piece of architecture, the house works nicely. It is built on a very solid ledge of rock next to a small stream. Its configuration is that of a steep-roofed chalet with a large dormer facing south onto a streamside deck. The solid rock makes an alternative sewage disposal system mandatory. In this case, the first floor is built around a Clivus Multrum. Greywater is pumped upstream to a small grove of trees. The Clivus fits neatly under the stairs to the second floor and provides a division between the living room and the kitchen-dining area.

Of course, the Clivus is illegal in New York (isn't everything) but Paul is one of those rare people who had the guts to go ahead and do things the proper way regardless of mindless bureaucrats. In this case, he just went ahead and installed his system and dared them to do anything about it. Since they have to have a formal complaint from a neighbor and there are none, Paul succeeded in getting his Clivus.

The house was actually designed and constructed by Paul's wife, Magdalena, with the help of Gordon Perry. The entire structure is built of roughsawn native pine—floors, walls, ceilings, and siding. It sounds overdone, but somehow is just warm and cozy. It is helped by soft indirect fluorescent lighting of Magdalena's own design throughout.

Fireplace with heat exchanger provides great quantities of heat; too much in fact.

A cedar-shake roof tops off the natural wood motif. The north and west walls are windowless while the south-facing dormer is heavily glazed to let in the sun. The combined effects of all the wood and the south-facing glass is to have an interior with too much contrast between the wall of glass and the rest of the house. Skylights on the north wall or some other means of distributing the light evenly are needed.

The house does stay warm, though. The entire frame is wrapped with Styrofoam on the inside of the studs, completely preventing any heat conduction to the outside. The tenant kept a log of indoor and outdoor temperatures for awhile. Typical entries:

January 8

6 A.M. outside	-8°F.	10 A.M. outside	4°F.
inside	72°F.	inside	78°F.

Paul is an avid advocate of wood heat and his "Thriftcharger" heat exchangers. He also makes smaller models which can be attached to woodstoves and furnace flues. His address is Box 42, Stone Ridge, NY 12484.

Kitchen faces deck overlooking stream. Clivus is at right behind the fluorescent light.

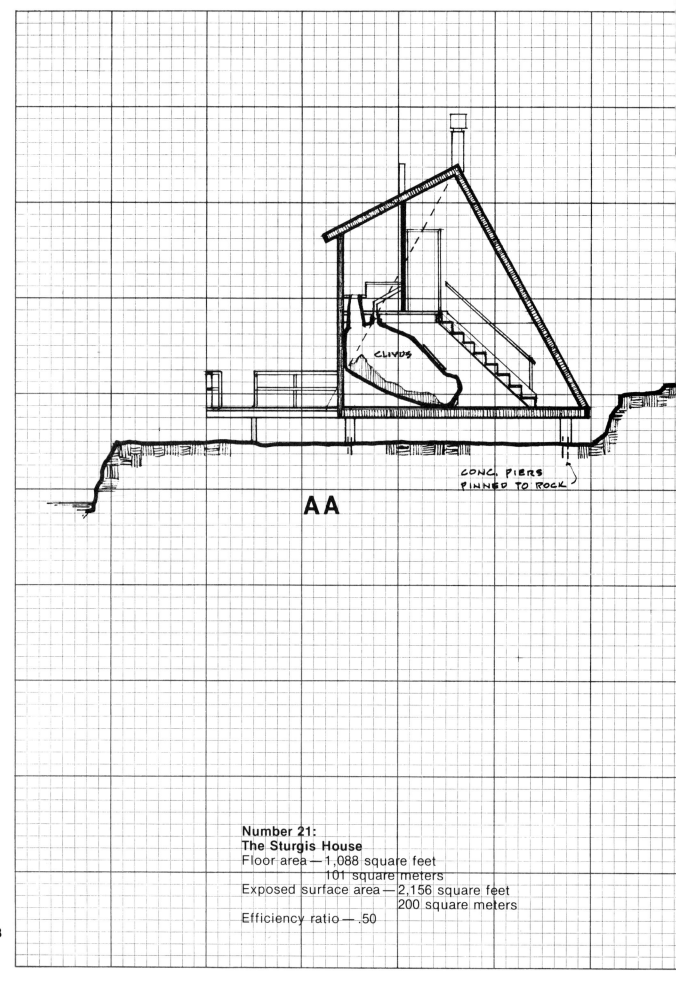

CLIVUS

CONC. PIERS
PINNED TO ROCK

AA

Number 21:
The Sturgis House
Floor area—1,088 square feet
101 square meters
Exposed surface area—2,156 square feet
200 square meters
Efficiency ratio—.50

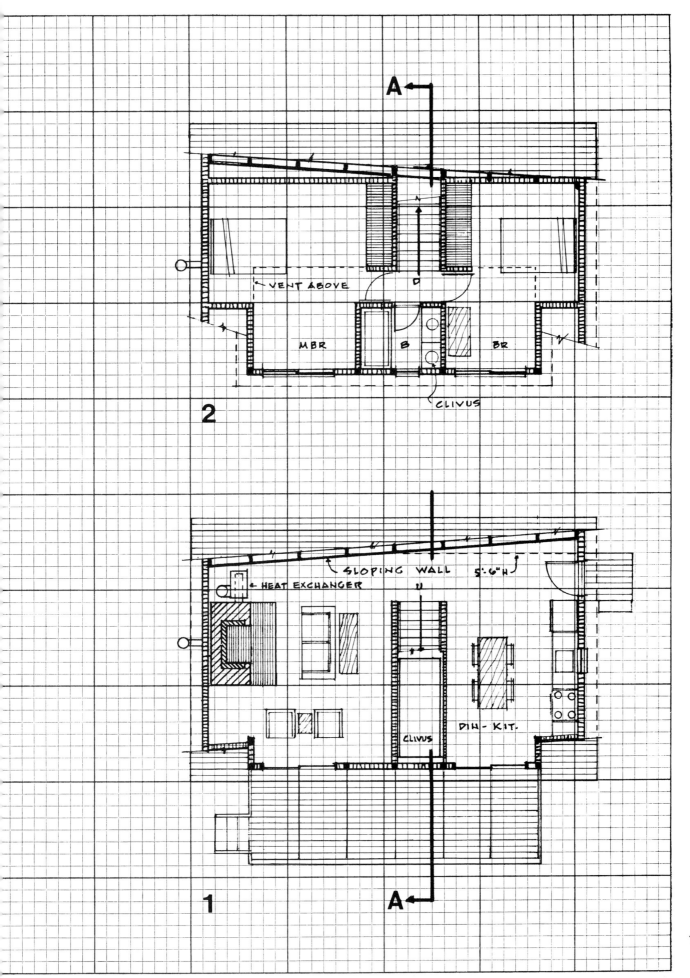

2 VENT ABOVE · MBR · B · BR · CLIVUS

1 SLOPING WALL 5'-6"H · HEAT EXCHANGER · CLIVUS · DIN- KIT.

A

A

Number 22: The Replogle House

This house is for Eric Replogle. Anyone for an almost free house? Eric came tramping through snowdrifts to knock on my door one day last winter. He had put in 20 years working in the city and was now eligible for a small pension and wanted to get away from it all and try something new. He bought a landlocked piece of property as remote as possible from civilization—or as remote as one can get here in the Northeast. Since there is no legal access, the property was quite cheap, but this also means no electricity, at least not from the power company. Fortunately, one of the neighbors is doing some extensive logging on his property, and in return for some help from Eric, he has agreed to let him have access so that he can get some logs out and materials in. Since Eric spent all of his savings on the property, he is trading work to build his house, and everything possible is being used from his land.

Eric had studied many books on low-cost construction before he visited me. We sat down and looked at all of my smallest designs with the idea of building something for virtually nothing. He picked a small house which I had originally designed as a portable, trailer-type structure. Eric said, "There's a nice old stone foundation out on the property which that'll fit right into. Cover it with a sod roof and no one will know I'm there." Since everything he's doing is rather illegal, it is important not to be too visible.

We visited the site and indeed there was a nice foundation. Unfortunately, it was in poor shape and would have to be rebuilt. Since insulation is very important for an underground house, it was good that the walls needed to be rebuilt. Otherwise, the site was perfect. It faced south and was cut into the hillside with the south wall of the foundation completely exposed and the north wall completely buried. It was just over a knoll so that there was no extensive area of surface runoff to cause leakage problems.

Old stone foundation half-buried in the hillside forms the beginning for this house.

Another glorious find: On our way back we stumbled onto the ruins of an old springhouse, well uphill from the house site. A trench and a bit of pipe will provide the house with running water, virtually free.

The old-timers really knew how to site houses, and this one is a beauty. Eric located it by getting loads of U.S. Geological Survey maps and pouring over them until he found an indication of an abandoned house which did not connect to any roads for miles around. Then he went for a long hike.

Eric has marked many trees for cutting. Some will be used for his own house, and others will be used to pay for absolutely essential materials which must be paid for with cash. He has gotten a bid for $600 from a sawmill for his trees.

While the ground was frozen this past winter, but before the snows got too deep, Eric loaded up materials on a sled and dragged in two large loads of them. Enough, he hopes, to build his house. Materials were scavenged or bought for next to nothing. I know of a place across the river from Manhattan where polyurethane insulation is dumped and then destroyed with a bulldozer. These are batches which don't meet specifications or are chipped or broken. Eric went down on a weekend and came back with a truckload saved from the dozer. A friend knew of a surplus house which had a large stock of insulated glass panes 22¼ inches square at $2 apiece. Eric bought 20. Local dumps were scrounged for plumbing fixtures, hardware, doors, windows, and anything else which might be useful. A real find at the dump a Servel refrigerator—in working order, or almost. It had to be recharged and have a small leak fixed. Repair bill: $35.

As a final stroke of luck a contractor friend asked me if I might know anyone who wanted to buy a large number of three-inch-thick oak scaffold planks. Eric offered him $100 and he took it in a hurry. I have the lingering suspicion that the planks had been removed from a job where the contractor was working, but Eric now has a deck to hold up that heavy sod roof.

Thus far, Eric has spent $437.63, much of that for gas and incidentals. Major expenses have been for sand, mortar, a large sheet of 20-mil plastic sheeting to cover the roof boards before placing the sod roof, and piping to build a rudimentary plumbing system. Oh, yes—he spent $25 on a kit for converting a 55-gallon drum into a stove and another $30 on a stovepipe oven. His floor will be of brick, recycled from the old chimney which had fallen down. Eric figures that there is enough stone leftover to build a chimney.

This house will be almost totally self-sufficient with minor exceptions. Eric will need bottled gas for use in summer for cooking and for the refrigerator. Eric found a gas range with a broken oven door at the dump

From the north, only the sod roof and steps leading down to the front door are visible.

and since he has the stovepipe oven, he will use the gas oven for storage. A small, 10-gallon industrial tank has had pipe fittings welded to it for use as a hot-water storage tank. A coil of copper pipe placed in the stovepipe will furnish the source of heat. In the summer, an old gas burner from a stove will be placed under the tank to heat it directly. One gaslight fixture is also to be connected to the propane system. The propane is stored in four 20-pound tanks which are light enough to be carried in by hand. There is enough wood on the property to keep Eric going for the next few centuries.

The sod roof is another quite unique feature of this house. Massive timbers with the aforementioned oak planks form the roof deck which has a rather gentle slope of $3/12$. Twenty-mil plastic sheeting has been placed over the planks. The sod itself is set in two layers; the first one with the grassy side facing the plastic, and the second one with the grass facing up. Eric is planning to use sod dug right from his land with an added sprinkling of a few very tough, hardy grasses, when he is finished.

Eric has a small travel trailer which he plans to use as livingspace until the house is finished. One sees articles about this sort of low-budget house occasionally. Frequently, they are not much more than upgraded shacks. In this case, the owner is a master craftsman and the results should be a fine, well-built house for very little money. My only real reservation about this particular house is waterproofing. Since the base of the foundation is in quite good shape and there is no sign of any

moisture penetration through the wall, Eric is just going to dig out the top part which has to be rebuilt anyway and put urethane insulation on the outside, and refill the dirt. I did suggest that he put a perforated drain on the inside of the wall to drain away any water just in case there is a spring flood.

This type of house is a very ecological solution for any south-facing site. It is possible to adapt many conventional plans, but the houses will work better if they are specifically designed for the site. For an example of this type of adaptation, see House Number 5. Also in chapter 12, I have included a set of plans for a hillside variation of my basic saltbox, similar to House Number 3.

The roof slopes up to the south, providing lofts and admitting sun.

Cliff Dwellers at Mesa Verda

Into the cracks in the table land
They tucked their pueblos, small adjustments
In the cliffline, nests of clay and stick.
Below the scorched mesa, embracing
The sandstone damp with sea memory,
They scooped out their cool cells for the drape
Of loosened limb, for the shape of love

They sketched their rooms in free hand: floors lift
Like strata, walls surprise like outcrops,
Bricks touch like spilled rocks that drifted
Into status, Here they hardly dreamed
Nightmares of the right angle, or schemed
The tautest distance between two points
Or heard the pressures of perfect cubes.

Walter James Miller from his book
Making an Angel (New York:
Pylon Press)

Number 22:
The Replogle House
Floor area — 580 square feet
                    54 square meters
Exposed surface area — 1,040 square feet
                    97 square meters
Efficiency ratio — .55

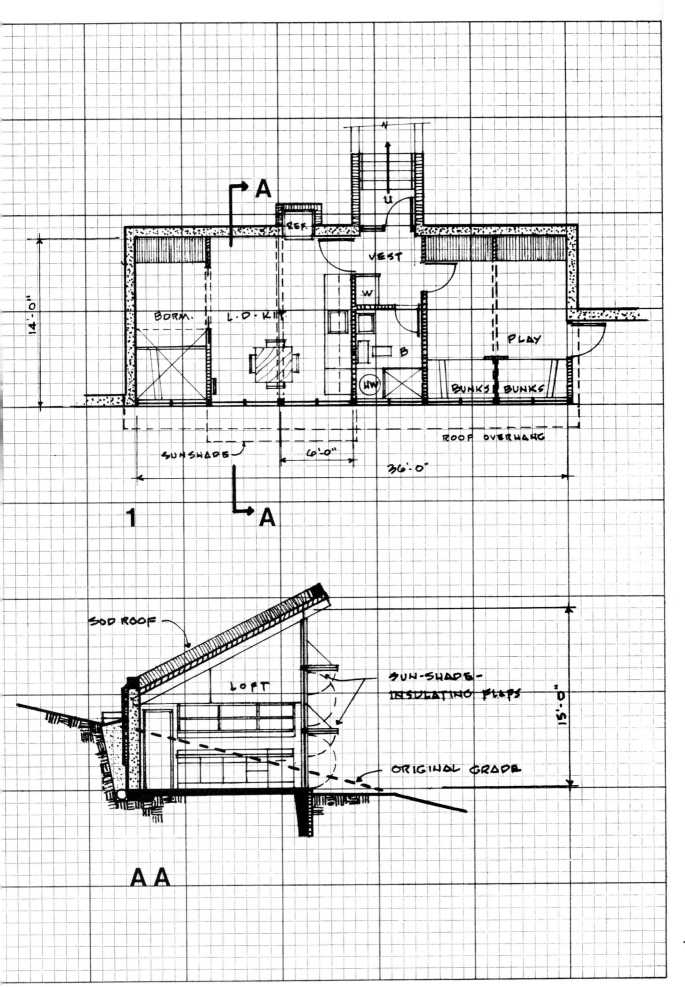

A

REF

VEST

W

B

HW

BDRM.

L·D·KIT.

PLAY

BUNKS BUNKS

N

U

SUNSHADE

6'-0"

36'-0"

ROOF OVERHANG

14'-0"

1

A

A

SOD ROOF

LOFT

SUN-SHADE-INSULATING FLAPS

ORIGINAL GRADE

15'-0"

AA

145

Chapter 4

Underground and Passive Solar-Tempered Houses

License plate on the car owned by David and Barbara Wright (House Number 25).

In this chapter I extend the principles which were presented in the last chapter. Most of the south-facing houses in that chapter had a conventional heating system which was considered as the principle source of heat. The houses were designed in such a way as to minimize the heat required from the conventional heat source. These houses, in contrast, are designed with heavier insulation, extra means of storing heat, and finally, devices such as insulating shutters for keeping the heat contained within the structure. This type of solar heating system is known as a "passive system." In these houses, we usually have a woodstove, heat-circulating fireplace, or other simple means for supplying backup heat.

Architect Malcom Wells has gained prominence by extending the principles of a south-facing, passive building to their logical conclusion. He buries the entire building. Natural lighting and ventilation are provided by means of light shafts and south-facing sunken courtyards. This is an excellent technique for using otherwise worthless property. Yes, the construction costs are more than for conventional construction, but it is possible to offset much of the difference using low-cost land. The completely underground house has the additional virtue of avoiding building code setback requirements. Usually these requirements are based upon the extent of the building *above ground*. Since your whole building will be below ground, you can frequently make use of an otherwise unsaleable lot. *Caution*: some codes prohibit living in a basement and the building inspector may decide that you can't live in your house. Check it out before starting.

If you do want to do an entirely buried house, I recommend consulting Mr. Wells directly. You will probably find him picking wild flowers on the roof of his office in Cherry Hill, New Jersey.

I do not mean to discourage the use of "active" solar heating. In fact, the solar hot-water heaters which I recommend in chapter 8 are very much active systems. They are just very much smaller than the systems needed to heat a whole house. At the moment, fully manufactured active systems designed and installed by engineers are out of reach for all but the very well-to-do. Most of the solar collectors are still quite expensive because they are largely handmade. As the market expands, competition and mass production should bring reductions in prices. In the meantime, many, many average citizens with no special training are going ahead and building their own systems. I feel, however, that you will get the most return for your time and money by designing the whole building itself as a solar collection system instead of adding expensive, maintenance-prone hardware to a conventional house.

Rapidly escalating heating costs are finally beginning to focus major attention upon systems that use energy from the sun. The best book out for the nontechnically informed layman is by The Department of Housing and Urban Development. It is called *Solar Dwelling Design Concepts.* * The overall explanation is well presented and the examples of work already done are well chosen, but the proposals for new houses are, with the exception of some nice designs by Total Environmental Action, awful. They are either schoolboy copies of traditional styles or slick, "modern" boxes. However, for a rather complete overview at rock-bottom prices, it is unbeatable.

My second recommendation is of a very different nature. It is entitled *Solar Heated Buildings, A Brief Survey* by W. A. Shurcliff. † The book is an exhaustive survey of several hundred solar-heated buildings. Buildings are usually explained in one or two pages of highly technical description. This book gives a rather complete idea of everything which has been done in solar-heated buildings to date. The variety of systems presented is mind-boggling. (Note that most of the older water-borne systems have notes such as "Collectors abandoned (replaced) due to deterioration after x years.")

The third book is *The Solar Home Book* (1976) by Bruce Anderson of Total Environmental Action.** Bruce has long been a very vocal advocate of passive solar systems, particularly of designing buildings so that they don't require so much heat. TEA also gives a series of weekend seminars on alternative energy for people who want to design and build their own systems.

There are three excellent periodicals in the alternative energy field. The first is *Solar Age,* a monthly by Solar Vision, Inc.†† It is quite good, but at $24 a year it should be. *Rain, Journal of Appropriate Technology* is an access and reference journal for resource-saving techniques. Many of

Professor E. S. Morse of the Essex Institute has devised an ingenious arrangement for utilizing the sun's rays in warming our houses; it consists of a surface of blackened slate under glass fixed to the sunny side of a house. The thing is so simple and apparently self-evident that one only wonders that it has not always been in use.

Scientific American, *May 13, 1882*

---

*Available for only $2.30 (at the time of this writing) from the U.S. Government Printing Office, Washington, DC 20402 (Stock No. 023-000-00334-1).

† Available from 19 Appleton Street, Cambridge, MA 02138.

**Cheshire Books, Church Hill, Harrisville, NH 03450.

††Route 515, Box 288, Vernon, NJ 07462.

One of the problems with solar energy is that it has been assumed that solar systems must be designed to be just as reliable and responsive as traditional energy sources. This adds large storage costs for solar systems. A modest life-style change to adapt human activities to solar availability would make some of this extra cost unnecessary. If families were willing to throw on extra blankets and not do the laundry on cold, cloudy days, far less expensive energy storage would be necessary and solar systems would be cheaper. In the case of electricity, it should not be impossible for a society to use less electricity on cloudy days.

Many persons perceive solar energy as ethically preferred to other energy sources. For this reason, they are willing to pay more and/or tolerate lower performance. This concern might be based on environmental concerns or on an interest in preserving fossil resources for the future.

Solar Energy in America's Future, A Preliminary Assessment, Stanford Research Institute for ERDA

my best sources of information have come from this magazine.* The third magazine is the old standby, *Alternative Sources of Energy.* †

Passive solar-tempered houses can avoid all or most of the expensive, complicated gadgetry of the active systems. However, they usually require "active" participation by the occupants if the gadgetry is to be eliminated. It is, of course, possible to design motorized moveable shutters which close automatically when there is no sun. Economically, manpower is much more desirable. Finally, I favor passive systems because I feel it is healthier for people to relate directly to their environment rather than having a set of automatic controls do their thinking for them.

These houses present a wide variety of methods of storing some of the sun's heat which penetrates to their interiors. The most common device is the solar greenhouse. It allows you to store large quantities of heat from the sun and transfer it to the house as necessary. Similarly, south-facing skylights will admit considerable amounts of solar heat. Both have to be separated from the livingspace at night by insulated panels or the heat loss will equal or exceed the heat gain. Ron Alward explains the principles of solar greenhouses more completely in chapter 17 of *Low-Cost, Energy-Efficient Shelter*. The size of the greenhouse which he presents is better suited to a large, older house than a small, energy-efficient one. Study the details in my chapter here for construction better suited to small houses.**

One of the great myths which has been deliberately circulated by the oil companies is that you have to have an expensive, automatic fossil-fuel heating system to back up any of the solar systems when a long period of cloudy, cold weather renders them ineffective. If you have built an efficient, well-insulated house, this is nonsense. Many alternatives exist, ranging from wood-coal stoves to a few electric heaters. See chapter 9 for detailed information on a wide variety of alternate backup systems which won't cost you a small fortune.

Most people still think that using the sun for heating is a very complex operation. All sorts of get-rich-quick schemers have hopped on the solar bandwagon to try to sell various badly designed solar collectors and various exotic accessories such as quadruple glazing. In fact, one such charlatan recently told one of my clients it is impossible to heat with solar energy unless you use quadruple glazing on all the windows. As an industry, the manufacturers of solar components are remarkably consciencious, at least so far. But watch out as big companies move into the field. Big companies are notorious for hiring pushy salesmen.

---

*Ten issues cost $10, and can be ordered from: *Rain*, 2270 N.W. Irving, Portland, OR 97210.

† Route 2, Milaca, MN 56353. The present subscription rate is six issues for $10.

**For more information on solar greenhouses, read Tom Lawland's *The Development and Testing of an Environmentally Designed Greenhouse for Colder Regions* (from Brace Research Institute, McGill University, Quebec, Canada; $1.25), or *An Attached Solar Greenhouse* by Bill Yanda (The Lightning Tree, PO Box 1837, Santa Fe. NM 87501; $2).

Even now, in some areas fast-talking salesmen of the type associated with used cars and real estate have moved in to try to convince people that they can work miracles just by installing a high-priced set of solar collectors on their house. Miracles just aren't there; it takes total planning of the house from the ground up, and then some.

This house is built on an island in Canada. Gregg Allan, a Canadian architect, has designed an interlocking series of passive solar techniques and backup heating systems that form a showcase for ecologically conscious solar design. Gregg believes that we should choose materials with great care so as not to use those which require great amounts of energy to produce. It is quite possible for a solar house to be an energy loss, not an energy gain to society.

Number 23: The Seaman House

Solar greenhouse extends across the entire south face of the house. Reflective foil-lined drapes close off the living area from the greenhouse at night. Similar drapes pull over the sloping glass roof. The pipe at bottom center is the air intake for the fireplace, vital for any fireplace to work well.

The solid metal roof faces north. The entrance is off center under the carport. Note the storage shed at the right.

To give you an example of what I mean, a local architect who was interviewed recently in our Sunday paper was bragging about his huge, gadget-laden $190,000 solar house. He claims to be able to save about $600 per year on his heating bills. Obviously, it will take a few centuries for that house to make a net saving. By contrast, Gregg has constructed an amazingly sophisticated house for $25,000.

The house is in an extremely severe northern climate, so Gregg did provide a water-borne storage system (2,000 gallons) connected to both a system of coils buried in the dark concrete floor and a heat exchanger located in the wood-burning fireplace-stove. The sun shines through the south-facing glass of the solar greenhouse and heats the water in the floor piping. Excess heat is stored in the aforementioned tank.

The fireplace-stove is located in the center of the house in a very massive stone chimney which in itself is another area in which heat can be stored. Note that I make a distinction here. While this unit looks somewhat like a fireplace, it has tempered glass on both faces and a controlled outside air intake. Finally, the roof contains specially placed skylights which allow the sun to warm the rear wall of the house which is masonry dug into the slope of the hill. All of these heat-storage methods plus very heavy insulation add up to a house which can maintain comfortable temperatures for three overcast days. The house is capable of keeping the temperature above freezing for over a week without any auxilliary heat source.

Gregg has given special attention to insulation on this house. The floor is insulated with 4 inches of urethane insulation which runs 8 feet deep to insure that every bit of heat trapped by the floor is saved. Part of the wall insulation consists of hay bales. These are very inexpensive and actually are very good insulators—an 18-inch hay bale is equivalent to 12 inches of fiberglass insulation. In this case, the hay is enclosed in a vapor barrier and then encased in metal lath and cement plaster. It's a nice idea, but I feel that the net result is that it costs more than conventional insulation. It is beautifully integrated with the design, and the massive walls are quite handsome. For the rest of the house, he uses 6-inch studs and conventional fiberglass insulation.

The water supply/waste system is equally unique. The house has no well or outside water source other than rainwater. It is designed so that

Two-foot-thick walls insulated with hay bales are in foreground. At upper left, are foil-lined light shafts which allow sunlight to brilliantly illuminate the north rooms of this house. Even late in the afternoon on a gloomy winter day these light shafts worked well.

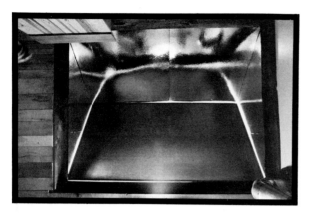

Light shaft with insulating baffle in closed position.

Light shaft with insulating baffle in open position.

it can recycle its water. The greywater from the house is run through a charcoal filter and then put through a solar still in the greenhouse to produce fresh water for the house. Human wastes are handled by a built-in-place composting toilet similar to a Clivus Multrum. People in areas of little water should take a good look at this system. So should some repressive health authorities.

Gregg is a member of that rare breed of architects who actually build the houses which they design. Until recent times, this was the way architecture was practiced. The architect was commissioned to build a building. This included everything: design, construction, and supervision. All of the major cathedrals in the world were built this way. But due to pressures from building trade unions and the American Institute of Architects, this is almost never done in this country. In many states architects can have their licenses revoked for building the house they designed.

Such an attitude is unfortunate because this integrated type of practice gives the architect more chances to experiment with new ideas. If he is doing something different which requires special care or very unusual techniques, he can personally execute the work himself to make sure that it is correctly done. Also, if it doesn't work, he knows exactly what was done, and there isn't the usual buck-passing between the various building trades. It is particularly beneficial in developing new and creative methods of capturing heat from the sun, because the architect can make sure that everything is done exactly as it is supposed to be. For instance, let's say that a contractor built Gregg's house and cheated on the foundation insulation. When the floor didn't store as much heat as it was supposed to, he could say, "See, the architect didn't know what he was talking about."

Construction of the house was a joint effort by the owners and the architect. Gregg and his wife worked with Mrs. Seaman and her daughter to build the house. They were very lucky in getting an architecture student on a work-study program to come for the year to help with the construction. I can't imagine a more useful way for an architectural student to spend a semester than studying with Gregg Allan.

Even though it had been cloudy for several days the house was reasonably warm when we arrived one cold, windy winter day. There

The master bedroom enjoys the view through the sloping south wall. To provide free air flow, the bedroom is open to the living room. Balcony rail is behind rocking chair. Massive stone chimney at left stores heat. Note in exterior view that masonry does not extend above roofline. In this fashion, all of the heat stored in the chimney is kept in the house.

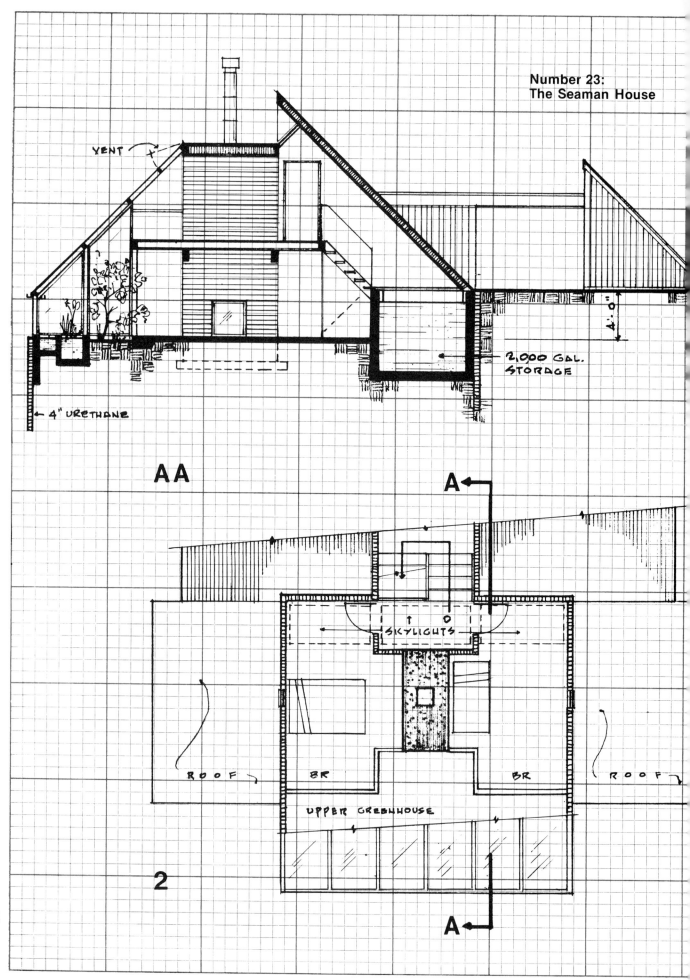

VENT

← 4" URETHANE

AA

2,000 GAL.
STORAGE

4'-0"

A

SKYLIGHTS

ROOF

BR

BR

ROOF

UPPER GREENHOUSE

2

A

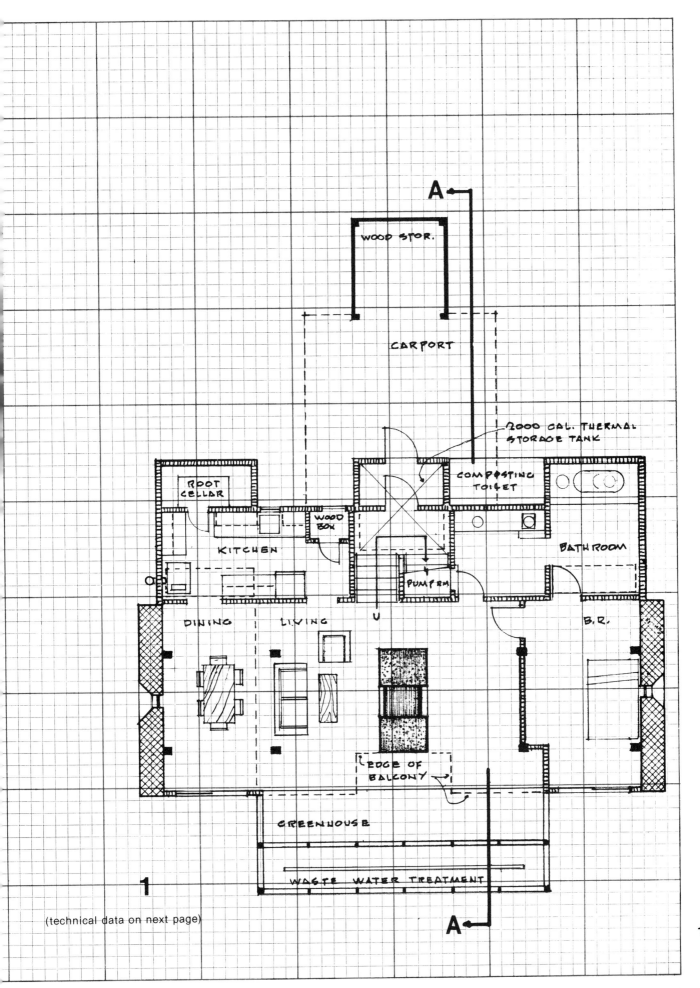

A

WOOD STOR.

CARPORT

12000 GAL. THERMAL
STORAGE TANK

ROOT
CELLAR

COMPOSTING
TOILET

WOOD
BOX

KITCHEN

BATHROOM

PUMP RM.

DINING   LIVING

B.R.

EDGE OF
BALCONY

GREENHOUSE

WASTE WATER TREATMENT

1

(technical data on next page)

A

Number 23:
The Seaman House
Floor area — 1,445 square feet
                    134 square meters
Exposed surface area — 2,290 square feet
                              213 square meters
Efficiency ratio — .64

(technical data for preceding page)

Still under construction is the combination washbasin-bathtub. Cast in one piece out of ferrocement, it is built into a shelf on the north wall of the house. The top surface, being prepared for a slate edging, is 36 inches above the floor. One faucet and one set of drain connections do double duty for both fixtures. The whole fixture is brilliantly lighted from above.

was no backup heat at all and the house temperature was in the 60's. Very comfortable for all of the people running around finishing construction. A fire was built and we had tea in front of the double-faced fireplace.

Gregg has been heard to complain that Canada is spending very little for solar research and is lagging far behind the United States. Singlehandedly, Gregg seems to be catching up. In fact, I'd say that he is way ahead of most of the architects here in the States. If I were to rank the houses in this book this one would be at or near the top.

A solar clock—otherwise known as a sun dial.

Number 24: The Perlberg House

This one belongs to Eric and Tee Perlberg and is located on the south side of a mountaintop in the Catskill Mountains. A contractor has bid $28,000 to construct the home, exclusive of roof labor, well, sewage disposal, and road. Construction is just starting as this is written. The Perlbergs are young professionals who plan not to have children. They are heavily committed to saving part of our fragile environment. Consequently, they searched for a long time before finding this dream site. The developer of this site is also a committed person who cares about his surroundings. Normally, I would advise anyone against buying a piece of property with deed restrictions. In this case, the restrictions are great! No firearms. No snowmobiles. No lots less than five acres. Houses no closer than 100 feet to the road. Certainly not the type of restrictions usually found in developments. A special arrangement was even made with the health department to allow Clivus Multrums. More on that later.

Siting presented a difficult quandary. All of us really wanted to dig the house into the side of the south-facing cliff. Unfortunately, by the time you got to where the house fitted in nicely, a road would have been nearly impossible. Also, the heavy snows would have tended to pile up behind the house making escape difficult if not impossible. Since both of the Perlbergs have to be off to work early in the morning and would not be up to a long hike to their cars, this site was reluctantly rejected. The final site is a natural clearing near the top of the hill where access

Completed Perlberg house.

from the main road is easy. The views from the top of the house are spectacular in any direction.

This house is literally wrapped around a solar greenhouse which extends to the middle of the house where it meets a massive brick chimney. The glazing for the greenhouse extends up into the second story so that maximum amounts of sunlight reach the chimney. This is made possible by the stepped seating in the sauna. A novel feature, a second-floor deck with removable deck panels, provides summer shade for the lower part of the greenhouse glass and the south-facing glass in the living room.

The house is designed as a heat trap to collect as much heat as possible from the sun. Exterior walls are 6 inches thick and are insulated with urea-formaldehyde which gives the exterior walls a Resistance Factor of 33.9 (a conventional 4-inch stud wall insulated with standard roll-type fiberglass has a Resistance 15.5). The insulation is quite expensive—it adds $1,200 to the house cost—but Eric and Tee feel that it is well worth the price. Roofs are all insulated with 12 inches of standard fiberglass. As another energy-saving technique, the house isolates the main livingspaces from the north wall by placing various storage and utility areas along that wall. The entrance is also on the north wall separated from the house by a vestibule with sliding doors between it and the house proper. In the summer, or in mild weather, these can be pushed back out of the way.

Way up on top is a third level containing a small study and a walled-in sun deck that will be usable much of the year. It also houses a solar water heater similar to Steve Baer's famous "Breadbox" design, a tank enclosed in an insulated box with operable reflective doors. In this case, we improve upon his design by letting the floor and back wall of the deck provide two walls of the enclosure. Since the roof deck is completely sheltered from the wind and is surfaced in black, the heater will be very efficient. Used plate glass and tanks were employed in the construction of the water heater, keeping the price competitive with a conventional new water heater. Keep that in mind when a sleazy salesman comes to your door trying to sell a $1,400 "solar" water heater.

All framing lumber for the house was shipped to the site on one truck and cost less than $1,300 delivered. Ward's Lumber of Jay, New York, filled our order in four days.

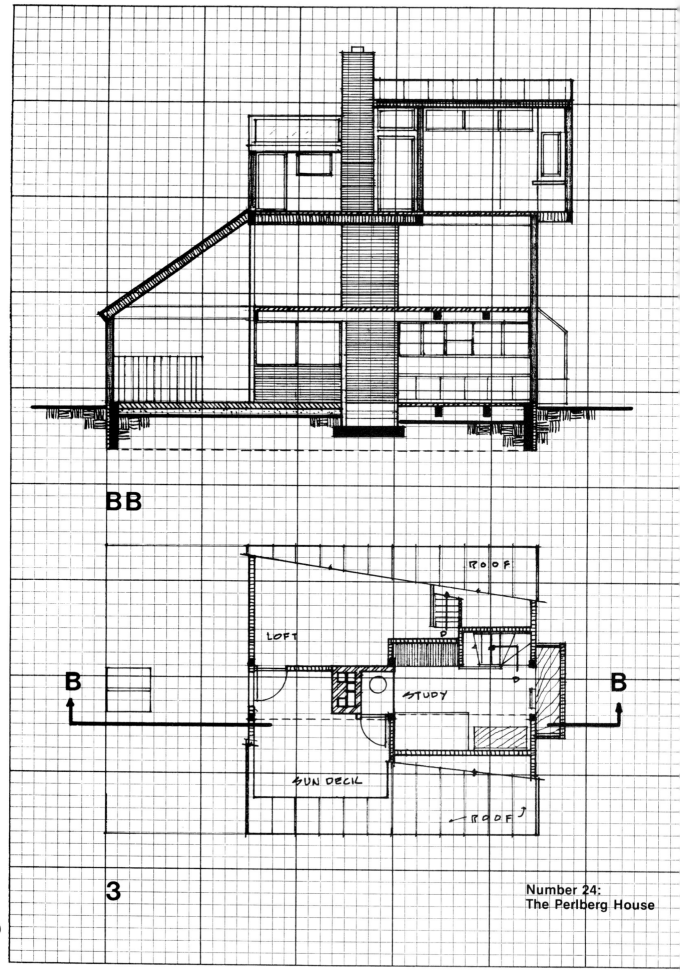

BB

B   B

LOFT

ROOF

STUDY

SUN DECK

ROOF

3

Number 24:
The Perlberg House

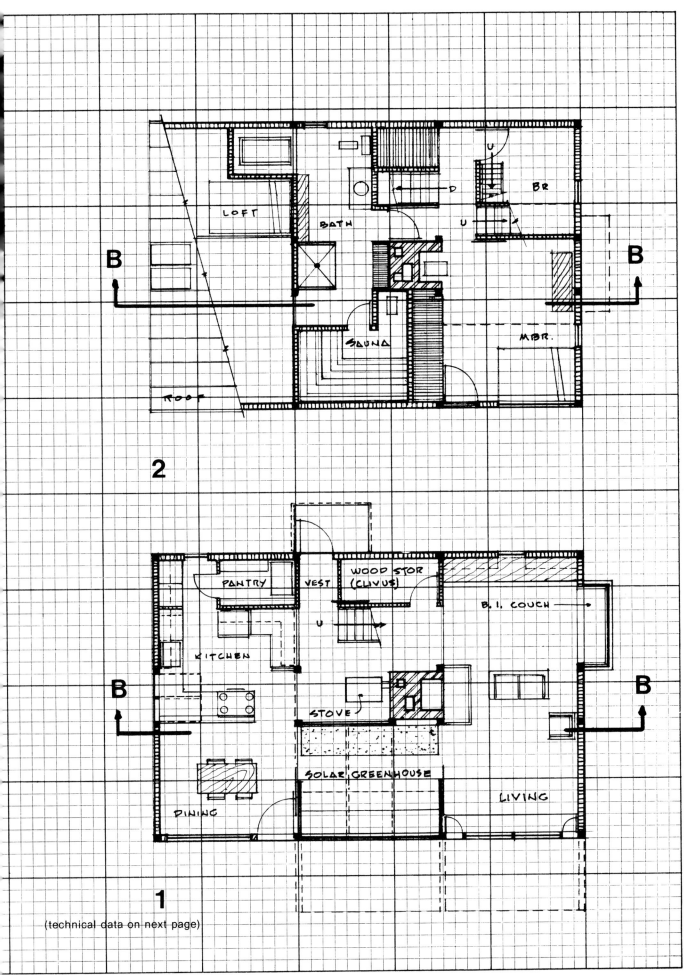

B ——— B

LOFT

BATH

D

BR

U

U

SAUNA

MBR.

ROOF

2

PANTRY

VEST

WOOD STOR
(CLIVUS)

B. I. COUCH ———→

KITCHEN

U

STOVE

B ——— B

DINING

SOLAR GREENHOUSE

LIVING

1

(technical data on next page)

Number 24:
The Perlberg House
Floor area — 1,866 square feet
                174 square meters
Exposed surface area — 2,652 square feet
                        247 square meters
Efficiency ratio — .70

(technical data for preceding page)

Materials throughout have been kept in harmony with nature. The ground floor is brick set in sand which in turn is over insulation. Much use is made of roughsawn wood inside and out. Flooring on the upper floors is native pine. The roof is standing-seam terne which Tee plans to fabricate herself. Eric, who is terrified of heights, plans to content himself by being go-fer. You can spend hundreds of hours running back and forth to hardware stores, lumberyards, plumbing and electrical supply houses, particularly when building on an isolated site. The less experience that you have in construction, the more trips necessary unless you try to plan ahead and think of everything to save trips.

The Perlbergs had a few problems with their sewage disposal. The health department went back on its promise. Well, not quite. They made just enough of a concession so that they couldn't be accused of lying: "If you put in a Clivus, we will let you reduce the size of the septic system by 10 percent." Since the standard septic tank required for this house is 750 gallons, and the next smaller one is 500 gallons, you can see where that leaves us. Flush toilets use a minimum of 40 percent of the water in a house. If we were allowed that commonly accepted figure, the 500-gallon system could have been used. As is, we would have to put in a $3,000 septic system and then add a $1,500 Clivus. Needless to say, they have effectively killed the Clivus. Since one difficulty with a Clivus is fitting it into a floor plan, I have shown the unit on the plan, but in the final version of the house, a wood storage room was substituted. I would have liked to fight this one through, but the Perlbergs were in a hurry for their house and it looked as if we might have to fight for years—and still lose.

Heating is provided by a large Lange #6302K woodstove which also incorporates an oven and cooktop. Backup is provided by some radiant electric heaters. The design of the house is such that all of the heat can be provided by the solar greenhouse and south-facing glass in sunny weather. Much to our amazement, the banker was enthusiastic about the heating system. She says that she has a new oil furnace in her house which has never been used because she heats with wood. Maybe there is some hope for sanity in the banking industry after all.

Since the Perlbergs both like an open fire, an efficient fireplace is located on the living room side of the chimney. This fireplace is constructed to act more like a stove than a real fireplace. In moderate weather, it alone can provide the extra heat which the house needs at night. Since all of the heating appliances exhaust into the massive chimney and additional heat is supplied to the masonry mass by the solar greenhouse, it will be possible for the chimney to store heat for the whole house for many hours.

The solar greenhouse will also be a valuable source of food as the Perlbergs are enthusiastic gardeners. Since the site is all rocky hillside (except for the original road which became a disposal field for the septic system) the greenhouse will be intensively used year-round.

Number 25: The Wright House

David Wright is one of the few architects in this country who saw the energy crisis coming and did something about it. Most of the pioneers in the solar field have worked with active systems. David was one of the few to specialize in passive systems. Since David also emphasizes compact, efficient houses and low cost, he is a prime candidate for inclusion in this book. David's first house for himself in Santa Fe, New Mexico, has received considerable publicity. It was quite appropriately named "Sunscoop."

As with all of his houses, this one relies upon mass to store heat from the sun. Although the house was equipped with insulated shutters for the windows, the Wrights found that they weren't necessary except in very severe weather—when the temperature dropped below 10°F. at night.

Since building "Sunscoop," David has moved to Sea Ranch, California. This second house is his latest effort, again for himself. David has discovered that the concept of solar-heat storage by means of a massive structure actually increases in efficiency as the structure gets larger. In his own case, he has considerably increased the size of his house. He has also used earth berms to shut out cold winter winds. Two sides of the house are completely buried and it has a sod roof. A few skylights gleaming in the midst of the grass are the only clue that the roof isn't just a gentle grassy slope. These face north and open to catch cool sea breezes in summer.

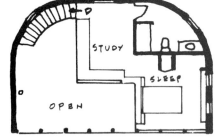

David Wright's first house.

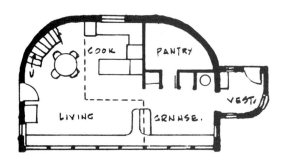

The entire south wall of the house is tilted to act as a solar collector. The two center panels contain flat, plate solar collectors which store water in a hot-water tank by means of gravity flow (water rises as it is heated); in this way, David provides ample hot water for the house without any automatic gadgetry. Since the house is long and narrow, the low winter sun can reach all the way in and strike the heavily insulated concrete back wall of the main livingspaces. Unwanted sun is shut out by means of reflective insulated curtains which can be drawn inside the windows. A series of top and bottom vents in the sloping glass wall provides air circulation in the summer and prevents overheating of the house.

View to the west overlooking the ocean. The small structure in the back center of the picture is David's study which extends above the main house for a spectacular view of the Pacific Ocean. The sod-covered roof of the main house is in the foreground. Operating skylights balance the light from the south-facing glass wall and provide cross ventilation.

A shot of the sunken courtyard taken from the garage roof.
The fully sheltered court is warm, even in winter.

Barbara and David stand on the knoll above the south-facing glass wall which is sunk into the ground facing a courtyard. This technique shelters the glass from cold winter winds and increases its efficiency as a solar collector. Collector coils for a solar water heater are behind the glass wall. They are visible through the glass immediately to the right of Barbara's shoulder. The narrow two-story glass wall at left overlooks the ocean.

The narrow west end of the house sweeps up to two stories to enjoy the view of the ocean. David's office occupies the loft-level room with the best view (architects always like to play king of the mountain). The ceilings on the low side of the roof slope are deliberately kept low to minimize the volume of the area requiring heat. Somehow, David got his house plans approved under the notorious California code, although he did remark that they came back from the building department looking as though they had been in a bloody battle. David figures that the house has enough heat-storage capacity to allow it to get through three-and-a-half days with no sun and still maintain a temperature of 65°F. or better. For backup, there is a woodstove constructed of a 55-gallon drum.

There is a detached garage (also semi-buried) which includes a guest suite. Maximum use of built-in furniture and the way the spaces visually flow into one another make the house seem much larger than its 1,000 square feet. Also, the fully sheltered courtyard created by the placement of the house and garage provides a warm outdoor space for mild winter days.

Interior of the living room. The brick floor stores heat from south-facing glass. Note the special insulating curtains which are gathered at the top of the windows. Operating vents are installed at the top of the curtains to allow air to circulate between the glass and the curtains; this gives an extra degree of control to the passive solar system. Backup heating (fireplace-stove) is at right.

A small second story contains David's study and overlooks the ocean. Don't make the same mistake the Wrights did and fail to install vents at the highest point of the house. This room needs them badly; it was too hot on a cold winter day.

The master bedroom faces on the sunken courtyard. The separate building across the courtyard houses garage, guest suite, and storage area. This extra building also helps shelter the south glass from winter winds. Since these areas are seldom heated, separating them from the main house also reduces the heating requirements.

Their cedar-lined bathroom gets light and air from an operating skylight. Note the built-in tub.

David tells an interesting anecdote concerning his local power company. Some clients had gone to the power company for an estimate for heating costs for electric heat for their new house before they met David. The power company had their engineers estimate the yearly heating cost at 1975 rates—$1,900 per year. Then the couple heard about David's passive solar-heated houses. They hired him to redesign their house. He added a great deal of mass and insulation and moved most of the windows to the south elevation. The house was designed to receive 85 percent of its heat from the sun. Electric heat was still to be provided as a backup. Just to check, the clients asked the power company to crank up its engineer again, who this time predicted a $2,500-per-year heating bill. David is anxiously waiting for them to blow all of their fuses when they come to read the meter and find that the actual usage is a tiny fraction of their estimate.

David is one of the few architects in this country who has had enough experience in working with solar-tempered houses to accurately predict the outcome of a project. Most architects design this type of system by trial and error if they attempt it at all. David warns of the necessity to

The simple, open kitchen looks out on both the courtyard and living room. The skylight further brightens room. Lights are simple G-40 bulbs installed in inexpensive chrome bases. The bases are by Lightoiler and are available at most lighting fixture stores. Simple porcelain pull-chain fixtures can be used with the same bulbs. The low ceiling makes for easy attractive storage of kitchen utensils.

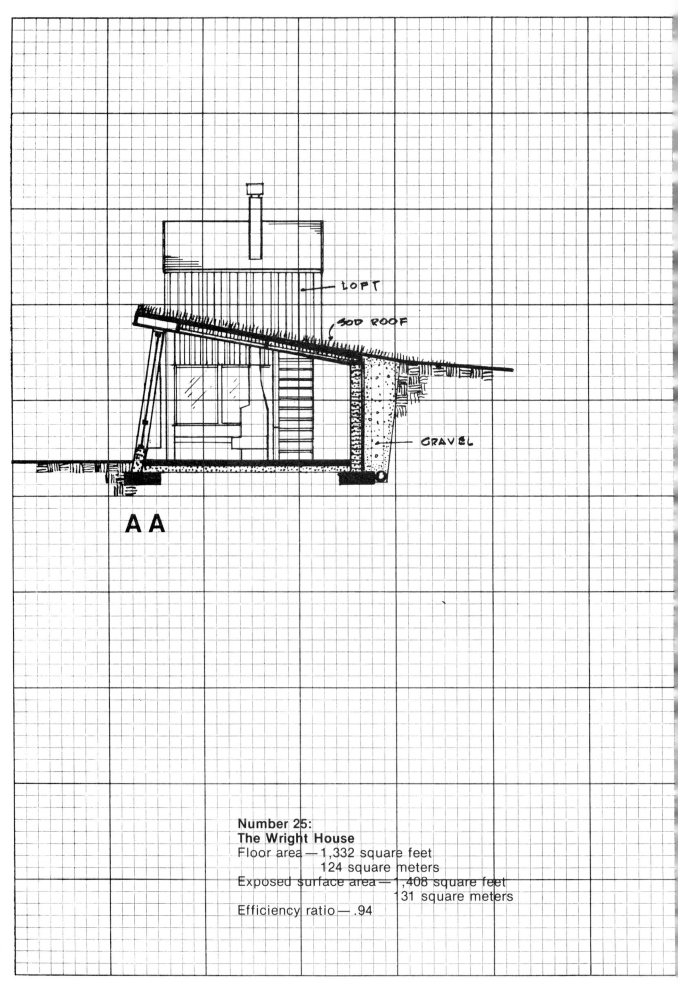

LOFT

SOD ROOF

GRAVEL

A A

Number 25:
The Wright House
Floor area — 1,332 square feet
124 square meters
Exposed surface area — 1,408 square feet
131 square meters
Efficiency ratio — .94

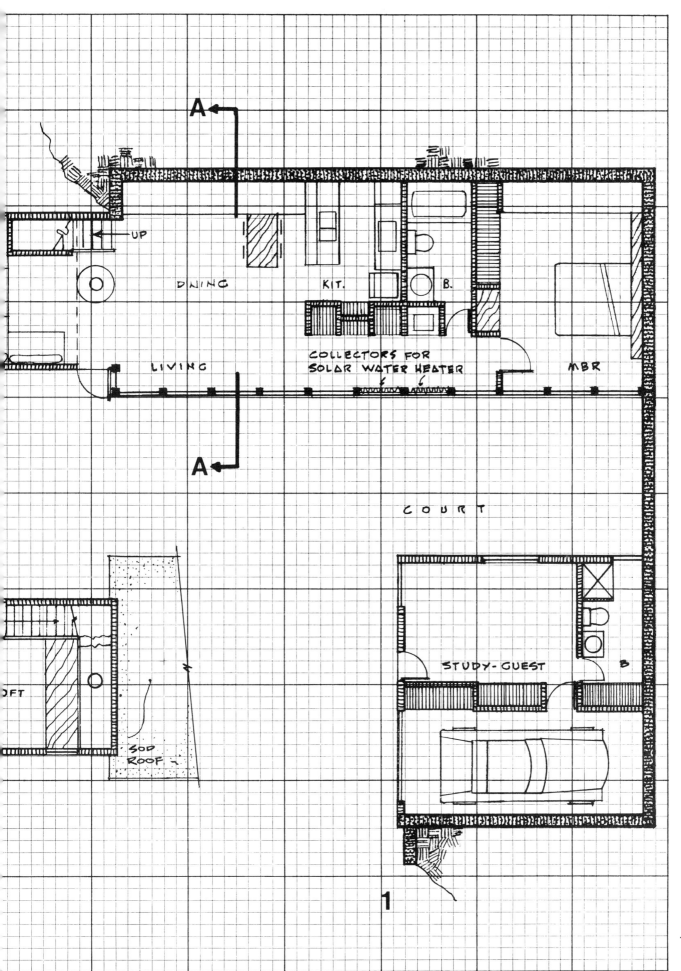

A

UP

DINING

LIVING

KIT.

B.

COLLECTORS FOR
SOLAR WATER HEATER

MBR

A

COURT

LOFT

SOD
ROOF

STUDY-GUEST

B

1

tailor your house exactly to the needs of your particular geographic location: "Up to now, we have had a national house style. This will change rapidly as energy shortages worsen." All of David's houses feature use of materials indigenous to their particular geographic location. His houses in the Santa Fe area are constructed using adobe as a principal building material. David foresees a time when all houses will be designed to fit in with nature, not necessarily because people want them that way, but because that's the only way they will be able to afford them.

Number 26: The Terry House

This one belongs to Karen Terry, one of David's first clients. Her first house steps up a hillside and is just as well known as David's "Sunscoop." After building and living in her own house, Karen decided to build a solar house on speculation.

This is one of the most perfect passive solar houses ever built. The mass of the house is so great that it has an estimated carrythrough of seven days before a backup heating system would need to be used. Karen says that she has never had to use the woodstove which was provided as backup for her own house. In this case, the bank demanded a 100 percent electric-heat backup system. When you consider that David is a world-famous architect with a perfect track record for building solar-tempered houses, don't be surprised if *your* local bank is a bit skeptical and makes you install a redundant heating system.

Unlike David's new house in Sea Ranch, California, which simply has the earth bermed up around it, this one is fully dug into the ground. That is part of its secret—massive concrete walls were required to hold back the earth. Quite appropriately, salvaged timbers from an old coal tipple are used as the main framing members for the house. The grade-level floors are all constructed of brick to provide both a finish floor and mass for heat storage. This is the only house of Wright's which doesn't have some extra heat storage such as a drum-filled banco (drums filled with water encased in adobe); yet it is also the only one for which he can claim 100 percent solar heating. As he points out, "Each one is improved just a bit from the last."

No one can pretend that his house is low cost. It was built as a showcase for passive solar heat and some of the techniques used were quite expensive. Also, since it was designed as a luxury house, it is set on a large, expensive piece of property ($25,000 worth). The sales price, including land, road, well, septic system, and the house, is over $90,000. Remember that this also includes mortgage interest and a profit for Karen and three friends who slaved mightily to construct the house. If you were doing this house yourself on an inexpensive piece of property, I would estimate that the cost could be cut to less than half of that figure; really hard work could cut it still further. David's houses re-

Karen's own studio-house steps gracefully up a hillside. Louvers are installed over the sloping glass windows in summer to shut out the sun. (See color picture on the cover).

quire lots of hand labor, which can save out-of-pocket expenses if it is your own house. But these cost a lot if you are hiring the labor or counting it in a sales price.

Karen is an avid enthusiast of solar living, but like most of us, likes beauty as well as function. Many people are turned off by solar designs because they are ugly; David's designs are not. Karen's own house steps gracefully down a hillside from a tiny sleeping loft located at the very top of the house. The canted glass sections of the roof do double duty as windows and a means of admitting solar radiation. As for the new underground house, people constantly comment that it is one of the finest integrations of solar heating into a house that they have ever seen. This house, too, is an aesthetic delight. Karen says: "It's sensual and curving, a beautiful house."

The insulated covering for the windows in this house is "Nightwall" which was devised by a clever, well-known solar pioneer, Steve Baer. This is just one of many of his solar devices which make use of very simple, low-technology ideas. In this case, magnets are attached to the window frames of the house. Matching magnets are attached to panels

Roughsawn wood makes elegant cabinets.

Karen's sleeping loft (half-circle cutout) is at the very top of her stepped house and overlooks the whole exterior. The bathroom is under the sleeping loft.

The stepped retaining wall with bench permits grade-level entrance at the side of the house.

Built-in bench (banco) adjacent to the fireplace encases 55-gallon drums filled with water to store heat from the sun.

The curving adobe wall provides a graceful transition between the buried section of the house and the full-height glass wall. Usually such grade changes are awkward unless expensive retaining walls and terraces are used. Note the retaining wall which was used to save the tree at the right (most contractors would have cut down the tree).

of Styrofoam which are simply snapped into place at night. One does have to provide storage space for the Styrofoam, and it will get dirty with time, but it is an elegantly simple system. Steve also makes "Skylids" which are automatic, sun-powered shutters for covering skylights and trapping heat inside your house. Another interesting design is "Bead-wall," a system of blowing Styrofoam beads between two panes of glass to provide insulation at night. In the daytime, the system is reversed and the beads pumped out of the space between the glass panes. Steve also has plans for easy-to-build solar water heaters which require hard work but little money.*

The south-facing brick terrace is enclosed by a curving adobe wall at bench height. Massive walls store heat from the sun. The semi-buried profile of the house along with the wing walls provides shelter for the glass and allows it to pick up a lot of heat from the winter sun. The glass is deeply recessed so as not to pick up summer heat.

*Steve can be reached at Zomeworks, Box 712, Albuquerque, NM 87103.

The pinwheel door is heavily insulated and was constructed of leftover scraps of wood.

North side of house is completely buried for protection from north winds. House uses native materials on roof here and elsewhere to blend with surroundings.

Inside there is a great deal of masonry mass to absorb heat. The tall Navajo-style fireplace is designed more like a stove than a fireplace. The opening is high and shallow to radiate as much heat as possible to the occupants of the room. Clerestory windows make the interior bright even though most of the house is underground. A ventilating skylight at the far right provides light and air for kitchen-dining area.

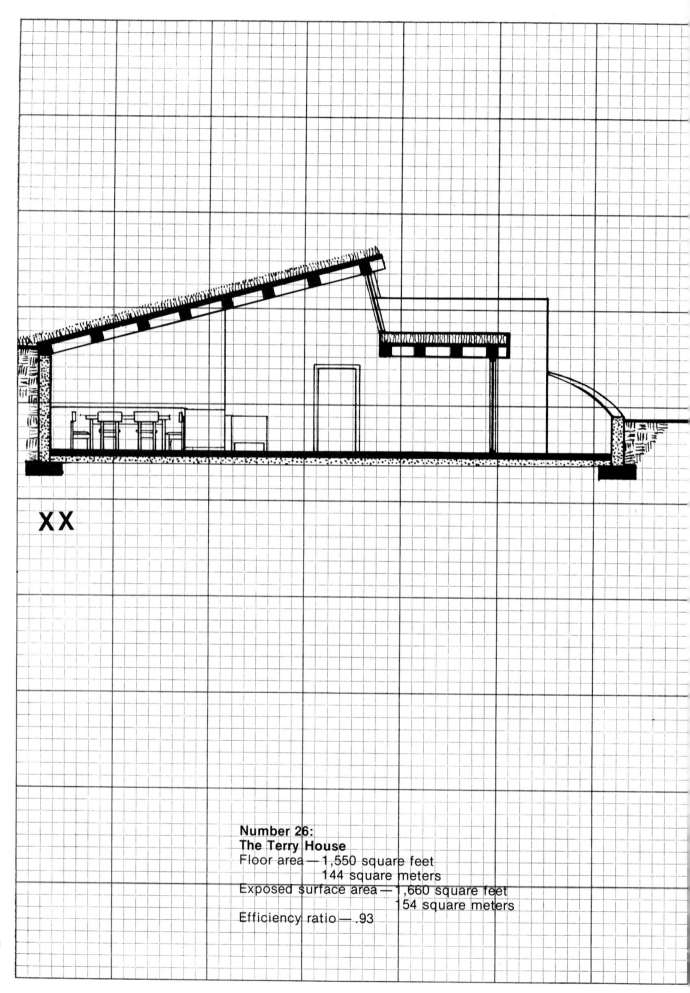

XX

Number 26:
The Terry House
Floor area—1,550 square feet
144 square meters
Exposed surface area—1,660 square feet
154 square meters
Efficiency ratio—.93

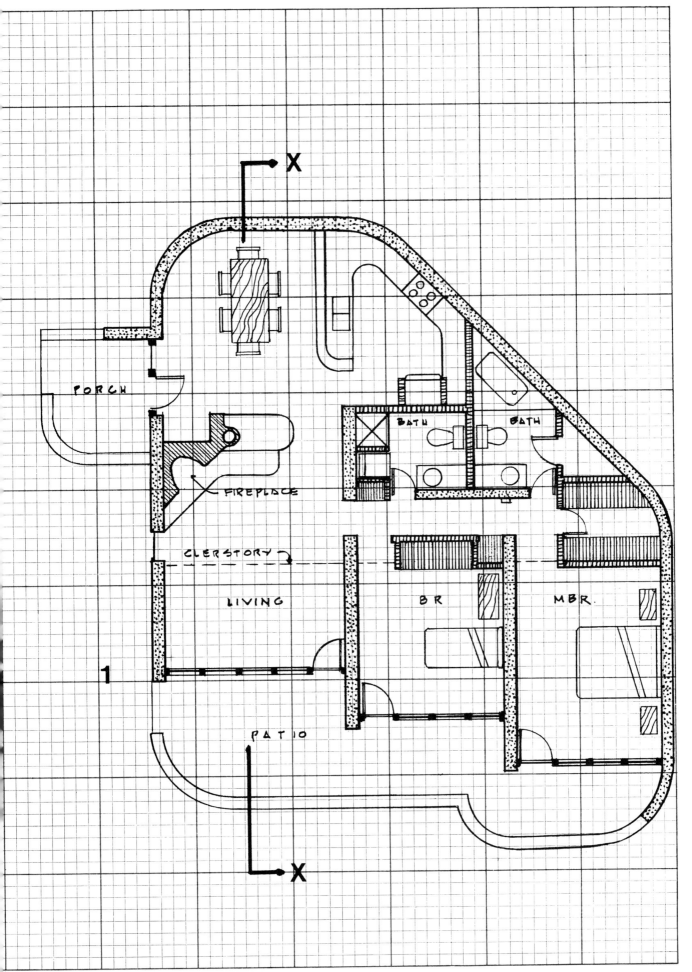

X

PORCH

FIREPLACE

CLERSTORY

LIVING

BATH

BATH

BR

MBR.

1

PATIO

X

Number 27: The Ondra House

This was designed and built by two architects, Mike Ondra and Mic Curd. It shows just how much innovative work can be done when the designers themselves have the skill to perform their own work. Many experimental construction techniques are used which would have been impossible or risky if the construction had been done by conventional contractors working from architect's plans.

This house is an extraordinary example of integrating the structure to a site and designing the building itself to absorb maximum amounts of solar energy. In this case, the design required exceptional skill, as the site is not quite ideal for solar heating. The house is partly buried into the west slope of a hillside. The buried portion of the house takes maximum advantage of the insulating value of the earth, while the south-facing glass areas absorb sunlight. The problem which requires so much skill involves the shadow of the hill itself. The south-facing glass area is more than adequate for heating the house, but early-morning heat gain is restricted by the fact that a portion of the glass nearest to the hill is in shade. The backup heater, a small Mørso wood-

The Ondra house nestles in a Pennsylvania valley. Unfortunately the hillside on the left prevents early morning sun from reaching the glass wall.

burning stove has been located in this glass area. The primary heat inputs from both the passive solar and the woodstove are located on the lowest level of the house. Heat is allowed to circulate by gravity up through the various levels of the house, assisted by a fan when necessary.

House is still incomplete in this picture. A set of coils for the solar water heater is to be installed on the blank wall at the top of the picture. A solar greenhouse will fill in the corner at the lower right.

The layout of the house is very skillfully executed. The stairway is located near the center of the house and serves as both vertical and horizontal circulation space. There are virtually no hallways or other waste space in this house—all of the room areas except for the stairs are usable as livingspace. The open staircase also performs admirably as air-circulation space to allow heat from the lower level to circulate throughout the house. Mike, his wife Lauren, and Mic all report that the house was very comfortable during this past very cold winter, at least most of the time. The exception was when they tried out an alternate woodstove. This was a very sophisticated stove called the Vermont Downdrafter. It is designed to be loaded up with a lot of wood all at once. The combustion process is very efficient and needs little attention.

Burning produces very little creosote buildup in the flue, a major problem with most efficient stoves. The problem which it does have, and it is a serious one, is lack of control. Once it is going, it puts out heat—lots of heat—and can't be turned down or off. All of the most efficient methods of heating with wood seem to suffer from this problem. If you remember the Sturgis system (House Number 21) was very efficient at the expense of loss of control. Mike feels that although the Downdrafter was a failure for him with his compact well-insulated house, it would be ideal for use as a basement-level wood furnace for an older, less-insulated house.

Mike and Lauren's house holds heat well because it has a 2-inch layer of Styrofoam wrapped around the entire exterior of the house, right over the top of a fully insulated stud wall. By using this system, heat loss by conduction through the studs is eliminated. The Styrofoam does double duty as insulation and a base for the special synthetic stucco compound which forms the exterior finish for the house. A thin application of the stucco is spread directly over the Styrofoam to form a permanent finish. To prevent any possible settlement cracks from forming, Mike embedded a layer of fiberglass mesh between coats of stucco.

A second unusual material is employed as a combination structural sealant and surfacing for walls made of concrete block. All of the underground walls, various outside retaining walls, and the base for the greenhouse are made by this special technique. The concrete blocks are merely stacked up to form the desired wall and then coated on both sides with a special epoxy compound made by Owens-Corning. The compound makes a tough film on both block surfaces and thereby welds them together into a very solid wall. This system makes blockwork very easy for the beginning homebuilder. The interior walls in the Ondra house which have been finished this way look just like rough sand-finish plaster. Where the walls are used as structural retaining elements, the cores were filled with cement mortar reinforced with steel rods. For non-retaining walls, though, the system is exceptionally easy. The coating comes in natural cement color, or for at a slightly higher price, in white.

This is the kitchen-dining area of the Ondra house. Incredible as it may seem, the small woodstove provided excessive heat for this very large house during one of the coldest winters in history, despite the fact that the large window is only single-glazed. The floor is concrete with coils to absorb heat from the sun.

By using standard concrete block merely stacked up in this fashion, Mike has designed a remarkable passive device for distributing warm air throughout a solar- or wood-heated house. He stacks up block to form a large centrally located, masonry return air column. The column extends almost to the ceiling and pulls hot air from the ceiling level through the blockwork by means of a circulating fan for distribution at lower levels. The warm air passing through the block column transfers some of its heat to the column which in turn radiates it back into the room. The duct system can be used to supply air to a remote part of the house or to add moisture through a humidifier. Mike estimates that a two-story column can be home built for around $200. If desired, the column can be combined with the chimney for the stove or fireplace as it is in his prototype. By using this column, Mike is able to overcome the most prevalent objections to wood and solar heat—heat stratification and buildup at upper levels. Heat which would otherwise be wasted is recycled to the living areas. True, this system does use energy for the fan and thereby might upset some purists who would prefer that all heat be supplied by exclusively natural, nonpower-assisted means. I feel that if it works well and is inexpensive, it should be strongly considered as a heating solution.

Mike and I got into a far-ranging conversation about different types of passive solar-heating systems. Our common lament is that virtually all

The Ondras reminisce about the development of their house.

of the research money goes for complicated, expensive systems which have little or no application for the typical householder who can barely afford a new house anyway, much less $20,000 extra for complex solar gadgetry. Mike relates many arguments with graduate-level physicists at MIT concerning obvious basic physical phenomena. One example was particularly interesting, as yet another "expert" had just tripped over the same question on the front page of the *Wall Street Journal*. Mike, who grew up on a farm as I did, had made the simple observation that hot water will freeze faster than cold. When he asked several different Ph.D.'s why this happens, he was brushed aside and told that he was mistaken; "Obviously the cold water will freeze first. Don't be silly!" I was able to explain the matter with ease. Heating water drives out gas bubbles and makes the water more dense; hence, it freezes more quickly. I learned this in a seventh-grade science class in rural West Virginia. Unfortunately, grants go to all of the hotshots at big universities who are so unattuned to nature that they can't even explain why water freezes. No wonder they design unrealistic solar systems.

Mike, Lauren, and Mic have also done their share of recycling old materials in this house. All of the doors came from an old hospital, complete with heavy-duty hardware. The countertops are a particular stroke of genius—they are recycled blackboards which Mike took to a blackboard company to have the surfaces reground. The company also made all of the sink cutouts and cut all the pieces to final size. The results are quite handsome, and since the company broke one of Mike's pieces of slate, they didn't charge him for their work.

It was particularly interesting to watch this house being lived in at a partially completed stage of construction. In this way, the occupants are able to react and make changes and adjustments to the design. The prime example in this house is the top floor which was added during framing stages when the Ondras discovered that they could create another large room just by extending the roofline a bit. Another area in which adjustments were made was in the greenhouse which has been redesigned several times, but not yet built. (See sketch for the final design.) By actually building the main house without the greenhouse they have been able to refine the design to be better-suited to the house than it was on the original plans. I was particularly interested to note that the south-facing glass wall has only single glazing. A second layer is planned, but they were quite comfortable in this extremely cold winter with only one layer. Of course, they do have insulating panels which are installed over the glass at night.

This sketch of the Ondra house shows the future greenhouse tucked into the southeast corner and the solar collectors that will eventually be installed on the roof.

A Clivus Multrum has been very skillfully integrated into the design, taking advantage of the stepped design of the old-type Clivus tank. This is one of the few house designs which I have seen which allows the toilet portion of the Clivus to be near the bedrooms while having the kitchen garbage chute located in a kitchen counter where it belongs. We discussed the problems of the Clivus. Although the Ondras have had no trouble with their own unit, there have been problems with others. A very serious potential problem results from using wood ashes in the Clivus. Coals can stay hot for many days in an ash bucket. In at least one case, the dried contents of a Clivus were set afire by coals in ashes dumped into the unit. I also know of people who have set fire to woods and compost piles in the same way. Be careful with ashes: coals can stay lighted for a *long* time.

There have been a few problems with this house. The concrete floor is designed with integral copper coils for heat storage in similar fashion to Gregg Allan's house. Unfortunately, the hillside cuts off the floor from direct sunlight until around midday, so it doesn't build up much heat. The coils have never been hooked up. Although they could be connected to a heat exchanger in the stove, the lower level tends to be a bit

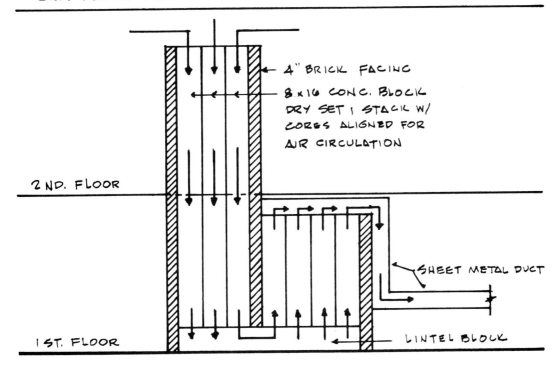

2ND. FLOOR. CLG.

4" BRICK FACING

8 x 16 CONC. BLOCK
DRY SET , STACK W/
CORES ALIGNED FOR
AIR CIRCULATION

2 ND. FLOOR

SHEET METAL DUCT

1 ST. FLOOR   LINTEL BLOCK

too hot, so their use is superfluous. A second minor problem involves Mike's homemade double-glazing. A small patch of condensation is trapped between the panes and moves around inside the glass, depending upon the angle of the sun. The Shelter Institute gives very fine directions for building your own without getting this problem. They seal the inner pane tightly to the window frame with silicone so that moisture from the house can't migrate into the space between the panes. One-eighth-inch thick felt is placed between the outer stops and the glass to seal the glass while allowing just a bit of air to circulate and prevent condensation.

Mike Ondra's masonry column allows you to recycle layers of hot air from the ceiling into the livingspace.

A view of the Ondra's kitchen. Garbage chute for the Clivus is in the butcher–block top at the left. A concealed fluorescent light is hidden in the bottom of a wall shelf. Open shelves for storage are at right.

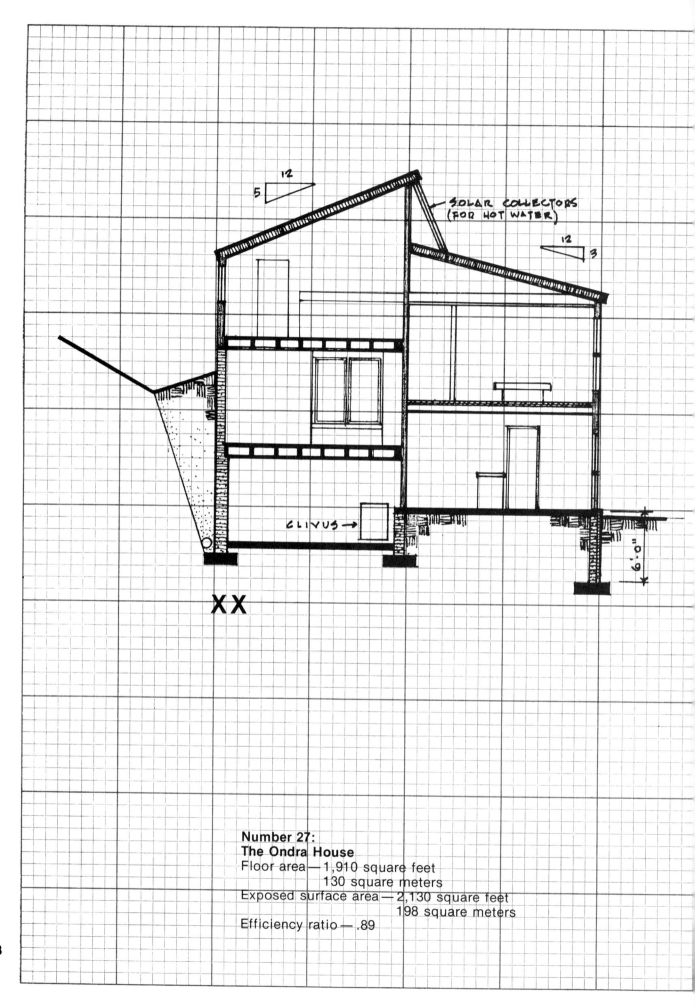

12
5

SOLAR COLLECTORS
(FOR HOT WATER)

12
3

CLIVUS →

6'-0"

XX

Number 27:
The Ondra House
Floor area—1,910 square feet
130 square meters
Exposed surface area—2,130 square feet
198 square meters
Efficiency ratio—.89

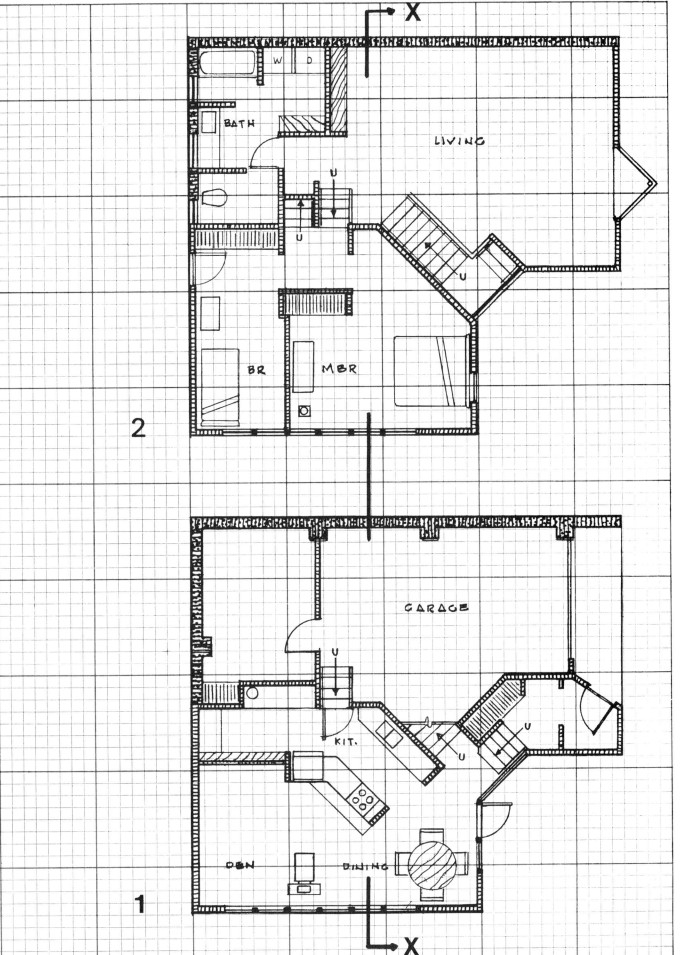

X

LIVING

BATH

U

U

BR   MBR

2

GARAGE

U

KIT.

U

DEN   DINING

1

X

Number 28: The Clock House

This one belongs to Liz and Jeffery Clock. It is one of the best solar-tempered houses in the book. And the irony is that it wasn't even deliberately designed to be solar tempered. It was designed by architect Jedd Reisner for his son, Hugh, who actively participated in the design phase and went on to construct the house himself. The idea was to build a very well insulated house which could be heated economically with electric heat. It just happens that the dramatic view of the Catskill Mountains is almost due south so that's where the major glass areas were put.

Four-foot-high stone wall provides thermal mass and makes this two-story house appear very low.

The house follows all of the best principles of compact design and use of mass within the structure. The lower part of the exterior wall is buried in the earth about three feet up on the walls. About four feet away from the house is a handsome stone wall which contains this earth berm. Since the house is only one-and-one-half stories high anyway, this further reduction in visual height makes it nestle quite nicely into its site. And, more importantly, the added earth insulation makes the concrete slab retain heat in winter and cold in summer. "Even though many of the windows are fixed, it's just like we had an air conditioner all summer," says Liz. Indeed, the day I visited was a spring day above 90°F., and the house was very cool. Operating windows were very carefully placed to take advantage of the chimney effect of the steeply sloping roof and prevailing breezes. The ridge of the roof bisects the square plan and soars up to the south view, providing space for the master bedroom on an upper level of an otherwise single-floor house. Frequently, diagonal geometric plans such as this produce oddly shaped, unusable rooms with much wasted space. In this case, the diagonal plan has been handled very skillfully and results in a very efficient plan.

Mr. Reisner likes to recycle old materials. The main roof beams came from an old house torn down to make way for "urban renewal." All of the doors and some of the windows are similarly recycled. The front doors are from the entrance to a Victorian mansion. An old boiler has been converted into a backup heating unit/fireplace. The front of the boiler was cut out and a firebrick base installed. Removable glass doors allow it to be used as a fireplace in mild weather and still function as an efficient stove in winter. The Clocks found that by simply placing Styrofoam insulating panels over the windows at night they could avoid using the electric heat. The only problem area is the kitchen which faces north. A coil is being installed in the top of the boiler to transfer some heat to the kitchen for next winter. It will be connected to a small radiator in the kitchen. In my own plans, I usually allow the kitchen and living room to flow together to avoid this problem.

Compact slab-on-grade houses often lack storage space. Mr. Reisner has solved this with another masterful stroke of recycling. He has converted a used air-freight container into a combination workshop, wood storage area, and general collection space for miscellaneous junk. Of course it would be better if we refrained from collecting excess belongings, but somehow they pile up. (One advantage of not building a basement is that you throw away useless items or don't acquire them in the first place.) The container does make an admirable workshop, though, and also provides plenty of dry area for wood storage so that

The large window and deck face south. An air-freight container which has been recycled into a shop-storage building is at the left.

wood can be easily gathered over the summer. Air-freight containers come with canvas tops, so a permanent roof was needed. The long wall of the container faces south and a continuous strip of clerestory windows was added along with a new roof to match the house. The container was painted to closely match the stain on the roughsawn natural siding of the house. The results are quite handsome and very low cost. Mr. Reisner acquired three of the containers at the same time. The other two were converted into a very nice apartment.

Insulation for this house is exceptionally heavy, prompted in part by the wholesale purchase of a truckload of polyurethane insulation. Six-inch stud walls are used for all of the exterior walls. Two inches of polyurethane board are set between the studs at the outside face of the wall. Standard 3½-inch fiberglass insulation is installed in the usual fashion inside the polyurethane. This wall slightly exceeds the insulating value of my highly recommended, urea-formaldehyde-insulated, 6-inch walls at less than half the cost. There are a couple of drawbacks, however. First and most important, urea-formaldehyde extinguishes fire; polyurethane burns intensely. Yes, it is buried in the wall in a relatively safe position, but if the house should get on fire it will go very quickly. The insulation was obtained wholesale from Atlas Insulating Products.* I have personally dealt with this firm and found them to be very reasonable, even for small quantities of material. If regular lumberyard prices had been paid for the polyurethane, it would have been no bargain. Polyurethane is the most effective insulation on the market and should definitely be used around and under concrete slabs-on-grade. Make sure that it is buried or protected with cement stucco. (See details in the working drawings in chapter 12.)

The Clocks had quite a time buying their house. Hugh had decided to move elsewhere and put the house up for sale. Three different bank appraisers looked at the house and scratched their heads and said, "Gee, that's a funny house. I don't have any idea what its market value would be." Finally Hugh got out all of the receipts and showed $17,000 worth of materials in the house. (Some of the used material items had to be "reconstructed.") With this evidence in hand, the bank allowed a value of $30,000 to be placed on the house.

The Clocks were somewhat apprehensive about the "electrically heated" house and laid in quite a store of wood. They have been pleasantly surprised. No frozen pipes, no dead plants, no huge electric bills. Everything works nicely. The only problems with the house so far involve the roughsawn siding which was put up quite green with neither battens nor shiplap joints. (These are the only methods of installation which I would recommend.) On the weather side of the house, the boards are cupping and twisting badly. Battens would have broken up the rather pleasant smooth surfaces of the house, but I feel that they should have been used to prevent the warping and twisting. The best thing the Clocks can do now is carefully replace just those which are badly warped, nailing securely with serrated nails to insure against further warping. Thoroughly dried boards will have to be used for the replacements. Fortunately, the condition is only bad on one of the small

*Ayer, MA 01400.

An old boiler has been converted into a "central" heating unit. Glass doors and a heat exchanger are to be fitted for next winter.

walls of the house. Those waist-high planting beds are nicely planted, partly I suspect, because they are at such a convenient height for working. They give the house its very unusual character and at the same time help keep it cool in summer and warm in winter. All in all quite an achievement, even if some of it was unintentional.

It must be emphasized that the Clocks are willing to live with some fluctuations in heat level. If they didn't, the electric heat bill could be quite high.

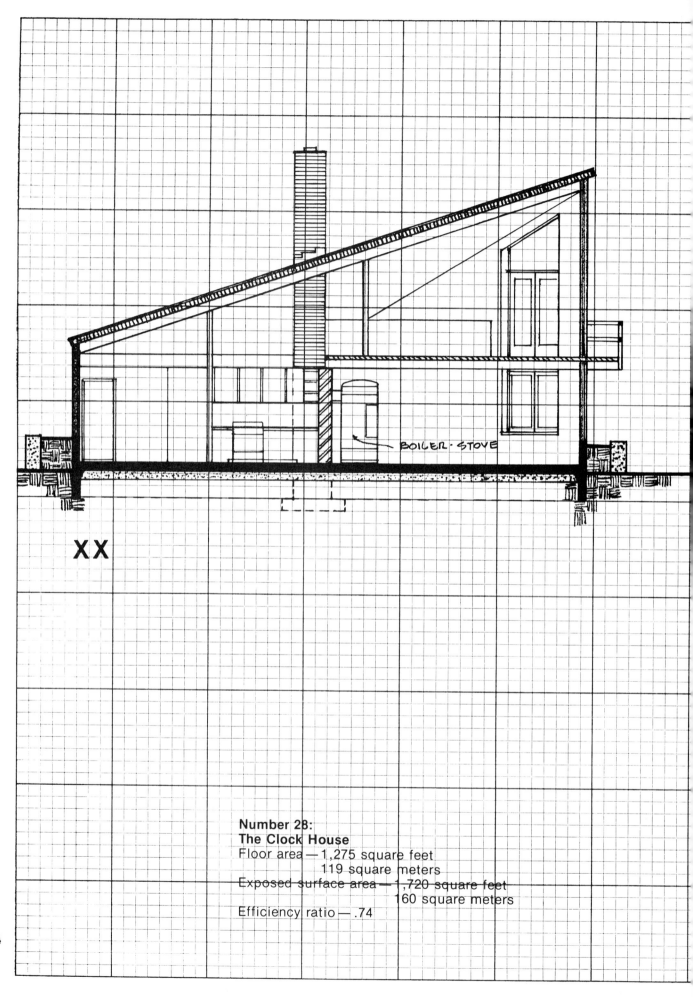

BOILER·STOVE

XX

Number 28:
The Clock House
Floor area — 1,275 square feet
　　　　　　119 square meters
Exposed surface area — 1,720 square feet
　　　　　　　　　　160 square meters
Efficiency ratio — .74

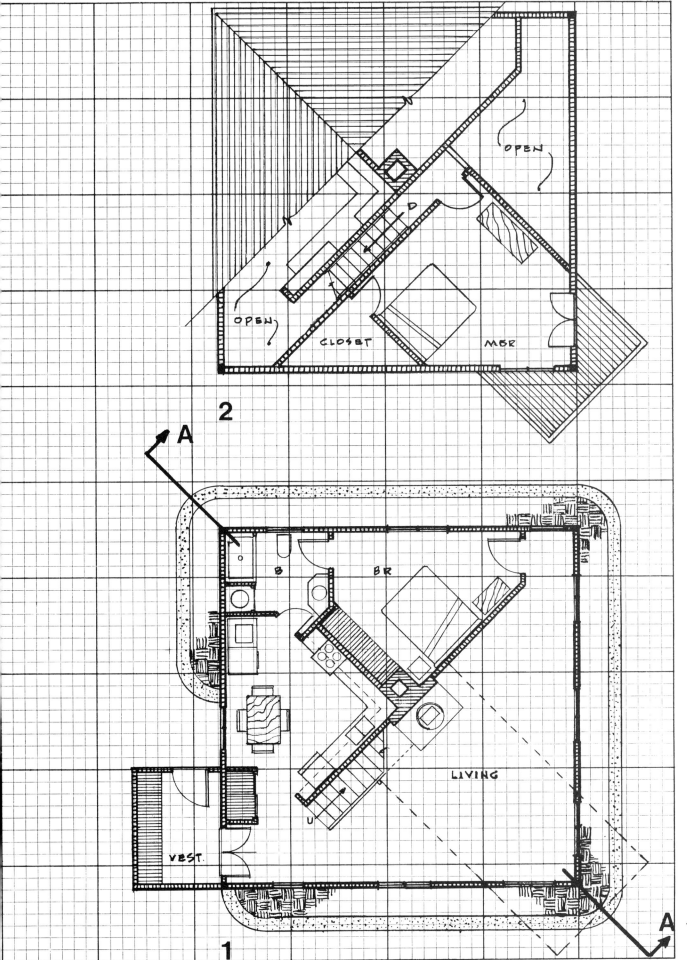

OPEN

OPEN

CLOSET

MBR

D

U

2

A

B

BR

VEST.

U

LIVING

A

1

Number 29: The Pergola House

Radically different from the others in this book, this house is designed for a hot climate, specifically southern Florida. Since fossil heating fuels are running short first, most attention has been directed to saving energy for houses in the North. In this house, I explore the possibilities for providing summer cooling as the primary load with a small amount of winter heating for chilly days. Make no mistake, as fuel supplies get tighter, such wasteful uses as air conditioning will be rationed or prohibited. Those who do not design their southern house to take advantage of the climate will roast.

Mr. Pergola read *Low-Cost, Energy-Efficient Shelter* and took it to heart. He wrote up a page of criteria for a house and mailed it off to 40 registered architects in the state of Florida. Zero results. He received only two replies. One said that the whole energy shortage was a fake contrived by the oil companies and the second one said that Mr. Pergola wanted a research project and he would bill him at $25 per hour. In desperation, Mr. Pergola wrote to me for help. He enclosed this sheet of criteria:

Dear———————,

It is my intention to design and build a "pole-frame constructed, low-cost, energy-efficient home" in the Pine Ridge section of Naples, Florida.

After considerable research I feel that dramatic changes created by future demands will cause tomorrow's builders to use a similar concept.

To facilitate maximum efficiency and cost savings in labor, construction, maintenance, and energy use I wish to incorporate the following ideas and devices:

  1. Construction of a two-story (28 × 56-foot) pole-type frame house with:
  > a. Upstairs—4 bedrooms, 2 baths, family room, large eat-in kitchen, screen and open porch
  > b. Downstairs—Playroom, ½ bath, den-shop, utility room, closets, storage (28 × 32 feet)
  > c. Downstairs—Open double-carport underneath main house (24 × 20 feet).

  (Pole construction negates expensive continuous poured foundation.)

  2. Framing 2 × 6s, 2-foot (O.C.) beamed rafter, floor, and ceiling joists using 4 × 8-foot modules for floors, interior and exterior walls, and roof. Natural cypress exterior including windows and doors. All other wood "treated" (e.g., floor beams 4-foot (O.C.) using 1¼-inch (4 × 8-foot) plywood flooring with 2-inch rigid insulation subflooring). Beamed roof system.

  3. Maintain a minimum Resistance Factor of 25 by using required insulation throughout, vapor barriers, tight construction, weather stripping on insulated windows and doors, etc.

4. Design home and carefully place windows to maximize thermal heating in winter and efficient air flow for cooling in summer. Use 4-foot roof overhang to shade windows. Use circulating fans and gable, soffit, and roof vents to aid ventilation and circulation.

5. Study house site for maximum solar orientation, air flow, beauty, privacy, sound, security, etc.

6. Solar hot-water heat.

7. Water-saving toilets, taps, showerheads, etc.

8. Fluorescent lighting (200 amp. electrical service).

9. Wood-burning heater (Norwegian/Jøtul, etc.).

10. Security and fire alarm system (Honeywell).

11. ALL "Energy-Saving" appliances.

If perchance you are familiar with this type of architecture and interested in designing a home along these lines I will be most pleased to hear from you.

Sincerely,

Jim Pergola

Pressure-treated posts are readily available at reasonable cost in Florida, so this house is designed for posts directly embedded in the ground. Since there are no snow loads in southern Florida a light roof structure of 2 × 6 decking spanning directly the eight feet between major supports was devised. The roof is quite unusual in that it is insulation and roofing combined. This is accomplished by spraying polyurethane foam insulation directly on top of the roof decking and then spraying it with an acrylic cap coating. In this way, we have a handsome finished ceiling which doubles as structure and a roof surface which doubles as insulation.

In order to save costs and build in less space, the lower level was modified from Mr. Pergola's original request. It now contains only a small utility core which separates the screened porch from the carport. Air is allowed to circulate freely under the house and is picked up by vents through the floor. A staggered ridge allows venting the hot air out at the very peak so that maximum advantage of the chimney effect can be achieved. Since the outlet area is considerably larger than the inlets, cool air from under the house is sucked up into the first floor. Highest velocity occurs right above the floor level where it does the most good. Overhangs are adjustable so that south-facing glass is sheltered from

This house sits up on stilts to provide maximum surface area for cooling during hot Florida summers.

the summer sun, yet can take best advantage of it in winter. The screened porch is completely sheltered by the house and open to breezes on three sides. It provides a cool evening escape if the house is too warm. Space is provided to add fans should they be needed.

Heating and cooling functions are supplied by a water-to-air heat pump of special design. Most commercial heat pumps are designed to work from air-to-air. If water is available, it greatly increases the capacity of the heat pump. This is an ideal climate for this type of unit. The particular one I chose has an integral heat exchanger to provide hot water during both heating and cooling cycles. The design of the house is such that it is hoped that the heat pump will not be needed except in extreme and unusual winter cold (such as in 1976/77) or in very hot, humid summer weather. The heat pump was actually installed to make the bank happy, not because we felt that it was a necessity. Provision is also made for a small woodstove in the main living area. Mr. Pergola is particularly concerned that he be able to be comfortable in his house even during extended periods of electrical blackouts which are almost inevitable in the near future.

Water conservation is also an important part of the design of this house. Special water-saving toilets which use only two gallons per flush have been ordered from the Adamsez Company in England.* In addition to saving water, these toilets are of simple, elegant design. It is interesting to note that the method by which these toilets save water is placing the tank high up on the wall so that the force of gravity helps flush the toilet. (Gee, didn't we used to have those in this country? Indeed and there is a company who will charge you over $500 for a replica!) Another thing about the English toilet is that the tank doesn't have all sorts of tricky mechanisms to foul up as the notoriously leaky American tanks do. Since the tank can be mounted high up on the wall, the toilet is shorter and there is more usable space in the bathroom. A simple, foolproof remote lever works the flushing action. All of the fixtures produced by this company are of particularly fine design and of reasonable price. I particularly like their washbasin which just hangs on the wall like a seashell. All of the piping is cleverly hidden in the wall instead of gathering dirt under the sink as in most primitive American designs. The prices were extraordinarily reasonable, even before the latest slide of the pound. If you have the time to order a year ahead, these fixtures represent a great buy.

In addition to providing natural ventilation, the offset roofline allows space for three children's bedrooms, and a family room to be tucked into a compact, two-level suite. Each of the children's bedrooms has an alcove just large enough for a built-in bed. In this way, the space usually wasted around a freestanding bed is eliminated. By arranging the children's suite in this fashion, I was able to conserve enough space to eliminate the lower level which Jim originally wanted. Of course, if he still wants to expand in the future, he can always enclose the screened porch.

I have also designed a second version of this house which is set on a concrete slab eliminating the lower level entirely. The roof construction has to be entirely different to support northern snow loads. The stairhall becomes a winter air lock to shut out the cold. This design would be suitable for areas with a moderate climate as the offset roof provides excellent summer cooling. I would not recommend it for areas in the far North with extreme winters because of its rather spread-out plan.

Number 29:
The Pergola House
Floor area — 1,700 square feet
        158 square meters
Exposed surface area — 4,060 square feet
        378 square meters
Efficiency ratio — .42

(technical data for next page)

*Adamsez Limited, Scotswood, Newcastle upon Tyne, England NE 99 2AA.

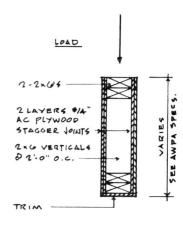

LOAD

2 - 2×6s

2 LAYERS ¾"
AC PLYWOOD
STAGGER JOINTS

2×6 VERTICALS
@ 2'-0" O.C.

VARIES
SEE AWPA SPECS.

TRIM

PLYWOOD BOX BEAM

Large span in the Pergola living room requires a plywood box beam (see plans on next page). Construction technique was described in House Number 15.

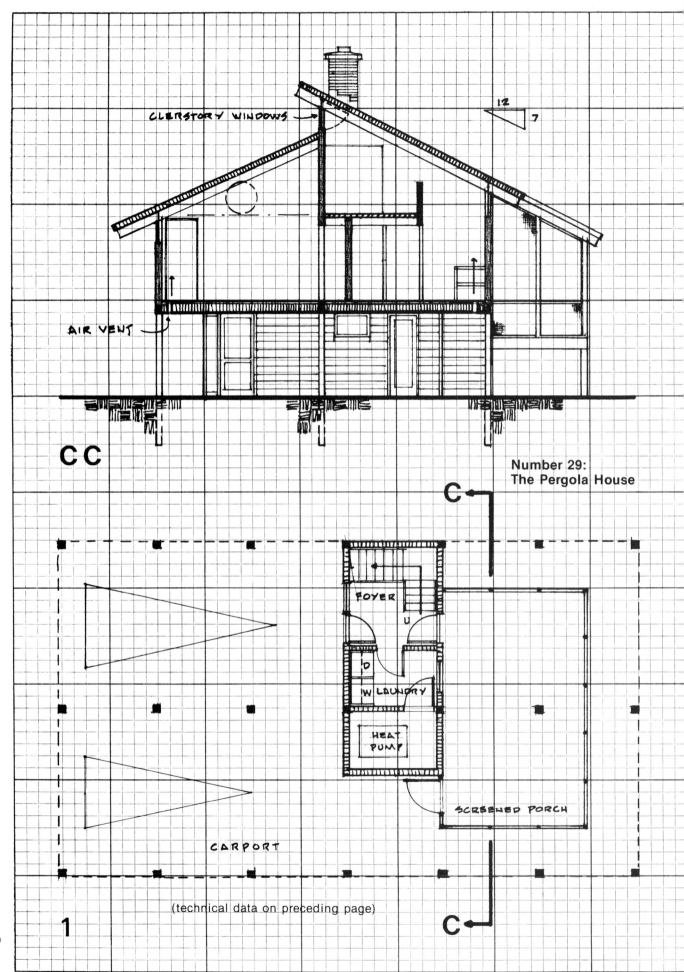

CLERSTORY WINDOWS

12
7

AIR VENT

C C

Number 29:
The Pergola House

C

FOYER

U

D

W LAUNDRY

HEAT
PUMP

SCREENED PORCH

CARPORT

(technical data on preceding page)

1

C

200

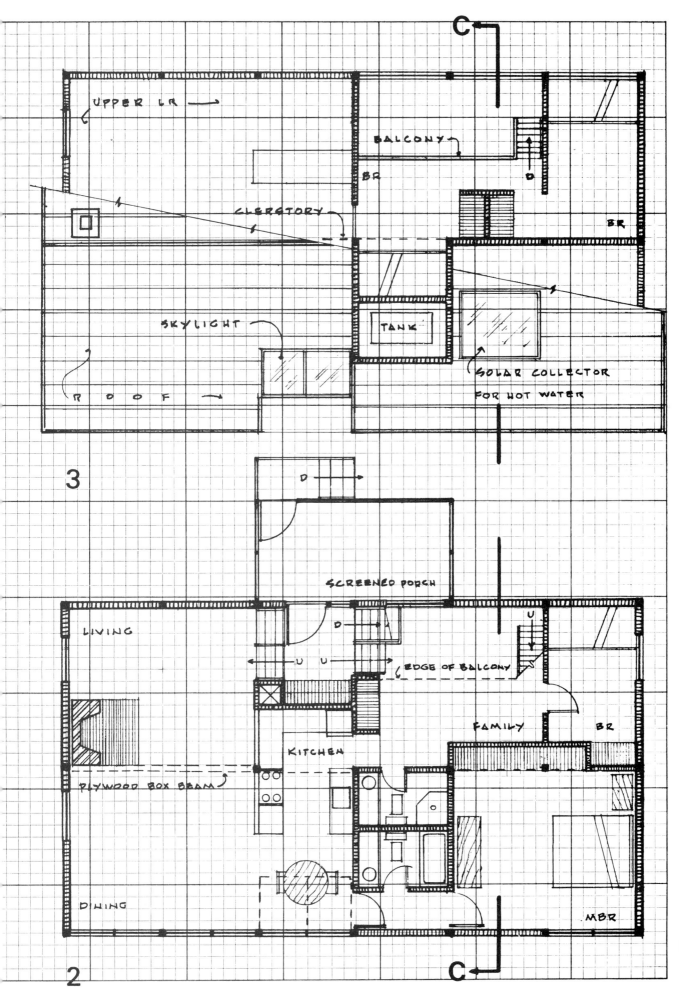

3

UPPER LR →

BALCONY →

BR

CLERESTORY →

BR

SKYLIGHT →

TANK

SOLAR COLLECTOR
FOR HOT WATER

R   O   O   F   →

D

SCREENED PORCH

D

U

LIVING

U   U

EDGE OF BALCONY

FAMILY

BR

KITCHEN

PLYWOOD BOX BEAM

DINING

MBR

2

House 30: The Modified Loomis House

This is my second house from *Low-Cost, Energy-Efficient Shelter*. The derivation of this design is of interest and will allow the presentation of some interesting variations for this design.

Several years ago I was approached by John Loomis who taught at a tiny, exclusive college. The college was so exclusive that it only held classes occasionally on Tuesday, Wednesday, and Thursday afternoons. The faculty was addicted to five-day weekends and the students invariably slept 'til noon, so midweek afternoons were all that were leftover. John, after going through several wives, was a confirmed bachelor. Several children were afloat in the debris of these marriages. He had taken an option on a remote, steeply sloping site. Could I design him a small house which could be built for less than $10,000? Of course.

John's only real requirements were a built-in Dutch oven and the total cost. I had a whole relaxed winter to design the house, an unheard-of rarity. After much trial and error, I came up with the idea of a four-post house, only 24 feet square. It had a simple shed roof which allowed for a couple of sleeping lofts for weekend visits from the children. In the very center was a brick chimney with a fireplace facing the living room and the famed Dutch oven built right into the fireplace flue from the kitchen side. John loved it and rushed right off to the bank to borrow money to build. The bank did not love it—too small. Besides, they thought it couldn't possibly be built for less than $10,000. I got two contractors to figure the house, and both figures *were* less than $10,000. Still no go at the bank. Since it was a very small rural town and that was the only bank, we gave up. Many years later, I discovered that the bank was afraid that the little college would fold and they would be stuck with a tiny house suitable only for a single college professor.

The plan lay dormant for several years until I was working on *Low-Cost, Energy-Efficient Shelter*. I had designed a saltbox especially for that book. At the last minute, it was decided that we really needed one more design for the book. One of the other architects had not had time to get his design together. So I dusted off the Loomis house, made it a bit bigger and fixed it up so that it would be suitable for a small family. Somehow, the plans got stranded in one part of the book and the house elevations were off in another chapter, but still many people ordered plans.

After some more thinking, I refined the house a bit more to make the spaces more usable and started including the alternate plan with the sets of working drawings which people ordered.

House Number 30:
The Modified Loomis
Floor area — 666 square feet
        62 square meters
Exposed surface area — 1,776 square feet
        164 square meters
Efficiency ratio — .38

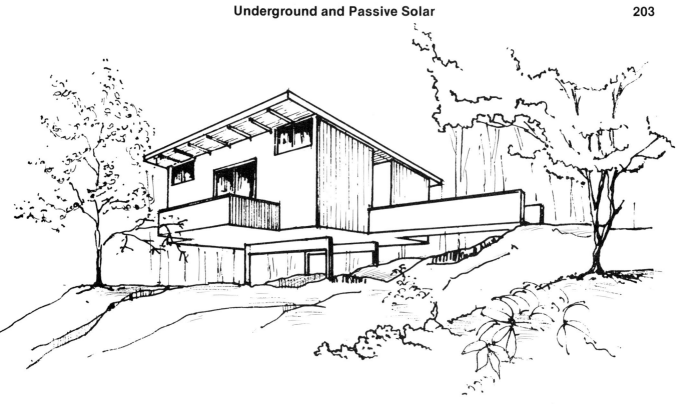

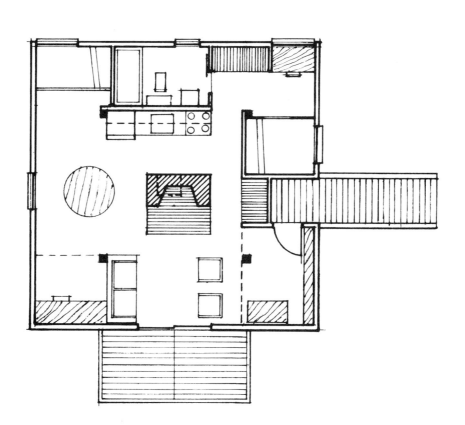

Many people still wanted something bigger. Twenty-six feet was the maximum that I could stretch the cantilevered floor structure for the four-poster. What if I set it on a slab-on-grade and made it bigger? Many people had also written asking if I had a solar-tempered house which used any of the principles which Eugene had described in his solar-tempering chapter. And everyone seemed to want a fireplace. It seems that if you are going to save money in building your own home, most people want to put some of the money back into the psychological warmth of a fire. I put in a masonry wall set back 6 feet from the south-facing glass wall. The sun strikes this wall and the mass of the wall stores considerable heat. Also, the heat from the flue of the stove or fireplace adds to the wall's storage capacity.

I included this larger house on my list of available plans. Two families have ordered it. Michael and Susan Moore are still running a raging battle with the bank and the code. We were inching a bit closer to building when the county health department issued a moratorium on all new building due to overflowing septic tanks.

The second order came from John Lundquist of Grant, Nebraska. The plans came back completely redrawn, bearing little resemblance to the original house. (I describe this transformation in the opening sentences of this book.) We sent the plans back and forth many times. After surveying his site, John discovered that there was a marked drop-off to the south. He decided to extend the house down one story on the south side and install passive solar collectors. As can be seen from the plans, the whole house has a different feeling than the original design. Mrs. Lundquist wanted a completely separate kitchen, complicating the plumbing somewhat. A small basement utility room doubles as a storm shelter for the nasty winds which they have out there on the plains.

John's house was especially designed to handle very hot summers and very cold winters. Flaps which are hinged top and bottom do double duty as sun shades in summer and solar reflectors in winter. A large air vent located at the top of the house opens to provide air circulation through the open plan in the summer. In order to make the bank happy, a heat pump was installed as the backup for heating and cooling. The solar collector is designed in such a way as to preheat the coils on the heat pump in winter so that it will use less power. John does not plan to use the heat pump in the daytime in summer; it would be turned on briefly at night to cool down the house.

Solar-tempered Loomis house under construction.

Sloping south wall stores heat in the solar greenhouse.

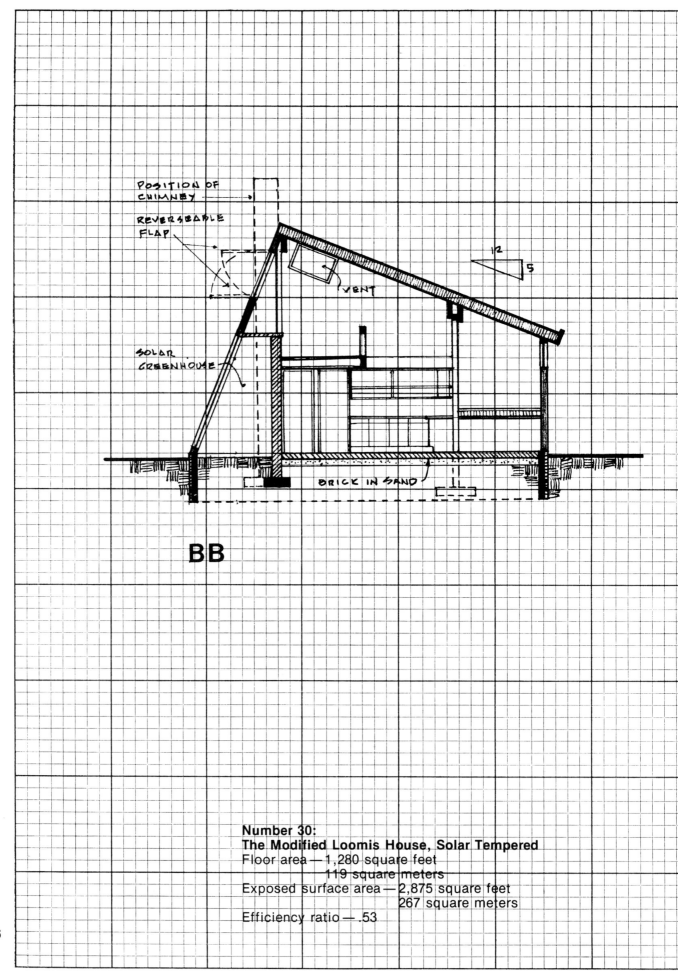

POSITION OF CHIMNEY

REVERSEABLE FLAP

VENT

12
5

SOLAR GREENHOUSE

BRICK IN SAND

BB

Number 30:
The Modified Loomis House, Solar Tempered
Floor area — 1,280 square feet
119 square meters
Exposed surface area — 2,875 square feet
267 square meters
Efficiency ratio — .53

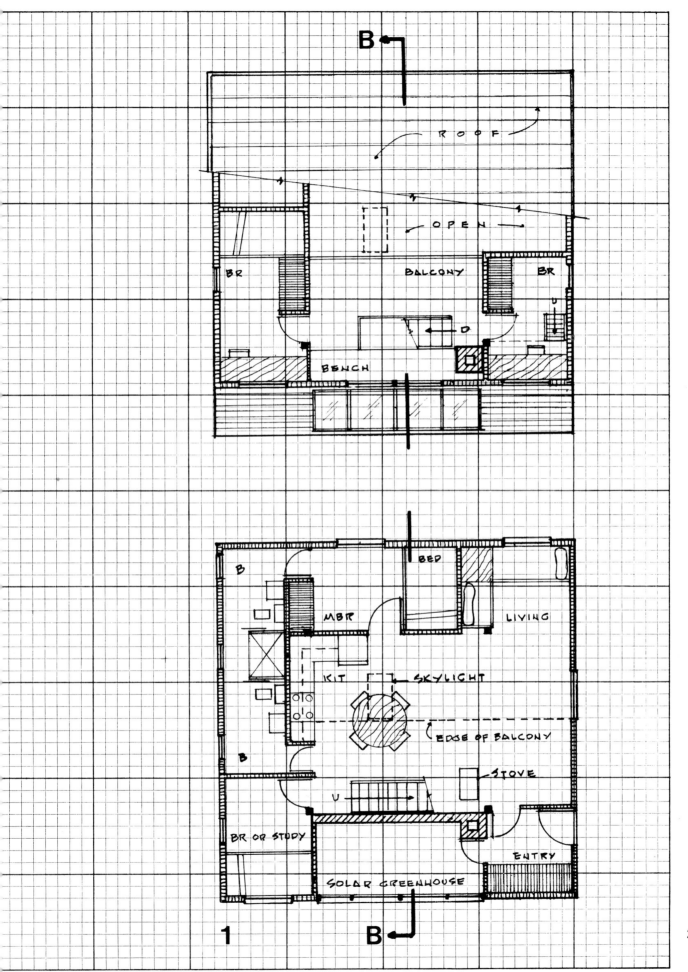

B

ROOF

OPEN →

BR

BALCONY

BR

U

D

BENCH

BED

B

MBR

LIVING

KIT

SKYLIGHT

EDGE OF BALCONY

STOVE

B

U

BR OR STUDY

ENTRY

SOLAR GREENHOUSE

1

B

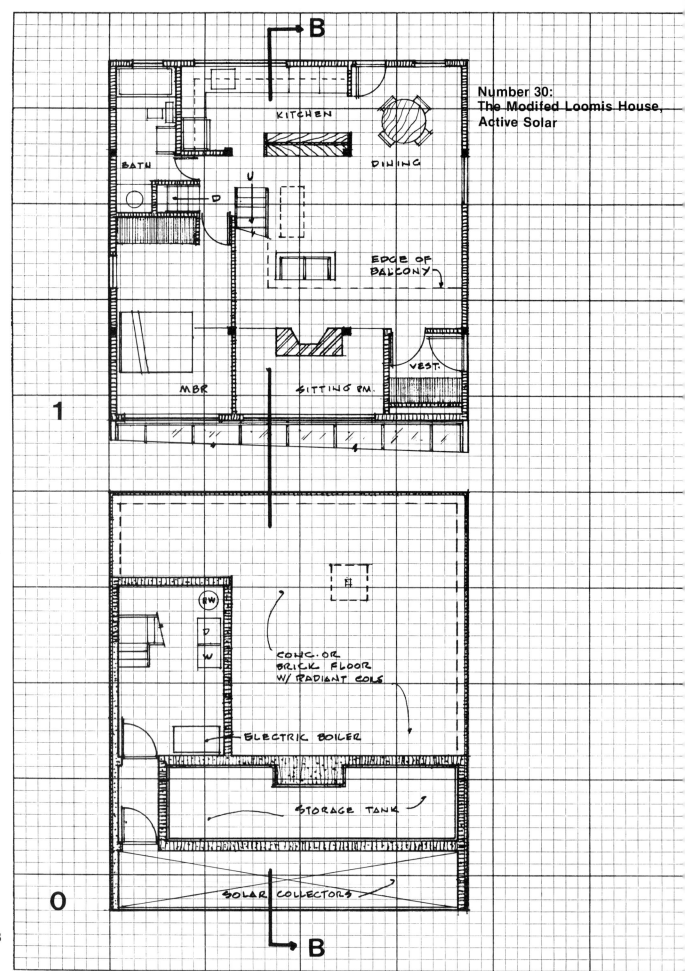

Number 30:
The Modifed Loomis House,
Active Solar

KITCHEN

DINING

BATH

U

D

EDGE OF
BALCONY

MBR

SITTING RM.

VEST.

1

CONC. OR
BRICK FLOOR
W/ RADIANT COILS

ELECTRIC BOILER

STORAGE TANK

SOLAR COLLECTORS

O

B

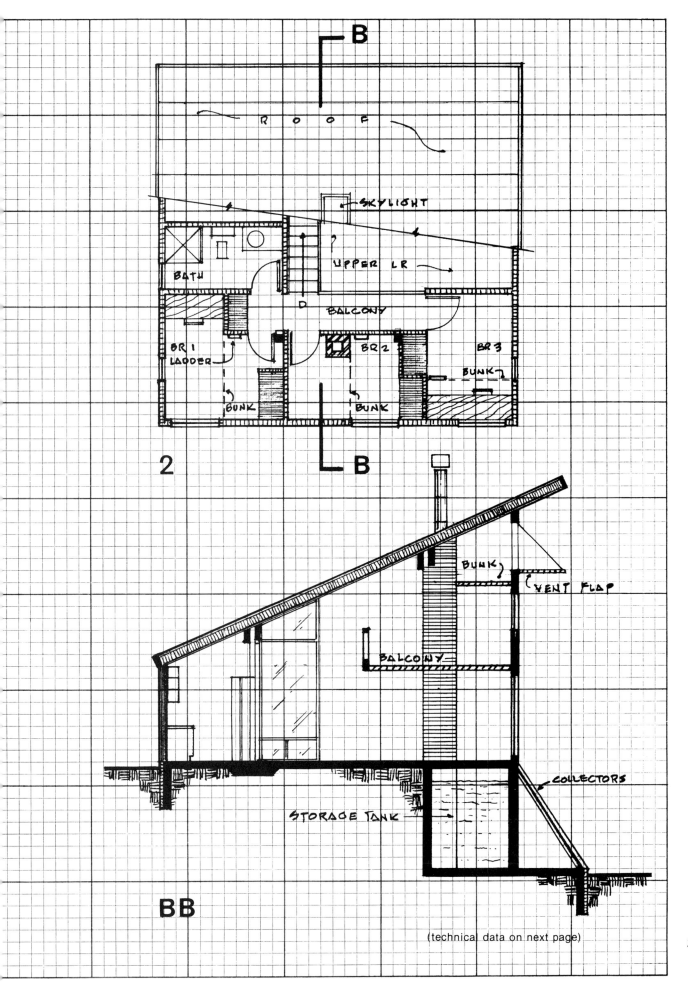

B

R O O F

SKYLIGHT

BATH

UPPER LR

D   BALCONY

BR 1
LADDER

BR 2

BR 3

BUNK

BUNK

BUNK

2

B

BB

BUNK

VENT FLAP

BALCONY

COLLECTORS

STORAGE TANK

(technical data on next page)

Number 30:
The Modified Loomis House, Active Solar
Floor area — 1,350 square feet
                126 square meters
Exposed surface area — 2,310 square feet
                            215 square meters
Efficiency ratio — .58

(technical data for preceding page)

One of David Howard's post and beam frames under construction. Note the chicken wire and Styrofoam on the walls near the bottom of the photo. They have been applied in preparation for plaster.

Part II

Design and Construction Principles

Chapter 5

Post and Beam Framing

Post and beam framing has been used for centuries because it is a simple and logical method of using the least material and labor to accomplish the most building. Strangely enough, many people regard it as a modern, unconventional building technique. The Pilgrims built their houses at Plymouth using this system, so it is hardly new to this country. It amazes me that such an easy and beautiful building method has been abandoned. Part of the trouble is that the system required large timbers both difficult to find and expensive to transport. (This makes it ideal for on-site work if you can cut timbers right on your property.) Another problem is that the connections between the various pieces require considerable skill if they are made in the traditional fashion. American workmen are not noted for their skill.

A traditional post and beam frame is heavy and requires a great deal of handwork to fabricate. If you have access to a lot of timber on your property, then it can be used to build your own house. Eric Replogle (House Number 22) is building his own frame that way, but much of the house is masonry, so framing will be simplier. There is a fine new book about timber framing on the market. It covers the history of the system and also provides a lot of details in case you want to do the work yourself. This invaluable reference is *The Timber Framing Book* put out by a group called Housesmiths.* Housesmiths also builds heavy timber-framed reproductions of early colonial houses. Some of the old designs—those which were nearly square and had a central chimney—are very energy efficient, particularly if insulated with modern insulating materials. If you want an authentic old house, these are the people to talk to.

David Howard of Alstead, New Hampshire, has evolved the post and beam frame one step further and has made it compatible with modern construction methods. Traditional frames were made by hewing actual tree trunks into posts or beams and then hoisting them into place. Since

*Chase's Pond Road, York, ME 03909.

the trees were usually just squared up, these frames are considerably heavier than necessary. David has engineered the frames into a complete building system and in the process has made the members considerably lighter. The members are still large enough to be quite dramatic, but their smaller size makes for cheaper transportation and easier erection. The frames are sawn from oak timbers which are either left roughsawn or dressed with an adz to resemble old hand-hewn beams. I prefer the former treatment as I feel that it is a more honest expression of how the members are actually made.

David has devised quite a number of design variations from his framing system and will fabricate a frame for almost any house you could imagine. His houses usually follow closely the design principles I advocate in this book. Since framing is the most difficult part of building a house, the Howard firm builds the frame only, and then turns the owner loose to finish the project.

All finished materials are applied on the outside of the frame so that the frame itself hides joints which may be difficult for the beginner. By the time the owners have enclosed their shell, they will have picked up enough carpentry skills to do a good job on the more critical interior finish work.

Running wiring and piping through the members of a post and beam frame is very difficult and expensive. David and I both solve the plumbing part of the problem by making compact bath-kitchen layouts which enable all of the piping to be placed along one wall. Since the insulated walls and roof are installed *outside* of the actual frame, wiring can be run in usual fashion in the Howard houses.

One of the major areas of cost savings in a post and beam frame is involved in the actual erection of the frame. Since there are many less framing members, the frame goes up quite quickly, usually in a day or two. This aspect of the frame gives a terrific psychological boost when working on the building. Seeing the whole frame go up in just a matter of hours encourages one to get going with the rest of the work. Whatever your building method, a house is a lot of work. The post and beam system provides an orderly, easy-to-understand method for starting the construction of your house.

The first major consideration in designing a post and beam house is the layout of your posts and beams. The distance between the major framing members is known as "bay spacing." Older houses and those of the Housesmiths and Howard tend to have very wide spacing between the major beams since they use heavy members. Ten- to twelve-foot spans were common. A typical 16 × 20-foot farmhouse would have been framed with six posts.

For my own post and beam houses, which were always built on a very low budget, I have devised a very economical, simple, framing system which uses light pieces of standard-size framing lumber laminated together to make heavy members. I do this because it is difficult to buy or fabricate heavy timbers without ready access to a sawmill. I laminate

Post and beam construction allows glass to extend right up to the ceiling and eliminates extra framing members over the windows. Ceiling beams are built up with standard-sized construction lumber. Posts are 4'0" (O.C.).

both posts and beams from three pieces so I can overlap the members at the wall and eliminate expensive custom joints. The simple straight cuts required can be made by an amateur.

There is another advantage to this system. Since the posts and beams are built up from smaller members, it is easy for one or two people to erect a frame. Traditional post and beam houses required large crews or mechanical equipment. Since these laminated beams are so strong, I usually space them 6 to 8 feet apart. I find that the beams make a convenient place to attach interior partitions and also provide a convenient tool for laying out the plan of a building. If the beams and partitions do not line up, however, the results are usually not very attractive. When installing a wall that *doesn't* line up with the beams, try to stop it short of the ceiling. Study the details at the end of the chapter to make sure that you understand this system. In my frames, unlike those of David Howard's and the Housesmiths, only the ceiling beams are exposed.

Two concrete slabs were poured to receive the prefabricated panels. Bases for 4 x 4 posts were embedded in the concrete. First panels are set in place and X braced.

Another major cost-saving feature of a post and beam frame is that the floor and roof can be constructed of heavy planks and thus form a structural floor or roof deck and a finished ceiling all in one operation. Anyone who has ever tried to patch a hole in a plaster ceiling or apply Sheetrock overhead will tell you how nice it is to have a wood ceiling. If you have to rely on a standard lumberyard, I recommend using 2 x 6 tongue-and-groove fir decking. It will span 6 feet safely for a floor; for a roof, the span can be stretched to 8 feet except in very heavy snow areas. In areas of severe winters, you will need to have a thicker roof structure to accommodate heavier insulation. A nice way to do this is to apply 1-inch roughsawn boards on top of the main structural members and then frame over the roughsawn with 2 x 12s at 24 inches on center (O.C.). If the roughsawn is applied at a 45° angle to the framing members, it can be nailed to both surfaces making a very solid roof. In this way, you can install 12-inch fiberglass insulation but still have the beauty of an exposed-beam ceiling. For moderate or southern climates, I recommend 3-inch polyurethane insulation board applied over the 2 × 6 decking.

More panels are installed along the center hall.

If you live near a sawmill, by all means use native roughsawn material for your floor and roof decks. Use 2-inch-thick stock for spans up to 6 feet. For floor decks with spans up to 8 feet, use 3-inch-thick lumber. If you need to have an 8-foot span, but can't get 3-inch roughsawn, you can buy 2½-inch-thick laminated deck which will do the job nicely. Or you can laminate the decking yourself (see House Number 4).

I have designed a series of houses (see House Number 29) which combines the best features of post and beam framing with the tilt-up wall system favored by some large contractors. In this method of construction walls are built in large sections and tilted in place by machinery. You can hire a contractor to build one of these houses for you. They have four freestanding posts in the center with the roof structure and a balcony cantilevered from the posts. This system has the major advantages of reducing the number of posts and providing uniform loading on each post. If you have a particularly obstinate banker or building inspector, you don't have to call this a post and beam structure since it technically isn't—the posts are freestanding and not attached to the walls.

When building a post and beam house yourself, accurate measurements are vital for a good job. Double-check all structural members to make sure that they are plumb, level, and properly spaced before fastening into place. When building a post and beam frame, set and plumb the corner posts first, brace them well so that they can't move, and then stretch strings between them for setting the intermediate posts. Bracing is really important on these houses. The old-fashioned heavy frames have diagonal braces notched into both posts and beams. These braces are one of the great charms of that system, but add considerably to the cost. I use plywood to provide an economical system of bracing. The book, *From the Ground Up*, gives exact instructions for calculating the amount of bracing needed for a post and beam house. *Be careful* as this is a serious structural calculation. Don't get carried away with a south-facing house and try to make the whole wall glass without any area for bracing. It can be done, but you should get the advice of a structural engineer.

Attachment of the members is another problem which I have solved by using new methods. For the light overlapped framing system, ordinary nails work very well. If you want to dress the frame up a bit, use cut nails. Another favorite trick of mine is to drill through the members and use 1-inch hardwood dowels dipped in glue to fasten them together. I always use a few nails to set the members in place and then drill and dowel them for a permanent fastening. Do not use this method for the four post houses though. The stresses are higher and steel bolts should be used instead. I use ¾-inch threaded rod and cut it to exact length with a hacksaw. Use double washers and tighten securely. If you are using green wood, you will have to retighten the bolts periodically. If exposed bolts don't appeal to you, substitute ¾-inch lag bolts for the threaded rods, countersink the heads and then plug the holes with dowel. This is also a nice detail for anchoring a wide, heavy plain floor deck. The lag screws will hold the floor down and prevent any warping. Nails, even heavy ones, may be pulled loose by the movement of the wood.

Another type of post and beam framing is called pole frame. In this variation, preservative-treated poles are used and embedded directly into the ground to form foundation and structure all in one. This system is excellent for making use of steep sites. If you build on a slope the raised floor causes additional insulation problems, so I would only recommend this solution for a moderate or southern climate or possibly as a vacation house. Of course, the embedded posts can be used on a flat site and will work perfectly well, but since I recommend using a heat-storing masonry floor when building on grade, I see no reason for spending the extra money for treated posts. There are several excellent publications which tell you how to build these buildings.* They are very

Posts are set in place and attached to panels. Note that doors are prehung in the shop.

All interior posts are set and outside wall panels started.

*From the American Wood Preservers Institute, the publications "FHA Pole House Construction" and "Pole Building Design." From Garden Way Publishers, (Charlotte, VT 05445),*Low-Cost Pole Building Construction* by Douglas Merrilees and Evelyn Loveday (1975). Also see *Low-Cost Energy-Efficient Shelter for the Owner and Builder* by Eugene Eccli.

well suited for farm buildings or garages where a finish floor may not be required.

Many people may try to discourage you from building a post and beam house. Aside from factory-built housing which has failed miserably in this country, this is the most efficient way to build. It is a particularly easy way for a beginner since it is logical and easy to understand. If you have any lingering doubts, just look at some of the post and beam houses in this book and the prices for which they were built.

Posts are installed at outside wall, roof beams are started and 2 x 6 decking begun. Note how the roof beams are made up of 2 x 12s attached to the sides of the post. Filler piece will be installed in bottom of beam after wiring has been run.

Beams in place all of the way across the house. Decking being installed.

A construction joint, post and beam frame, showing dowels.

A construction joint, post and beam frame,
showing through bolts.

Roof decking almost finished; roofer is standing on the upper-level roof deck which is hidden at the top of the house.

Shell of the house complete. Polyurethane
insulation has been sprayed over the 2 x 6
decking.

Finished roof and trim in place. Small structure in front of house hides heat pump.

Chapter 6

Ecological
and Economical Materials

A wise choice of materials is important when building a house if it is to be economical in both its primary costs and in maintenance expenses in the years to come. Since materials comprise over half the cost of a typical house, significant savings can be made in this area. But let us not save money at the expense of our fragile environment. Remember that many otherwise desirable materials may use excessive amounts of energy in production, transportation, or both.

Brick, Stone, Concrete, Slate

One example is brick. It uses great quantities of energy in the firing process and then, because it is heavy, more energy in transportation. However, brick, along with other masonry materials, is valuable because of its capacity for storing heat for long periods of time. We now have a conflict of a desirable material versus the excessive energy needed to manufacture and deliver it. How do we resolve this conflict? Simple—buy used brick. If you can find an old brick building being demolished, you can frequently salvage bricks for almost nothing. But whatever you do, don't buy used brick from a commercial brickyard. Used bricks are considered decorator items and are priced accordingly. Your best bet is to buy either from a wrecking company or a small speciality shop which deals only in used brick. Our local shop sells "seconds" for four cents apiece—if you pick them up and load them yourself.

In some parts of the country, there is another easy, often free, option—native stone. The stonework shown in the picture was obtained from the excavation for a new building. It had been blasted out for a foundation. Working with stone takes lots of time and patience, but is relatively easy, and there are some really good books on the subject.* If you

The Club of Rome's projection of when we will run out of common materials, based on known reserves and rate of consumption trends:

gold	1982
redwood	1983
silver	1986
mercury	1986
tin	1990
oil	1993
copper	1994
lead	1994
gas	1995
tungsten	2001
aluminum	2004

*The Owner-Builder's Guide to Stone Masonry by Ken Kern, Box 550, Oakhurst, CA 93644, and Building Stone Walls by John Vivian (1976), Garden Way Publishing, Charlotte, VT 05445.

collect your stone from a streambed, don't use it for a fireplace because it will explode when exposed to intense heat. One of my lesser architecture professors once built a dandy exploding barbeque pit.

Another basic building material which is ecologically sound is concrete. Since it is made mostly from local materials and employs people from your community, you will also help boost the local economy. Concrete is very useful in making a massive floor which stores heat and keeps your house warm. A nicely troweled concrete slab makes a perfectly serviceable finished floor. A coat of clear polyurethane varnish will make it easier to clean and a few colorful area rugs add the final touch. (Don't use too big a rug, however, or you will affect the slab's ability to radiate heat.)

If you want a more interesting finish for your slab, slate works well. I don't mean to suggest the nasty multicolor stuff which comes precut in jumpy rectangular patterns. A much cheaper and infinitely more desirable slate is available from masonry yards in large irregular slabs which can be broken into smaller random pieces with a sledgehammer. The colors are quite handsome—blue black, soft moss green, and a medium clay red. I would recommend using only one color; it makes a much better looking floor. The slate must be set on a 1½-inch-thick mortar bed and takes a lot of hand work. The concrete slab must be depressed about 2 inches in the area where you want to use the slate, or you will have a dangerous tripping spot where the floor changes materials. It is particularly handsome for an entrance hall or bathroom.

A section of a two-foot-thick stone wall constructed with stone salvaged from an excavation.

Maybe all of that work doesn't appeal to you, but you still want something other than grey concrete. There are literally thousands of thin composition-flooring materials on the market but they are patterned with all sorts of hideous imitations of terrazzo, or other "real" materials. One company—Kentile—gives you an alternative. It makes ⅛-inch-thick, vinyl-asbestos floor tiles in solid colors. No glittery flecks, ugly patterns, or other tasteless designs. You will probably have to go to a big city tile dealer or have your dealer special-order these tiles for you, since most dealers don't bother to stock them. Even Kentile's patterns tend to be in better taste than the competition.

Wood

A hand-hewn beam. It *is* possible to make your own.

If you build a post and beam house as we recommend, you will use considerable quantities of wood. Try to buy from local sawmills, not from lumberyards. In this way, you put the money directly into your local economy, not into the pockets of big business elsewhere. Most such mills sell only roughsawn (unplaned) lumber. It has many advantages. Roughsawn is more attractive than planed lumber and the costs of planing and long-distance transportation are eliminated. Because of its rough surface, it takes stains and preservatives more readily. Paint should be avoided as a finish. Preservatives and penetrating stains do a much better job of protecting the wood, and for less money. Note that I said penetrating stains. Many paint companies have started selling so-called "pigmented" stains which are really just dilute paint. They also peel off like paint and have to be frequently recoated, which is why the paint companies are pushing them. They are of little or no benefit to the wood. The best preservatives are Cuprinol and Woodlife, and they can be easily applied with a common garden sprayer. Both come as a clear chemical that doesn't materially change the color of the wood. If you want a color, Cuprinol is available with added pigments in several pleasant colors.

One of the best uses for roughsawn lumber is as siding. Since most roughsawn is available only as green (not kiln-dried) lumber, there is considerable shrinkage and care must be taken to cover the joints. There are two easy ways to do this. The first is simple board and batten. The battens cover the cracks between the boards as they dry and shrink. Be careful to nail the battens only on one side of the crack or they will split as the boards under them shrink. A second method is the shiplap joint. This costs you a bit for milling the edges of the boards, but you save the material costs and time of installing the battens. The difference is primarily one of aesthetics.

If you have the time to buy ahead, you should consider allowing your green lumber to air dry before you use it. Six months to a year is the recommended period. It must be stacked in a dry place with spacers about three feet apart between each layer of boards to allow air to circulate. Lumber dried this way is much more stable than the kiln-dried stuff from your lumberyard.

If you do buy lumber from a commercial lumberyard, try to buy the cheaper grades and sort it carefully when you pick it up. Third-grade oak flooring, for instance, costs even less than asphalt tile and, in my opinion, is much more handsome than the more expensive grades of clear oak. I think it adds considerably to the character of a floor to use this material. This flooring comes in shorter lengths and has lots of color variation. Also, if you stain your interior trim instead of using paint, you can use common pine which costs half as much as clear. Minwax Colonial Pine is a very handsome stain, and a coat of paste wax seals the wood. If a very dark finish is desired on cheaper grades of wood, try creosote. It gives a very rich finish which considerably upgrades the wood. Some people may be allergic to it and it gives off an odor for several months, so use it with care.

Plywood and pressed chipboard are two excellent and ecological uses for wood. Both are much stronger than the wood in its original state and they use logs more efficiently than just cutting them into boards. Neither of these materials is very attractive in its native state except when veneered with a finish wood as is frequently done for cabinetwork and furniture. Plywood is the stronger of the two and is a good choice for roof sheathing or as a sidewall sheathing where bracing is required. Chipboard takes paint well and is used where a good finish is required. A new product which combines the advantages of both materials laminates the two materials together into one sheet. Both, however, are considerably more expensive than roughsawn lumber. If you are doing your own work, it will pay to use as little of them as possible. If you are hiring the work done, the sheet materials go up much faster and save labor.

Plywood can also be used as a finish siding material and sheathing combined into one. This system saves a lot of time and labor and also one layer of materials. Exterior plywood sidings come in cypress, cedar, and fir with grooves cut in to resemble planks. The former two are naturally weather-resistant and require only a coat of clear Cuprinol. The pattern is called Texture 111. I prefer, however, to use the plywood in smooth sheets and then apply battens to the outside. They are fake, as actual joints only occur every four feet, but this makes a much better-looking job. Use Johns-Mansville construction adhesive and nails to install the plywood and battens. The adhesive does a fine job and lets you cut way down on the number of nails.

Use appropriate materials. Metals conduct heat rapidly and should be avoided where wood or other materials can be used instead. Aluminum, in particular, is an ecological disaster. One of the primary reasons for the proliferation of new generating plants, atomic and otherwise, is the inefficient use of energy by American industries. This, in turn can be traced to widespread use of aluminum. Aluminum refining requires astronomical quantities of electricity. Artificially cheap power has encouraged the development of such absurd products as aluminum siding, gutters, windows, and doors. All of these products are better made of wood. One exception to the use of metal is a product called Terne.*

Board-and-batten siding.

Roofing Materials

*It is manufactured by the Follansbee Steel Company, Follansbee, WV 26037.

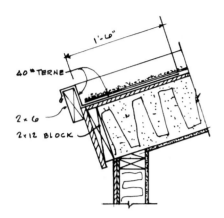

Built-in gutter.

This is steel sheet with a protective coating of lead. Unlike aluminum, which deteriorates rapidly, this is a permanent material. It should be used for all flashings and makes a nice looking built-in gutter. Built-in gutters are much better looking and last longer than the ugly tacked-on kind. Since building-in a gutter is a lost art, I have included a detail here.

With the costs of asphalt shingles rising daily due to their oil content, you may want to consider using Terne metal for your roof. The material costs less than asphalt, but the installation is very labor intensive. The metal has to be bent into pans, then painted, and finally installed on the roof by means of double-crimped seams. The pans for the standing-seam roof should be fabricated by a sheet metal shop, as this is a bit tricky for the amateur to do. A special machine called a brake is used to make neat bends in the metal. You can rent brakes, but you have to be very accurate when working with them so that the pans fit together well.

Two of my clients who are fond of these roofs are getting together and doing all of the installation work for their roofs. A sheet metal shop will do the initial work of bending the pans, but they plan to take over from there. Fabricating one of these roofs for yourself is a time-consuming project, but when you are done, you have a permanent roof which will last hundreds of years, as opposed to an asphalt roof which must be replaced after 15 to 20 years. Also, the sound of rain on one of these roofs is one of the most delightful I know.

Standing-seam roof installation. A "professional" roofer started this roof; I finished it. Note the crooked seams at the left done by the roofer versus the straight seams on the right made by an amateur.

If all that bending and crimping sounds like a bit too much, you can still have a factory-made metal roof. Several of the houses in this book have V-crimped or corrugated galvanized-iron roofs. If painted,* this material should last 20 to 30 years—up to twice as long as an asphalt roof. In certain areas with industrial fumes and near salt air, galvanized iron will deteriorate rapidly and should not be used. If your roof was built perfectly square, this roof is probably the quickest and easiest roof for the beginner. The sheets are simply overlapped and nailed to the roof deck with lead or soft plastic-headed nails.

The cheapest durable roof you can install is double-coverage roll roofing. It is made from the same material as regular asphalt shingles but is manufactured in 3-foot-wide rolls instead of small shingles. A conventional shingle roof rots out where the fake notches are cut in the asphalt, but since this roofing doesn't have the cutouts, it lasts a lot longer. Very clear installation instructions are printed on the paper wrapping for the roll roofing. Follow them exactly. For very low-sloping roofs such as porches, this is the best low-cost solution.

Roofs offer an excellent opportunity for recycling materials. Slate and tile can both be recycled since they never wear out. Sometimes the nails corrode and are difficult to remove in one piece. It may take quite a bit of shopping to find a large enough quantity of slates or tiles in good condition to cover your roof. This is also an extremely labor-intensive job. The slates and tiles have to be cut with a power saw equipped with a masonry blade (this can be rented from a tool rental shop). These

*Tinolin is an ideal paint for Terne roofs. It's a good, old-timey, oil-based paint that comes in a variety of colors. It's available from Calbar, Incorporated, 2626 North Martha Street, Philadelphia, PA 19125.

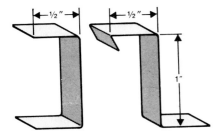

Pans formed for installation.

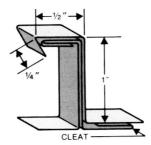

Installed with cleat.

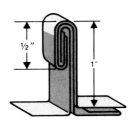

Finished seam.

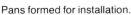

CLEAT

Details for standing seam roof.

roofs must have heavier framing to carry the extra weight of the materials.

Plaster has become a victim of high-priced labor unions. Most people would rather have plaster than Sheetrock if they could. Since labor is the major component in plastering costs, plaster can even save you money if you do it yourself. Except for ceilings and corners, plastering is an easy, do-it-yourself project. Since I advocate wood ceilings, you don't have to worry about that problem. The plaster to which I refer is a rough-finished natural grey plaster, not the smooth white finish which is difficult to apply. Plaster can either be applied over gypsum lath (similar to Sheetrock) or Styrofoam. If you apply 1½ inches of Styrofoam to the inside face of the studs, it will make an excellent base for plaster. Here are the detailed directions which David Howard provides to his clients:

Plastering Tips

1. Use perlite-base plaster (80-pound bags)—"Gypsolite" or "Structolite."
2. Use a 5½-cubic-foot mixer (rent it).
3. Use *good tools.* (A good plastering trowel is $6 to $8; a good haug is $5.)
4. Test each group of bags. Make sure plaster is *fresh* and all of the bags have the same number—old plaster will set very fast and turn brown.
5. Clean all tools and mixer after *each* batch.
6. Let plaster set for one-half hour after mixing—then apply.
7. Plaster has the right amount of water in mix when it's a bit soupy and if you squeeze a handful it will all come out through your fingers.
8. Apply two coats.
9. Always do one complete area on second coat.
10. Start at the edge of a wall. Put a line of plaster on edge of trowel and press into corner. Release pressure on trowel before removing it from wall.
11. Room temperature should be 50° to 80°F.
12. Let plaster set about one-half hour—then smooth. Let it set two hours and when slightly hard, dress it a bit smoother.
13. If day is hot and dry, sprinkle a little water on plaster each hour for three hours.

14. When plaster gets a little hard in the wheelbarrow, add a bit of water to it.

15. Start in an area you won't see (behind a counter or in a closet).

Sheetrock

Sheetrock, if applied on the inside of a well-insulated wall, does store some heat from the room. If you are installing it yourself, you should strongly consider using two layers of ⅜-inch material rather than the single layer of ½-inch material which is more commonly used. In this fashion, you not only provide extra mass for heat storage, but also get a very superior wall finish which rivals plaster for quality. In this system, the Sheetrock is applied with screws and panel adhesive. Joints between the two layers are staggered making the seams almost completely invisible and providing a very flat surface. Full details for this excellent system can be obtained from one of the major suppliers, such as U.S. Gypsum or Gold Bond.

Hardware, Plumbing Fixtures, Etc.

Ours has become a throwaway society. If you are willing to spend the time, almost anything you might need for your house can be found used or at salvage yards. Sometimes, you can even find a whole house and buy all of the parts you want. Many wrecking companies just take a wrecking ball to a house and then cart everything off to the dump. If you keep your ear to the ground, maybe you can find one of these and slip the contractor a few bucks to let you strip out doors, windows, stairs, plumbing fixtures, and the like. These items are some of the most expensive in a house and it is a good investment to go looking for them. Most of these older products are also of such high quality that you couldn't find them today at *any* price. For example, the front door of the Gummere house is 2½-inch-thick solid oak with a fine brass lockset. The door would cost new around $450 and the lockset about $200. The door, including the lockset, cost only $20 at a salvage yard.

A used stainless steel, restaurant-size bread-mixing trough recycled as a bathtub.

An even more worthwhile recycling method is to buy a whole house and dismantle it for materials. Many people have old buildings on their property which they want to get rid of. If you don't have any luck looking on your own, try placing an advertisement in a community newspaper such as *Bylines, Pennysaver,* or *Want Ads*. I have found this to be quite effective. If you use care in dismantling your old house, you may be able to get most of the materials for your new one. Note that such things as wiring, asphalt shingles, and old piping (other than copper or brass) are better left alone.

Hardware and plumbing fixtures are such expensive items that everyone should try to buy them used. The best brands are Russwin locksets and hinges and Kohler plumbing fixtures and faucets. Be very picky; check everything for wear. Take along a can of WD-40 and spray the parts of locks and hinges and check to make sure that they work properly before taking them home. Check faucets for worn stems or missing parts. Make sure that you get *all* of the pieces necessary to attach your plumbing fixtures to both supply and waste piping. Sometimes they have obsolete-size piping which is virtually impossible to match. Also, make sure that you buy a cast-iron tub. A steel tub isn't worth taking home even new. The old cast-iron jobs were deeper and contoured to fit the body rather than made to fit some Madison Avenue idiot's idea of what will sell. A copper or brass tub, on the other hand, is worth a mint as an antique. If the owners don't know what it is, take it and run. Remember, you can easily sink one of the old roll rim-type, cast-iron tubs into the floor if you build a slab-on-grade house. In this way, you can have an elegant sunken tub for very little money.

When you *do* buy new materials, buy wisely. Purchase in large quantity and buy all of any items of a kind which you need at one time. A good example is nails; they are much cheaper in 50-pound quantities than by the pound at the hardware store. In some cases, it pays to go directly to the manufacturer or to the nearest large city. For instance, a sheet of Plexiglas costs over $120 at our local rip-off glass shop. The same 4 x 8 sheet costs less than $50 at a plastics supply house in New York City. Almost exactly the same prices apply to a 34 × 76 sheet of tempered insulating glass. The same glass shop wanted $120, while the manufacturer, the Economy Glass Company of Boston, charged less than $40. When buying sheet glass, try to standardize sizes and buy a case. (Glass comes in even-inch sizes in all reasonable sizes; for instance, 22 x 28 inches). You can even construct your own double- or triple-glazing. Good instructions for doing this are given in *From the Ground Up*.

Sources for Used Materials:

Contractor's Salvage
Taunton, MA 02780
Taunton is also home base for Glenwood Range Company so look around for a used one while you are there. This is the best salvage yard I have found.

Webber Wilson
Chambersburg, PA 17201
One of the largest suppliers of used stained and leaded glass windows in the country.

The Wrecking Bar
292 Moreland Avenue, NE
Atlanta, GA 30307
They have a large collection of stained and leaded glass salvaged from buildings.

Ball and Ball "Whitford"
463 West Lincoln Highway
Exton, PA 19341
Here you'll find old-style hardware, rim latches, shutter hinges, strap hinges. Expensive, but the price may be worth it in order to match old work. Many items made to custom-order only.

Plexiglas and Glass

An old roll-rim, cast-iron tub enclosed with cedar and Plexiglas.

Locating wholesale outlets takes loads of time and effort on your part, but if you don't have the extra money, your time is well spent.

For large glass areas requiring shatterproof glass, Plexiglas is an ecologically sound material, despite its use of oil-based chemicals. Your alternative is tempered glass. Tempered glass must be fired after its initial manufacture to produce its special characteristics. Since this is normally done at a separate plant, handling charges as well as large amounts of energy are consumed in its manufacture. Economy Glass Company does all its own operations and hence cuts prices sharply.

I strongly recommend Plexiglas for the beginning housebuilder. Unlike glass, it can be easily cut with common hand tools and does not have to be special-ordered at astronomical cost for special sizes. It is also safe and easy for one person to work with. Special effects such as greenhouses can be cheaply fabricated with ease. Plan window sizing carefully, keeping overall sheet size in mind. A nominal 4 x 8 sheet is actually 52 x 100 inches. The skylights which I show on the plans are usually 52 inches long so as to use the material without waste. Plexiglas or tempered glass should be used in all areas where breakage could be a problem, such as skylights, large panes which are located high above the floor, and in any area where someone might walk through the windows. Plexiglas scratches easily and must be handled with care. Leave the masking in place until all fabrication is complete. Do not use conventional cleaning agents for cleaning. A dandy product called Silver Brite* does the job very well at low cost; it is also great for any shiny, but scratchable surface.

As a final thought, remember that everything you use that is already made means that energy and labor aren't required to manufacture the items again. You save money and you save resources.

A lovely walnut latch design for a Dutch door. It's available from David Howard.

*Available from Fred Silver and Company, Incorporated, 145 Sussex Avenue, Newark, NJ 07103.

Chapter 7

Windows, Doors, Skylights, and Insulating Flaps

Windows

The size, shape, and placement of doors and windows are especially important in establishing the character of your house. The doors and windows should be the very soul of your house. The units available commercially are aesthetic disasters. Unfortunately, the designers of these mass-market items have virtually no taste or sense of proportion. Many people sense this and want something better, but are at a loss as to how to proceed. The first step is to make sure that you have exhausted all of the local wrecking yards mentioned in the last chapter. This is by far the easiest and cheapest solution.

Before we get into building your own, I do want to call your attention to some fine commercial windows which are available at a reasonable price. The first is a versatile little awning vent made by Andersen Window Company; it is intended for use as a basement vent and is listed in lumberyard catalogs as such. This great little window comes in three sizes, all 2-foot × 8-foot long and ranging in height from 1 foot 3 inches to 2 feet. These windows cost less than $24 each. They open to two positions and can be lifted out for cleaning and even reversed since they have hinges top and bottom. They are miraculously free of any breakage-prone cranks or other tricky hardware and are one of the best buys available in the building industry. They are prime-painted white and come with single glazing and a screen. These windows work nicely as operating vents above or below fixed glass panes and also are good for kitchens, baths, and clerestory windows (see the picture of the Hess house).

The second windows are traditional multipaned casements and double-hung units which are available at very low cost direct from the factory.*

---

*They are made by the Riverside Millwork Company of Penacock, NH 03301. The trade name is Rivco. Another company which will make any size or style double-hung window is R & R Windows and Interior Supply Company, 268 Penn Street, Brooklyn, NY 11211.

A fixed pane of insulating glass provides a magnificent view for less than $60.

This bay window is a stock Rivco unit from Riverside Millwork Company in Penacook, New Hampshire.

The company will also make almost any size or shape multipaned sash. Keep this in mind if you have to replace an old sash or want one made to match some that you already have on hand. There is one drawback to dealing with this excellent company. They only ship their windows within a 100-mile radius of their factory. Otherwise, you will have to pick them up yourself and costs could be prohibitive if you live a sizeable distance from the factory.

Simple window sash can be constructed using exactly the same technique as I describe for doors later in this chapter. Before you actually build any windows, make sure that the size and placement are correct. Badly placed windows are a permanent mistake, particularly in a small house where you have no room to waste. High windows let daylight penetrate far into your room. If you have a low ceiling as shown in our post and beam houses, it is possible to simply hinge the windows at the top and swing them right up out of the way. In a room with a high ceiling, the windows can be lowered to eye level and have shelving placed above them. The sash can be swung up against the shelves or ceiling and hooked in place. You can use either new or salvaged sash. The screen can be installed on the outside and no special hardware is needed except for the cam-type latches. Again, use sponge-type compression weather stripping to seal tight against the weather. Think carefully about your furniture placement before putting in those windows. High windows give you much more space for furniture.

The traditional favorite for houses is the multipaned, double-hung window. The scale and rhythm provided by these windows is unbeatable. In order to get nice ones, you almost have to buy them used. New ones frequently have bad proportions. They do not ventilate very well as you can only open one half at a time. The combined use of high ceilings on the south wall and 6-inch-thick walls provides an excellent opportunity to revive a great window from the past. It is called a triple-hung window. There are three sashes installed in similar fashion to the double-hung window, but going all of the way to the floor. Since each

A window built on the job and on Blaine hinges. The top of the window drops as you push it out for perfect ventilation.

Three used window sashes have been triple-hung to form a new floor-to-ceiling window.

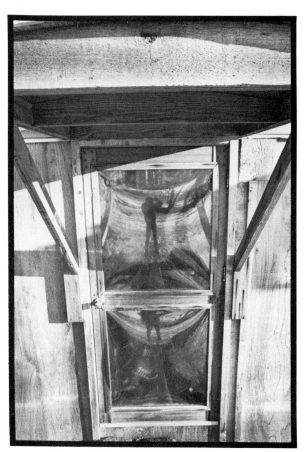

A homemade door of cedar with inflated vinyl glazing.

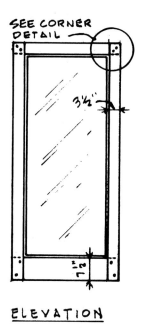

SEE CORNER DETAIL

3½"

ELEVATION

sash runs on a separate track, all three can be pushed together providing very flexible use for the window. It works well as a door to a deck as in the picture. If you find window sash which you like at a wrecking yard, buy extra top sash and you can make these windows. One disadvantage is that they are as hard to weather strip as are double-hung windows. Insulating shutters or other such devices are necessary for these windows.

Many of the houses in this book show large panes of safety-tempered insulating glass. These have been designed to use standard replacement glass usually used in aluminum sliding-glass doors. You do not want to use the sliding doors themselves. They leak air, transmit heat rapidly through the aluminum frames, and are a security problem.

Sometimes these doors can be bought on sale at reasonable prices. If you live in a southern area or plan to install insulating flaps over the doors, they might be a good buy. It is a lot less work to just install the sliding doors rather than build your own. The standard replacement glass for these doors runs $40 to $60 direct from the factory. The Gummere house (Number 9) has a two-story window wall with owner-built doors. The glass for this wall cost less than $400.

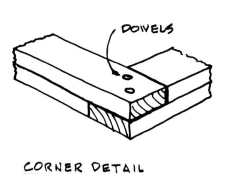

DOWELS

CORNER DETAIL

Doors   Doors are one of the most wasteful building components. Home-built doors are better than those in lumberyards and much cheaper. The worst thing about commercial doors is their poor insulating qualities. We solve that by using a polyurethane foam core. A simple frame is made up of 2 × 2s or 2 × 4s; the cavities are filled with foamboard and the unit is surfaced both sides with ¼-inch tempered Masonite, plywood, or coreboard. The door should be glued together and the surfaces nailed with screwtie nails. I have built doors and insulating flaps as large as 8 feet square using this technique. For larger sizes, use a 2 × 4 frame around the entire perimeter. Members should be set with the 4-inch dimension parallel to the face of the door. For heavy doors, I recommend strap-type utility hinges, through bolted. Compression-type sponge weather stripping should be used to seal against the weather. Simple, cam-action latches should be used to insure that the door or flap seals tightly against the frame.

Exterior doors should always be constructed new for northern climates, unless you plan insulated covers for them. While I favor recycling old doors where possible, there are some other possibilities.

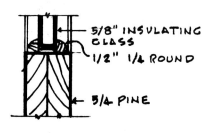

5/8" INSULATING GLASS
1/2" 1/4 ROUND
5/4 PINE

GLAZING DETAIL

Simple home-built glass door constructed of two layers of wood overlapped at the corner.

One nice technique which is particularly nice for large interior doors is to glue together 2 × 2s. Use the lumberyard variety with slightly rounded corners. The rounded corners of the individual boards not only provide a nice texture, but spare you the difficulty of having to line up the boards precisely or alternatively sand them down after assembly. No clamps or special equipment is required, just apply glue and nail the boards together one at a time with serrated nails. The sketch here shows an old-fashioned crossbuck door which was fabricated from scraps of 2½-inch decking. A very heavy, but nice door. Use your own imagination; the possibilities are limitless.

Sometimes you may want glass in the door. If you want only a small pane, it can easily be framed into the door as it is being built. The picture here shows an oak door which is double-glazed with Plexiglas. It was constructed entirely with hand tools and employs a unique method which I use to make both doors and window sash. In this case, two layers of ¾-inch-thick oak were used to construct the door. The oak on one face of the door is ½-inch narrower than on the other face, thereby allowing room for the glazing. The boards are simply overlapped at the corners (one side of the door has horizontal joints; the other side has

A two-inch-thick insulating door, opened and braced with a board here, is constructed with a polyurethane insulating core. Small Plexiglas windows give a view of the valley to the north when the door is closed.

A door framed in solid oak leads to a south-facing deck. The door is double-glazed with Plexiglas. The glass sidelight is a standard-sized, Blaine tempered insulating-glass unit.

Heavy door constructed from scraps of 3-inch decking. Since the material is very heavy, one of the diagonals from crossbuck has been omitted.

vertical ones). The two layers of the door are glued together and fastened with nails. I also used two dowels per joint at each corner. With this technique, no fancy joinery is needed at the corners and simple hand tools can be used. Notice that this particular door has very narrow side rails requiring a circular extension to accommodate the lockset. Since the two sides of the door are offset by ½ inch it was easy to make a strong attachment for the circular lock block. Materials for the door cost less than $50 and it took about half-a-day to build.

One major problem for an amateur owner-builder is getting hinges and latchsets attached properly to doors and windows. Mortising in hinges and locks can be quite tricky and is better left to a skilled carpenter if you are not very handy with tools. There is an easy alternative, however. That is to use surface-applied hinges and latchsets. Both are much stronger than conventional-type mortised units as they do not require weakening the door or window to apply them. The surface-type latchsets are commonly available at salvage yards and are known as "rim"-type latchsets. Surface-type wrought iron hinges are available new from Stanley Hardware Company, normally available from a local hardware store, although they may have to be ordered for you.

A four-inch-thick homemade door with a handmade latch (outside view).

The same homemade door (inside view).

Skylights Skylights are the easiest, most efficient way to admit light and heat from the sun in both old and new houses. The reason that so few skylights are used is that factory-built units are ugly and expensive and most people don't know how to build their own. In fact, they are easy to build. As in the case of windows, placement of the skylight is important. Consider the path of the sun and make sure that it will fall where you really want it. Skylights can make otherwise unusable attic spaces bright and cheery without adding expensive dormers; they also admit much more light than a dormer. South-facing skylights can be a valuable source of winter heat. In order to work properly, they must be insulated at night. Any of the methods which I describe later in the chapter for insulating windows can be used. The light-tight shade is my favorite

Skylights brighten an attic.

Top edge of a piece of Plexiglas is slipped under the existing roofing, just like a big shingle, to form a skylight that doesn't leak.

as it can be operated with a long cord and doesn't require climbing or gadgetry.

Skylights, even the factory-built ones, have a very bad reputation for leakage. This is because they are always built up on a curb which forms a perfect spot for leaks. In my houses, I install a sheet of Plexiglas just like a big shingle. Plexiglas (acrylic plastic) is the ideal material for skylights. If installed properly, it will not break and it transmits less heat than glass. The easy solution to leaky skylights is to slide the top of the skylight under the roof shingles at the top of the skylight opening and let the Plexiglas overlap the opening about 4 inches at the bottom and sides. Seal the plastic in place with clear silicone and anchor it with roundhead screws and washers spaced exactly evenly (about 1 foot apart) around the perimeter of the skylight. Seal the screwheads with the silicone and you are finished. If you like, you can install a second layer of Plexiglas from the inside. Make sure, in addition, to provide a thermal barrier for use at night.

Insulating Flaps

Insulating flaps constructed in similar fashion to the doors I mentioned earlier can be used for a wide variety of purposes. The south elevation of the Lundquist house (mentioned on page 204) shows a 4-foot × 6-foot flap fitted with hinges top and bottom. It has several uses. It is primarily used as a summertime vent. If opened from the top, it forms a small balcony and gives access to the roof. If opened from the bottom, it lifts up and forms a sunshade. The solar-tempered shed house (Michael Moore, House Number 30) shows another double-hinged flap. This one covers south-facing glass. In the winter, it is opened from the top to reflect sun onto the glass; in the summer, it is opened from the bottom to act as a sunshade. This picture shows an example of a flap in use as a door to a deck. This flap was installed on the north elevation of an existing house to provide access to a deck. More livingspace was provided in summer without adding an ugly and energy-wasting addition to a nice little saltbox.

With energy costs rising every day, it pays to carefully provide ways of preventing heat from escaping through your windows. Glass is a notoriously bad insulator. Even double-glazing, which adds greatly to your costs, leaks a lot of heat. Some companies are even promoting quadruple-glazing (at astronomical costs). There are better, much cheaper ways of solving the problems of heat loss through glass. Let's examine some of them. Storm windows are an easy partial solution and avoid the excessive costs of double-glazing. If you are using used windows, try to buy enough of them to use in two layers, or at least look to see if standard wooden storm sash are also available. Since the "home improvement" companies have made a big business of selling combination aluminum storm/screens, used wooden storm sash can be had very cheaply. If you have odd-sized sash or an old house and you can't find enough used storm sash, you should consider using ⅛-inch Plexiglas as a second layer of glazing. It can be installed either inside or out, over the surface of the sash or fitted into a convenient groove in the window frame. With double-hung windows, you may want to screw the Plexiglas directly to the sash. Install it on the inside of the bottom sash and the outside of the top sash; this way the windows work normally. Sometimes, this method can do double duty by reinforcing old sash which might otherwise have to be replaced.

Double-glazing by itself is not an adequate thermal barrier. In order to prevent massive heat losses to the glass by radiation at night, some sort of night covering should be devised. On the solar-heated and solar-tempered houses, we show insulating flaps which are installed on the outside. In other designs, you may want to install similar devices on the inside of your windows. *Low-Cost, Energy-Efficient Shelter* shows ways of installing various thermal curtains.

If you are on a really tight budget, just get some ½-inch Celotex insulating board from the lumberyard and cut panels to fit your windows. You can leave the north-facing panels in place all winter and take the south ones down in the daytime to let in the sun. These panels can be easily painted or covered with fabric.

Another useful material for insulating panels is called Styroboard. It is available at art supply and hobby shops. It is a ¼-inch-thick sheet of Styrofoam with a smooth white paper laminated to both sides. It comes in 30 × 40-inch sheets which are ideal for covering double-hung windows. The nice feature is that some light does come through so you are not entirely shutting out natural light. These boards are light, easy to cut and put up and take down. If you want to really do a super insulating job, make two layers and put a spacer around the edge thus creating a ¼-inch air space between two layers of board.

If you already have drapes, you should consider lining them with the insulation used for quilts or sleeping bags. Provide a way to seal the drapes tightly to the window frame. An easy way to do this is with Velcro fasteners, but any easily detached fastening system will do.

Another possibility is to use light-tight shades. These are of very dense fabric and shut out all light. They are normally made to order and come with side tracks which insure that the shades are lightproof. This same feature makes them an excellent heat barrier. Use them for inaccessible windows or skylights. They make a big difference.

A very fine material for home fabrication is available from the Shelter Institute. It is a 54-inch-wide roll fabric similar to "Space Blankets." This very light and easy-to-handle material cuts heat loss through glass dramatically. Its reflective surface actually radiates your body heat back at you so that you feel warmer than the thermostat would indicate. This is just one more example of the effectiveness of radiant heat. I explain radiant heat in more detail in chapter 9.

Caulking

All of your hard work building doors, windows, and insulating flaps will be for naught if you don't do a thorough job of caulking joints between materials to stop air infiltration. Really good caulking compounds are not normally available at retail stores and have to be ordered. The very best caulking is Mono which is manufactured by the Tremco Company.* If you need a clear sealant for glass or Plexiglas, silicone caulking is the answer. Do not buy the inferior American brands, though. They are overpriced and come in cheap cardboard tubes which tend to disintegrate. Rhodorsil† is a French brand which comes in a superior plastic cartridge with resealable tip so that the remainder of the silicone won't solidify.

Mono has to be warmed before you can use it and it has a nasty odor when first applied. If you are doing all of your construction work yourself, you can apply caulking between materials as you install them instead of the usual method of applying a bead along a crack after the building is finished. By applying a good high-quality caulking before assembly, you can simplify construction details and make use of butt joints where otherwise you would have to make some difficult overlapping-type joinery. You will have to do a perfect job of caulking though, or the joint will leak air and water.

*Tremco Company, Clifton Avenue Extension, Clifton, NJ 06013.
† Rhoda,Incorporated, 600 Madison Avenue, New York, NY 10022.

Chapter 8

Kitchens, Bathrooms, and Waste Disposal

Your bathroom and kitchen are basically institutionalized systems for wasting over 100,000 gallons of water a year. Typical North American households use four times as much water per capita as other civilized countries, even those that use flush toilets. The bath-kitchen-laundry complex and its attendant water-supply and waste-disposal systems are responsible for well over half of the cost of a new home. Until recently, water supplies, like many other resources, seemed infinite. Due to continued depletion of forest areas, the water table throughout the country has been steadily dropping for years. Several years of abnormally wet weather have obscured the problem in the industrial Northeast. Other parts of the country recently have been brutally reminded of our past wastefulness. We can no more afford to squander water than we can oil or gas.

The severe drought conditions in late winter and spring of 1977 have produced changes that no amount of lobbying by conservationists could have accomplished. Many places have written or are writing new codes which require water-saving plumbing fixtures. This makes things easier for everyone since it will promote the sale of more efficient fixtures all over the country. A health department official near New York City even suggested to some clients that they could use a Clivus Multrum composting toilet on their steep, rocky site where a septic system will be very difficult if not impossible to install.

A few years ago, some Department of Housing and Urban Development staff members created a panic in housing circles by releasing a report advocating the elimination of running water in low-cost rural housing. Their report showed that almost 40 percent of the budget of a low-cost house was devoted to the well, pump, bathroom, kitchen plumbing, and the septic system. The Nixonian bureaucrats were properly horrified and promptly disavowed the report. The conclusions of this report plus recent water shortages point the way to some areas for major savings in a new house.

The combined effects of our wasteful use of water and the rapidly nearing completion of the interstate highway system have produced another nasty factor which must be considered in discussions of disposal of wastewater from the private house. The same lovely people who ruined all of those miles of wilderness are busy looking hungrily around for something to do with their gas-guzzling machinery and beer-guzzling workmen. They must find something to do, but something which will not bring the ecologists down upon them. A few badly maintained septic tanks can easily provide the answer. The same big company who is angling to get the three billion dollar job of putting in a central sewer system runs out and "finds" the defective septic tanks and uses them as propaganda to reinforce the need for replacing them with a sewage disposal system which leads to a central treatment plant. This might be a nice way to put some unemployed people to work if it didn't cost so much taxpayers' money and waste so much energy which we don't have to spare. An excellent book called *Septic Tank Practices* (1976) by Peter Warshall* goes into detail on methods for fighting the "big sewer" lobby. It is an excellent general reference which should be read by anyone who has to be concerned with a septic system.

Waterless Toilets

Let's start by examining some of the alternatives to the flush toilet. Obviously, there is enough material here for several books. An excellent new one is called *Goodbye to the Flush Toilet* (1977) by Carol Stoner.† It goes into great detail on the subject. I give a very simple explanation of a plumbing system which emphasizes those methods which I feel do the most for the least cost both to the consumer and the environment. As Goldstein and Moberg say, "From just about any environmental point of view, a privy of sound construction which is properly maintained represents an excellent solution to the disposal of human excreta."** It is also a very inexpensive solution.

There are many other ways of disposing of human waste without a water-borne system, but all of them require either more attention or much more expense than the old-fashioned pit privy. It may astound many people to know that over 30 percent of the rural households in this country are still using outhouses. One of my friends has one done up in great splendor; it is fully insulated, and equipped with an electric light and a small radiant heater. Both are controlled by a switch from the house. There is also a nice window at eye level so one can look at the forest beyond. And finally, a magazine rack, since one is tempted to linger.

Various composting privies and toilets are now the vogue in environmental circles. The lowest cost design was devised by Sym van der

*Available from Peter Warshall, Box 42, Elm Road, Bolinas, CA 94924.

† Available from Rodale Press, 33 East Minor Street, Emmaus, PA 18049.

**Wastewater Treatment Systems for Rural Communities*, Steven Goldstein and Walter J. Moberg, Jr., Commission on Rural Water, Washington, DC.

Ryn, the California State Architect, for the Farallones Institute, and it is essentially a modified outhouse design with two compartments. The drawback to this system is that it does require constant maintenance by the owner if the contents are to be successfully used as compost material. Since the American public is notoriously bad at maintaining *anything,* I can sympathize with health departments who are reluctant to allow the use of the composting privy. In fact, one of the major objections to privies in general is that they are frequently allowed to get into such a state of bad repair that flies get into the pit, possibly because they are often used by very poor tenant families who have little or no incentive to repair or replace them. Health authorities should take a positive approach and send crews around to upgrade privies instead of outlawing them.

Now we take a giant leap in both cost and controversy to devices called composting toilets. The acknowledged leader of the pack is the Swedish-designed Clivus Multrum.* Scandinavian countries all have very rocky terrain which will not accept conventional septic systems. Since the Swedes are very practical and care a great deal about their environment, various composting toilets have been in use there for years. The largest, most expensive, and most foolproof is the Clivus. It is so well publicized by now that even most health departments will grudgingly acknowledge that it does satisfactorily dispose of wastes.

Unfortunately, they have another out to prevent you from using the Clivus. It is called "greywater." This is all of the rest of the wastewater from the house except that from the toilet. Theoretically, the greywater does not contain a significant number of dangerous organisms but it is possible for the greywater to become contaminated. It then needs a septic system or other treatment to be safe. Gregg Allan's system of filtration and solar distillation works well (see House Number 23), but I'm sure that it would run into rough sledding with officialdom.

The conservative health department approach is as follows: "Of course we'll let you put in the Clivus, but you also must install a full-size septic system to take care of the greywater." As soon as the householder finds out what he has to pay for a full conventional septic system on top of the $1,500 for the Clivus, he promptly forgets the Clivus.

Virtually every one of my recent clients has expressed serious interest in using the Clivus, but none has as yet been installed for a variety of reasons, usually rejection or evasion by the health department. Another problem is the bulk of the unit—it is about 7 feet high, 8 feet long, and 4 feet wide. One client had an existing house and didn't have to have approval for its installation. Unfortunately, since the house is a one-story house sitting on solid bedrock, there was no convenient way to install the big Clivus.

For those still unfamiliar with the beast, I offer a brief description: It is a large, prefabricated fiberglass box with a bottom surface sloped at about 30° to the horizontal. Bathroom and kitchen wastes and other organic material are deposited through two openings near the top of the

The solar greenhouse being constructed here will distill the greywater from the house so that it can be reused. The process works like this: greywater is filtered through charcoal beds and then condenses on the underside of the sloping glass roof where it is collected in the gutter at the eaveline and recycled to the house. Drought-stricken Californians and health departments take note. The access door to the greenhouse is in the center of the picture.

*Available from Clivus Multrum USA, 14A Eliot Street, Cambridge, MA 02138.

unit. Air is supplied to the wastes through a network of tubes (see picture) and forced ventilation takes place by means of a vent stack through the roof. After a couple of years, finished compost is removed from the bottom of the chamber.

The units seem to be almost trouble-free. One problem is starting up the composting cycle. This takes time, and the ratio of input of human waste to organic refuse must be carefully watched. Many owners report a buildup of liquid at the bottom of the unit in early periods of operation. A second possible problem is an infestation of fruit flies which get in on kitchen scraps and then multiply. Care must be taken to put scraps into the Clivus immediately and not let them sit around. Lem Tucker, Paul Sturgis's tenant, reported that his difficulties with the fruit flies eventually subsided: "It's simple," says Lem, "you just spray your ass with Raid before you sit on the thing." Extensive testing by a wide variety of authorities in several countries has assured us that the final product is indeed safe and harmless.

Several efforts have been made to combat the related problems of high price and great bulk of the Clivus. The simple, obvious solution would be for Clivus to make available fiberglass forms for casting the unit in concrete (it is standard practice in the building industry to rent fiberglass formwork). Various competitors to the Clivus—all of which are smaller and cheaper—have been recently introduced. Two of the best known are the Ecolet (or Mullbank) and the Mull-Toa. Both of these units employ heating units which run almost constantly, consuming power, but these heating units do not use very much electricity, and the toilets are small enough to fit into the space required by a normal toilet. Finally, they cost about half as much as the Clivus. There are other

A Clivus Multrum composting toilet lying on its side, showing the ventilation system inside. The privy which it replaces is in the background.

systems available, but most use considerable energy and produce no compost material to offset their energy use. For a more complete listing of alternates, see *Goodbye to the Flush Toilet.*

McGill University, an early pioneer in ecological water and toilet systems, has taken yet another approach. They have devised a home-built copy of the Clivus which is constructed of concrete block. It's called the Clivus Minimus and is illustrated in their book, *Stop the Five Gallon Flush.** This is definitely not a do-it-yourself type project unless you are a real expert on composting toilets. McGill has built several with complete success, but they still consider them experimental. The development of the composting toilet is somewhat parallel to that of solar heat four or five years ago.

Water-Borne Systems   Dr. Witold Rybczynski, of the McGill Minimum Cost Housing Group, emphasizes that the composting toilet is not for everyone. It requires attention and awareness as to what is taking place inside of the unit on the part of the user. Dr. Rybczynski compares tending a composting toilet to growing a garden. Both require that very simple uncomplicated tasks be performed for success. And they require careful attention and timing. If possible, some or all urine should be kept separate from the unit, particularly when the compost process is just starting. One reason that the Clivus Multrum is priced so high is that the company provides full instructions for their clients on how to use the units and will also help out if the balance gets upset. But don't try to talk to your local plumber about any problems. He'll just tell you that you are crazy to want one of them anyway.

Now let's examine the possibilities for water distribution and cost savings in water-borne waste systems. Most American houses are designed with little or no consideration for economies in the plumbing layout. Baths, kitchens, hot-water heaters, and laundry facilities should be placed back-to-back along the same wall in as compact a layout as possible. In two-story houses, fixtures should be aligned vertically on the same wall. Supply piping should be under the kitchen counter or otherwise exposed so that it is accessible. *Do not* bury the piping in the wall. Energy shortages which will produce power and/or fuel cutoffs during the lifetime of your house may produce freeze-up conditions. With this factor in mind, make absolutely sure that you or your plumber slopes the entire supply piping system to one easy drain point. Good, well-positioned drain valves are much more important than the useless little chrome things which plumbers install under all the fixtures (many codes which were, of course, written to make more work for plumbers will require these redundant valves).

My sketch shows how two bathrooms can share a common shower. It also shows you how all of the plumbing can be placed back-to-back along one wall to form a very compact mechanical "core."

The same back-to-back system makes drainage lines shorter, easier to install and eliminates extra vent pipes. I have designed my own back-

*Available from McGill University, Minimum Cost Housing Group, School of Architecture, Box 6080, Montreal 101, Quebec, Canada.

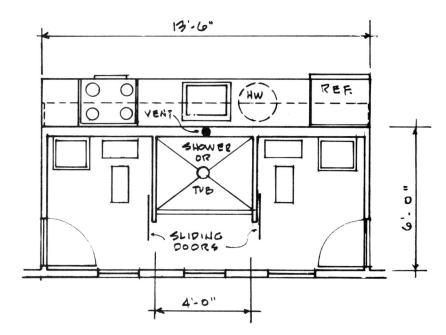

A compact layout that backs the kitchen up to two bathrooms that share a common shower.

to-back system which uses conventional plastic pipe fittings to make a very basic system at rock-bottom cost. This system employs a squat-type toilet similar to the one advocated by Ken Kern in *The Owner-Built Home* (1972).* In my case, though, I eliminated the special trap which must be ordered and made my system with PVC pipe. Only one trap is required for the entire system and serves at the toilet, shower drain, and sink, all in one.

In the simplest version, the toilet is flushed from the kitchen sink, thereby eliminating all mechanical gadgetry and using only 2 gallons of water per flush (an average flush is 5 to 7 gallons). In addition, the toilet only needs to be flushed for feces, as urine is washed away by normal usage of the sink. The showerhead is located directly over the toilet/shower base and can be used to rinse off the base. I recommend using a poured concrete base coated with epoxy enamel. This entire waste piping system was put together with less than $20 worth of plastic piping.

A final advantage is that there is only one trap for the entire system and it is protected by being buried underground. In this case, the one trap can be in close proximity to the septic tank and will be further protected by the heat generated by the decomposing matter in the tank.

"Gee, that's a nice idea, you have there, but what if we want to be able to flush the toilet without filling the sink? And how about a washbasin in the bathroom?" These are typical comments visitors make when they see my system. So I went back to the drawing board and took care of the deficiencies—without in any way compromising the original system. The washbasin drain is open and simply drains onto the concrete toilet/shower. Flushing the toilet is a bit more complicated. For about $50 you can still get one of those great old oak toilet tanks that hang on

*Available from Charles Scribner's Sons, 597 Fifth Avenue, New York, NY 10017.

My minimum plumbing system that has one drain for sink, shower, and toilet.

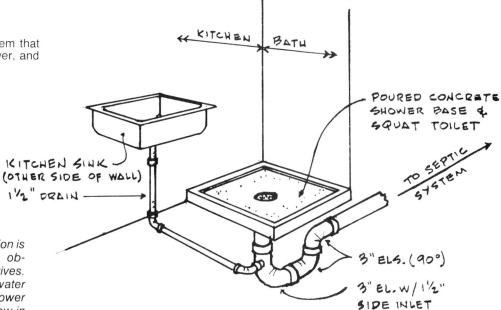

KITCHEN | BATH

POURED CONCRETE
SHOWER BASE &
SQUAT TOILET

KITCHEN SINK
(OTHER SIDE OF WALL)

1½" DRAIN

TO SEPTIC
SYSTEM

3" ELS. (90°)

3" EL. W/ 1½"
SIDE INLET

Man's natural attitude during defecation is a squatting one, such as may be observed amongst field workers or natives. Fashion, in the guise of the ordinary water closet, forbids the emptying of the lower bowel in the way nature intended. Now in this act of defecation great strains are imposed on all the internal organs. . . . It is no overstatement to say that the adoption of the squatting attitude would in itself help in no small measure to remedy the greatest physical vice of the white race, the constipation that has become a contentment.

F. A. Hornibrook, *The Culture of the Abdomen* (New York: Doubleday, 1933), pp. 76.

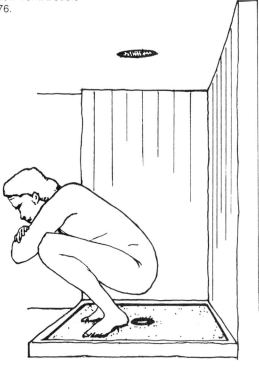

By using the squat-toilet design for my bathroom and thereby saving space, I was able to make room for a sauna. Sauna heater (lower left) is a cast-iron galley stove.

the wall. This is hooked up to the pipe from the kitchen sink and still permits water from normal sink usage to wash away urine, but gives you the option of flushing the toilet. Double-Kaye Plumbing Supply Company* sells just the tank, and a plastic high-level toilet tank is available from Adamsez Limited of England† for less than half the price of a wooden tank, but many times the hassle. I'd spend the money for the wood cistern any day. If you keep a sharp lookout at junkyards, you just might find a used one. Either of these systems will enable you to reduce the water consumption in your household to less than 10 gallons per person per day, and even less if need be. The system is well suited to any small design which has the bath and kitchen located back-to-back.

Now that we have reduced the water and waste output to a bare minimum, what do we do with the water after it leaves the house? How about a small septic system? Yes, a septic system. They are actually a quite efficient method of disposing of wastes with minimum damage to environment, but there are two very major problems concerned with these systems. The first is overloading. When these systems were originally designed, such horrors as garbage disposals and automatic dishwashing machines hadn't been invented. The automatic washing machine also adds its toll to the system. Garbage disposals are such a disaster that many codes require that systems be enlarged by 50 or even 100 percent to accommodate the residue which, ironically, makes fine compost. (Friends of mine have disconnected their garbage disposal from the septic system, have hooked it up to a 55-gallon drum, and take the kitchen wastes and water that collect there and apply them to the garden. If you are absolutely addicted to a garbage disposal, you might consider this solution.)

If the soil and drainage conditions are adequate, the septic system will work just fine, but you can't install one in a very wet area because the soil can't absorb water. Very dense clay, very steep hillsides, and ledge rock close to the surface are also no-no's for a septic system. These can be circumvented by bringing in tons of new soil and recontouring, but this is expensive and messy.

It is possible to dig a septic system out by hand; in fact, it's preferable. Heavy machinery compresses the soil and cuts down on its absorptive abilities. Never let anyone dig a disposal trench when the soil is wet, whether by machine or shovel. The movement of the smooth metal against the surface of the soil effectively seals up the pores of the soil and cuts down on the effectiveness of your disposal field. Sizing of the tile field is a very complicated process depending upon too many factors to discuss in this chapter. A simple meander-type drain field is shown here for illustration purposes only. Again, I recommend Peter Warshall's excellent book, *Septic Tank Practices*. It has information in it that the average health inspector has never dreamed existed.

Finally, septic systems are not foolproof forever. They do have to be pumped out occasionally, roots must be kept out of the pipes, and

Out-of-sight, behind-the-wall plumbing is responsible for the simple elegance of the Adamsez wash basin.

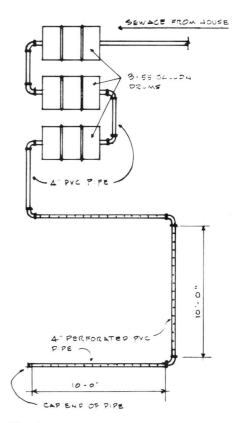

Simple drum-type septic system. Meander type should be sized to suit family and soil requirements.

*Double-Kaye Plumbing Supply Company, 450 West Broadway, New York, NY 10012.

†Adamsez Limited, Scotswood, Newcastle upon Tyne, England NE 99 2AA.

damaged pipes mended. Keep all machinery away from them. I never will forget looking out the window of one of my houses just in time to see the landscape truck disappear from sight into the remains of the brand-new septic tank. Moral: use only masonry septic tanks and keep all trucks away. Finally, draw a thorough map showing exactly where the tank and field are located. Measure to the corners of your house or some other permanent reference point so that you can locate the system when necessary.

If you are only building a weekend cabin, or basic living unit for one or two people, you don't need to put in a full-sized septic system. Notice that I said "don't need to." You may be forced to put in one whether you want to or not. If you are very lucky and out in some remote area where the curmudgeons can't get you, you may want to consider my minimum system. It is actually based upon very sound design principles, probably more sound than a lot of the commercially available septic tanks. Install piping to three 55-gallon drums as shown in the sketch. Coat the drums thoroughly with asphalt emulsion before installation, the insides, too, if possible. If you can get hold of drums with a removable end, so much the better; if not, your task is a bit harder. Seal all joints between the plastic pipe and the drums with Johns-Mansville Ductseal which will form a permanent flexible joint. (This is a very handy product to use for all mechanical sealing purposes.) If you are in a very remote area where you can't get trucks or machinery readily, this system may be your only way out.

Let's say that all of my pleas are for naught or that the building inspector, bank, or other official says that you have to have a conventional system. At least work very hard to see that it uses the least amount of water possible. All major manufacturers of toilets now make models which use less water. The most promising is one by Gerber which has a two-position flush handle: up for urine, down for feces—one gallon and three gallons, respectively. Either of the high-level toilet cisterns which I mentioned earlier in the chapter will also be suitable for reducing the water consumption of your toilet.

Plumbing   If you are using recycled faucets which I recommend, place an Eaton or Noland in-line flow control valve in the piping ahead of each faucet. Use a good high-quality Speakman showerhead; they can be adjusted to give an excellent spray pattern while also saving water. Speakman also makes some of the finest kitchen faucets available. Since the kitchen faucet gets some of the hardest use in the house, it is sometimes better to buy a new one. If you can find an old Kohler though, forget the Speakman.

Used plumbing fixtures are becoming quite popular, so you may have to do some hard shopping to find what you want. Plumbers make much of their money on materials, so be prepared to have your plumber turn up his nose at your old fixtures. Also, plumbing fixtures are designed by engineers whose primary function is to make as much money for the fixture company as possible. Hence, you will be faced with a bewildering array of assorted pipe sizes. Shop carefully at your salvage yard and make sure that you have all of the fittings necessary to hook up both the faucets and your drains to standard-sized modern piping. Since the professional plumber is going to give you a big hassle about almost everything, you should strongly consider doing your own plumbing. To do this, you will have to study the subject; it is a bit complicated. I would not recommend that you try anything more complicated than one of my very simple back-to-back systems unless you have some experience. There are many books out on the subject, but unfortunately, most of them just cover the whole spectrum of plumbing without making any judgements or specific recommendations. One rather thorough book on the subject is *The Encyclopedia of Household Plumbing Installation and Repair* (1975) by Martin Clifford.*

Materials for your plumbing piping should be selected with care. Plastic should not be used for supply piping except for a summer cabin or basic living unit. It is very easy to install, but it is fragile and tends to rupture with shock or freezing temperatures. I recommend ½-inch Type L copper for your supply piping. For a small system such as I advocate, ½-inch-diameter pipe will be more than adequate for the whole installation. Solder-type fittings can be easily obtained from salvage houses for a small fraction of their new cost. Copper pipe itself is lower in cost than the fittings, and for the small quantity involved, you will be better off to purchase it new. Clifford skips over the specifics of how to sweat copper pipe fittings together. In olden days, it used to be a disaster because the homeowner had no choice but to use a small, somewhat inadequate propane torch. The new Mapp gas torches (yellow tanks) produce a hotter flame and put the homeowner on a par with the professional. The only real trick to joining the fittings of copper pipe is to make sure that both surfaces to be joined are shiny bright and that flux is applied liberally to both surfaces. Heat the joint thoroughly and let the solder "flow" into the joint. Good luck.

For drainage piping, the beginner should use either PVC (ivory color) or ABS (black) plastic pipe. Most codes won't let you mix the two. The hardest task for the beginner will be the actual layout of the pipe for both the supply and drainage piping. With the plans available for order in chapter 12, I include a simple dimensioned layout for very basic, back-to-back bath-kitchen piping layouts. Check your local codes before you start work. Most will let the homeowner do his own work on his own house, but some won't. Also, they may require you to use cast iron for the drainage system. This is definitely not a job for a beginner.

Water Heaters

Almost 15 percent of the energy used in a typical household goes for heating water. This is an area where you can easily save. If you are doing your own plumbing system, you should incorporate a solar hot-water system. *Low-Cost, Energy-Efficient Shelter* has an excellent chapter on such systems. My favorite is not mentioned in the chapter, though. It produces more water than many other designs at less cost. The rub is that you have to manually open and close insulated doors in the morning and evening, but if you are doing that anyway with insulated solar flaps, it won't be too much of a chore. This heater is the "Breadbox" design by Steve Baer. It is simply two long tanks painted black and surrounded by an insulated box with flaps which open on the

*Available from Crown Publishers, 419 Park Avenue S, New York, NY 10016.

This small, German, instantaneous water heater uses fuel only when the water is turned on.

front and top. We are installing one on the Perlberg house with slight modifications so that the flaps can be operated from inside the house. Steve also has some of the best plans for a more conventional, do-it-yourself solar water heater.*

Even if you don't use solar energy, try to get an efficient hot-water heater. Electricity uses three times as much fuel as on-site fossil-fuel heaters, although it does make some sense for a backup for a solar heater because of its simplicity and low initial cost. If you need very little backup, it is the obvious solution. Check out a gas heater very carefully. Most of them simply have a hole straight up the middle of the tank, a typical wasteful American solution. Some of the more expensive ones have a convoluted inside chamber for better heat transfers. Rheem and Rudd make some of the best heaters, and if you can find a junked one, it may pay to buy it. Check the recovery capacity on the label; if it is higher than the standard ones in the store, you have a find. Mrs. Rice (House Number 16) once discarded a 20-gallon Rudd heater and replaced it with a new 40-gallon Sears. Guess what? The Rudd produced more hot water per hour than the Sears, and the Sears promptly broke down and took weeks to get repaired.

The real find would be one of the old "sidearm" heaters. In those, the burner and heating coils are completely separate from the storage tank. These are the most efficient units of all. They are still sometimes used commercially, so if you look hard, you may find a used one or stumble upon one tucked away in a warehouse somewhere. Repair parts are still generally available. The most likely repairs would be a new tank (those are standard and should be easy to replace) or the thermocouple for the thermostat, also standard. The older ones did not have automatic controls and could be dangerous. Automatic control kits are readily available for all gas burners.

For my own hot water, I use a coil very similar to the sidearm heater built into the stovepipe from my woodstove. It feeds a small storage tank which also has an electric heater. I use the electric heater sparingly in the summer. I find a swim outdoors much more refreshing than a shower any day. A teakettle provides water for dishes and other purposes, so the electricity rarely gets used.

Showers and Tubs   Showers require less hot and cold water than tubs, so you should strongly consider installing only a shower. At the very least, install a showerhead in the tub and encourage people to shower rather than take baths. Most bathtubs and showers are enclosed with a variety of unpleasant materials which are supposed to keep the water out of the surrounding walls. Most of them eventually leak. I have a favorite material which is also used by David Howard and other ecologically oriented architects. It is cedar. David uses standard weatherboards applied horizontally which makes a very easy application. I prefer vertical V-grooved, tongue-and-grooved boards. I have also seen cedar shakes used for this purpose. All are good. Any of them require careful workmanship and thorough sealing at the joint with the tub and at the corners. Clear silicone sealant is best for this purpose. Make sure not to

*Write to Zomeworks, Box 712, Albuquerque, NM 87103, for price list.

let the wood get wet before you apply it or the sealant won't stick. A coat of clear Cuprinol will prevent the wood from staining, but also seals in the nice smell of the wood. Some may prefer to let it get stained and give it an occasional light sanding to clean the surface. In order to make a neat job of the shower piping, it may be necessary to violate my earlier warning and bury it. For this and any other piping which might freeze, such as lines from a remote solar water heater or pipes entering the house, there are small portable urethane foam kits called Insta-foam Froth-Pak Kits.* The material is one of the finest insulations available and ideal for getting into or around tricky piping. It is highly flammable and toxic, so stick to small quantities on pipes. When used for house insulation, it *must* be covered with a fireproof material such as Sheetrock.

The modern kitchen has become overladen with gadgetry and expensive cabinets. Most of this is unnecessary, particularly if you are trying to save money. Consider open shelving instead of enclosed cabinets. You will find that kitchen items are much easier to find and the items themselves can be quite decorative. Try a floor-to-ceiling storage unit of very shallow (4- to 6-inch deep) shelves. These are great for canned goods and a wide variety of other kitchenwares. A nice place to put these shelves is on one side of the refrigerator. In this way, you can box in the refrigerator and make it less obtrusive. Make sure that you don't restrict the air circulation, though. (See chapter 10 for instructions on making a refrigerator more efficient to operate.) Drawers are very useful for small items and somewhat difficult to build. Amos Molded Plastics of Edinburg, Indiana, makes a nice system of one-piece, molded drawers which come complete with guides. These drawers are designed to accept a wooden front piece, so you won't have plastic showing in the kitchen. They make things very easy for the amateur carpenter.

If you do build your own cabinets (which I highly recommend), there is a good set of details included in *Low-Cost Homes for Rural America* (1972) by L. D. Anderson and Harold Zornig.† A good source of supply for all of those nice concealed hinged, drawer slides, lazy susan turntables, etc., is Craftsman Wood Service Company.** They also stock every conceivable variety of hardwood from oak to zebrawood just in case you want to do up the kitchen in real style. (I, personally, find that ordinary #2 pine with a stained finish makes quite handsome kitchen cabinets.) The lazy susan which I mentioned earlier is great if you have a dead corner in the kitchen. Most people try to fit doors to them and thereby ruin their effectiveness.

Plan your kitchen very carefully so that it will work well. It's not the amount of space that counts, but rather where the space is placed. A simple straight-line kitchen takes only about 10 feet to have a really workable layout. Most of the houses in this book have well-planned compact kitchens. Study the layouts for ideas.

* 2050 North Broadway, Joliet, IL 60435.

† Available from Dover Publications, 180 Varick Street, New York, NY 10014.

**2727 South Mary Street, Chicago, IL 60608.

Kitchen Shelves and Cabinets

Shallow open shelves are excellent for kitchen storage. Plants thrive in the solar greenhouse beyond. The glass back makes shelves light and airy.

Countertops   Kitchen countertops are one place where you can save a lot of money. Factory-built plastic laminate (Formica) tops have become almost prohibitively expensive. I recently made a novel Formica top, though, for less than $10. Surplus houses frequently sell sink cutouts from lab equipment and commercial countertop companies for very little money. I got a batch of these scrap pieces, trimmed them neatly into rectangles, and put them together to make a countertop. In order to conceal the joints between pieces, I cut strips of dark-colored Masonite and coated one edge with several coats of polyurethane varnish. Then I assembled the pieces into a one-piece top. The front edge was finished off with a 1 × 2 piece of solid oak. If you want to make your own Formica top, I recommend a solid-wood edge strip. Not only is it handsome, but it keeps you from having to make a tricky edge with the plastic and will protect the edge from chipping.

One of my more inventive clients made his countertop from old white marble toilet stalls. I think that is a bit much, but you might want to put in a slab of marble for a mixing center. It's great for working pastries and the like, or, it's particularly good near the stove as a place to put hot pots.

My favorite way to make countertops is to laminate together short pieces of wood. The wood strips should run from front to back of the countertop and be trimmed with a solid strip along the front edge. If the piece has some depth, say 3 inches, it can hide a structural support for the counter (see photo). I have successfully used scraps of maple flooring and scrap 2 × 6 decking which I recommend for floor decks. Any of the wood materials should have several coats of polyurethane varnish, thoroughly rubbed between coats. Oak is not a good material for countertops, as any ferric metals (like cast-iron pans) will cause black stains which are very difficult to remove.

A final plea for building your own is that you can make the built-ins suit your own needs. A friend who is 6 feet, 6 inches tall built his cabinets to a 40-inch height instead of the standard 36 inches. "Old-fashioned" ranges had cooktops which were at 33 inches so that you could see into the pot and stirring was made easier. I frequently see bathroom washbasins at 33 inches or 35 inches above the floor instead of the usual "plumber's standard" of 31 inches. The 31-inch height is a compromise for adults and children and the result is suitable for neither. Either give the kids their own basin set to their height or a stool to get up to the adult-height basin. The entire construction industry is hamstrung by this type of herd instinct. Nothing is ever questioned.

A countertop assembled from scraps of recycled Formica sink cutouts.

Chapter 9

Heating and Ventilation
Using Nature

I consider this to be the most significant chapter in the whole book, so read carefully. We constantly hear cries of "fuel shortages." Nonsense! We use vastly more fuel per capita than any other country in the world. Countries such as Sweden with much colder winters use only 60 percent as much heating fuel per person. The shortage is not of fuel but of competent designers and engineers who can design buildings which do not waste so much heat. Heating is likely to be the costliest item in a homeowner's budget. It shouldn't be. A small, efficiently designed house, well insulated and thoroughly sealed against air infiltration, needs very small quantities of fuel for heating. If the house has south-facing windows with proper insulating shutters its heating needs can be reduced to about 10 percent of the requirement for a conventional sprawling ranch house. Similarly, if proper use is made of the forces of nature in hot climates, electrical needs for air conditioning can be considerably reduced. In this case, we need wide roof overhangs to shield the house from the summer heat and careful attention to siting and window placement to take advantage of natural cooling breezes. In areas where there are both cold winters and hot summers, the overhangs have to be lowered or made adjustable to work properly for both seasons.

It is past time for all of us to speak out against energy waste in all of our buildings. Sprawling, badly designed schools with fixed single glass and no insulation can affect the amount of your taxes drastically. If your place of work is similarly designed, it means that fuel costs gobble up money which could otherwise go for salary increases. It is time for the public to take the system in hand and stand up to those who would continue excessive energy use when easy solutions are at hand.

Before we consider actual methods of heating, let's examine some ways of reducing the actual *amount* of heat needed. The location and orientation of the building as well as surrounding plantings play an important role in the amount of heating and cooling which is needed. Jerome Kerner covers this aspect in great detail in chapter 5 of *Low-Cost, Energy-Efficient Shelter*. Be sure to study this information carefully before buying a lot or finally locating your house.

I have stressed throughout the book the importance of keeping a house compact and using heavy insulation. This is where it really pays off. In this chapter, I will refer often to the concept of radiant heat. If the interior surfaces of your house are designed to retain heat and radiate it back to the occupants, you will feel warm at much lower temperatures and thereby save fuel. Heating engineers will tell you that most heat is lost through the roof and that wall insulation is of secondary importance. Don't believe them. A 6-inch-thick stud wall filled with urea-formaldehyde foam will make a significant difference in heating needs. Similarly, a masonry wall exposed inside the house with polyurethane insulation on the *outside* will retain heat from the house and radiate it back to the occupants. In chapter 3 I explained how houses can be built using this heating principle. Remember that radiant heat from any source can make the occupant of a room feel warm even though the surrounding air is quite chilly. For example, try standing in the sun on a cold day in a sheltered area. You feel warm even though the air around you may be below freezing. The loss of radiant heat from the body is one reason that we tend to turn up the thermostat on a cold day. If your outside walls are extra cold the body loses heat more rapidly and needs a warmer air temperature to compensate.

Control of humidity is also quite important to comfort. Humid air is able to hold much more heat than dry air, so compensate accordingly. If you have single-pane glass, you can't do too much about humidity as any excess will immediately condense on the cold surface of the windows and then turn to ice. To be really effective, you need three layers of glass. Either use the double storm windows which I mention in chapter 7 or some sort of insulating flaps. A good bit of moisture is needed to really do the job. A constantly boiling teakettle such as my grandparents used to have will help. If you use a brick floor set in sand as I recommend, pour water liberally on the surface and let it evaporate. If you have an unsealed basement slab, you can pour water directly on that floor also (David Howard uses this method to keep his oak frames from checking in the winter).

One major consideration, both winter and summer, is proper dress. My grandfather used to work in the oil fields of the late 1800s. He was outside the year round. He learned from daily experience to dress to suit the weather, both in summer and winter. In extremes of winter and summer, he always wore a hat: a light, wide-brimmed one to keep off the summer sun and a tightly knit stocking cap to keep out the winter cold. In the winter, he always wore woolen long johns, a wool shirt and pants, and a vest. He wore the vest in the morning until the fires were going and the house was warmed up. In mild winter weather, the vest served as an outside garment. In severe weather he donned a topcoat. In summer, he stripped down to one layer of light-colored, lightweight clothes. Also, he wore suspenders rather than a belt so that hot air wasn't

A wall of hay bales encased with cement plaster makes a novel and extremely well-insulated wall, equal to 12 inches of fiberglass. Alex and Neal look at each other through the window.

trapped at his waist. I lived with my grandparents as a child so I remember all of this well. How many men do you see these days dressed in a heavy long-sleeved shirt with a tee shirt in summer and who then turn around and wear a short-sleeved shirt open to a bare chest in winter? Then come bitter complaints about hot hot or cold it is. Women are similarly lax in dressing properly for the weather. If you dress properly and insulate your small house well, you will find that 60°F. is a perfectly agreeable indoor temperature.

Now let's examine the merits of the various heating fuels available to us. The sun is free, and it will probably be there for awhile—unlike some other fuels. Rate it as an A1 priority. In this country, coal exists in great abundance. Anthracite coal burned in an efficient unit provides a low-cost reasonable source of heat. It will probably be less affected than wood by the periods of dire shortage ahead. Wood is, of course, the easy and readily available standby. Unlike coal, oil, and gas, it is a renewable resource. However, a massive shift to wood heating such as is now taking place will create shortages. They may not be permanent, but they will drive the price up. A hedge against shortages and price rises is to have your own woodlot. A plot of about five acres of hardwoods should provide plenty of wood to heat a reasonably sized house. Make sure that you cut your wood ahead so that it is properly seasoned and burn it in an efficient heat source.

The use of electricity as a heat source is a much more complicated matter. Direct-resistance heating as recently promoted by the power companies is a disaster. About 20 years ago, I met a mechanical engineer who was an associate of the late Frank Lloyd Wright. He warned quite accurately that the moguls who control the electric power companies would mount a massive advertising campaign to force electric space heating down the throats of unsuspecting homeowners. The public, by sad experience, now knows better. Since installation costs of electric heat are relatively low and heaters can be set selectively, electricity does make some sense as a backup for wood or passive solar systems. Also, there are some efficient sources of electric heat such as heat pumps. I will discuss them in detail later in this chapter. You should bear in mind that the electrical distribution system in this country is quite extensive. It is likely that major efforts will be made to continue to provide some electricity, no matter what. It may therefore pay to provide some small part of your house which has electric heat capabilities as a safety factor for emergency shortages of all other fuels.

At this stage, oil or gas cannot be seriously considered as the only source of heat for a new house. Indeed, we can reasonably expect restrictions upon new connections for their use. Conventional oil- and gas-fired furnaces work most efficiently when they are maintaining a uniform temperature.

It is better to consider them as backup systems to maintain a base temperature of 50° to 60°F. and use another heat source to bring the house up to daytime temperature. Setting the thermostat back by 10° to 15°F. at night does save fuel, but the sudden prolonged demand when the thermostat is reset in the morning offsets much of the saving.

A good way to use these units is to use them as a backup with the thermostat set at 55° or 60°F. This way they can run efficiently and other sources such as a cookstove (highly recommended), solar glazing, a small woodstove, Rumsford fireplace, or the like can be used to provide extra heat during the daytime.

A recent article in a major newspaper on the subject of furnace efficiency and thermostat settings revealed that the so-called experts know little or nothing about the subject. Follow-up letters to the editor proved conclusively that everyone was wrong. What it does show is that furnaces and conditions vary too much to make generalizations. Instead of offering silly theories as engineers do, I offer a solution. Just install an electric clock (an ordinary, run-of-the-mill household kind will do nicely) on the circulating pump or circulating fan, depending upon whether you have a water or air system. Then experiment with various temperature settings and night setback schemes. Pick the combination which provides the maximum amount of comfort for the minimum amount of fuel.

One thing which will help if your furnace runs a lot is a heat exchanger installed on the flue pipe to recover some of the heat normally exhausted up the chimney. These should be used only if you have a good tall chimney with a strong draft. Otherwise, they can cause incomplete combustion and be quite dangerous. The latter problem is most likely with oil burners. Oil burners should receive regular service to insure efficient operation.

How do we supply heat sparingly to efficient houses? Unfortunately, the commercial heating market offers nothing obvious which does the job. The problem is that these heating units are designed by creatures called mechanical engineers, and I have only met one truly competent mechanical engineer during my 20 years of practice in the field of architecture. He doesn't have either a college degree or an engineers' license. What he does possess is that elusive quality known as "horse sense." He is also an experienced workman who can actually install the systems he designs. The inability to do this is a major failing of most professionals in the design field. How many architects have actually built a house? (All architects represented in this book have done so.)

Heating systems available on the market today are designed by engineers who are a very different breed from this practical designer. Since competent professionals gravitate only to challenging areas of design, the heating engineer is one of the lowest men on the totem pole. Abundant supplies of cheap energy meant that heating plants could be wasteful, badly designed, and consume unnecessary quantities of fuel. Now that priorities have changed, we can hope that a new group of engineers will replace the fossils who produced those absurd units.

The "wisdom" of the cheap energy era was not to bother with adequate insulation, but to design a huge system to distribute heat around the perimeter of the building. Obviously, much precious fuel was used to heat the outdoors. Now the equation has changed. Excellent insulation and a central source of efficient heat are to be preferred. Since this is an entirely different approach, careful analysis is necessary in order to choose a system wisely. It is also necessary to design houses more compactly in order to make heat from a central source a valid option.

A major, usually overlooked consideration in the design of heating systems involves the use of radiant heat. Most mechanical engineers simply don't understand that this source exists. It doesn't fit their standard calculations, so it is completely ignored. According to heating calculation tables, the radiant heat from sun streaming through south-facing glass doesn't exist. Its effects can't be easily recorded in standard heating terms, so it is ignored. An open fire burning wood or coal is another obvious radiant heat source. A mechanical engineer will actually *increase* the size of the heating plant for each fireplace in your house.

Fireplaces

In all fairness, there are good reasons for this. No fireplace is a really good heat source, but most people are attracted to an open fire and it is better to have a fireplace that uses heat efficiently than a wasteful one. Modern fireplaces, like most houses, are heat-wasters. The truly fine fireplace designs of earlier days have been forgotten. An efficient fireplace allows as much heat as possible to be radiated into the room from the hot back wall of the fireplace. Accordingly, an efficiently designed Rumsford fireplace is shallow and unusually high to give off much more heat to the room—not like the deep, low, and wide so-called modern fireplaces. These fireplaces are named for Count Rumsford who designed them about the time of Ben Franklin and are still to be found in many old houses. People rarely use them because they think they are too shallow to work. I have heard many comments to the effect: "That must have been designed for coal; it's too shallow for wood." Indeed, they *can* be used to burn coal and since coal burns hotter, a small fireplace sometimes will do nicely.

I include two designs for Rumsford-type fireplaces. The first was taken from my grandfather's house and is suitable for burning wood or coal. It is quite small and could be used in a small room or as a supplemental heat source for a larger room. It requires a very small amount of fuel to give a nice fire. One further attraction—it is so small that a standard 8×8 flue will provide sufficient draft. In any fireplace, the area of the opening from the fireplace into the flue cannot exceed the area of the flue itself or the fireplace will tend to smoke. In the case of the Rumsford, smoke escapes by means of a rather narrow slot across the entire width of the fireplace located immediately behind the lintel. This gives the fire a chance to transfer its heat to the curved back wall which in turn radiates the heat to your room. The position of the slot creates a high velocity of air right at the face of the firebox and keeps the fire from smoking. Provided, of course, that there is a proper smoke shelf, the chimney is the right height, and a host of other factors. This is all explained in great detail in the book *Wood Heat* (1976) by John Vivian.*

*Rodale Press, 33 East Minor Street, Emmaus, PA 18049.

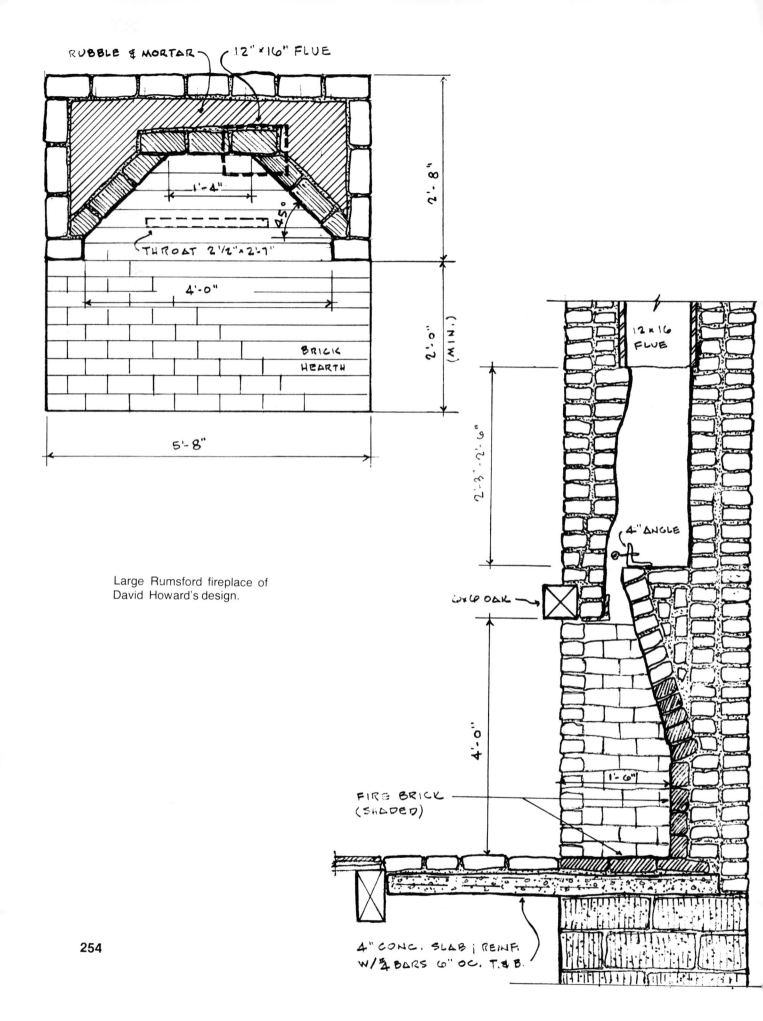

RUBBLE & MORTAR

12"×16" FLUE

2'-8"

1'-4"

45°

THROAT 2½"×2'-7"

4'-0"

2'-0" (MIN.)

BRICK HEARTH

5'-8"

Large Rumsford fireplace of
David Howard's design.

12×16 FLUE

4" ANGLE

2'-3"-2'-6"

6×6 OAK

4'-0"

1'-6"

FIRE BRICK
(SHADED)

4" CONC. SLAB; REINF.
W/ ¾ BARS 6" OC. T.& B.

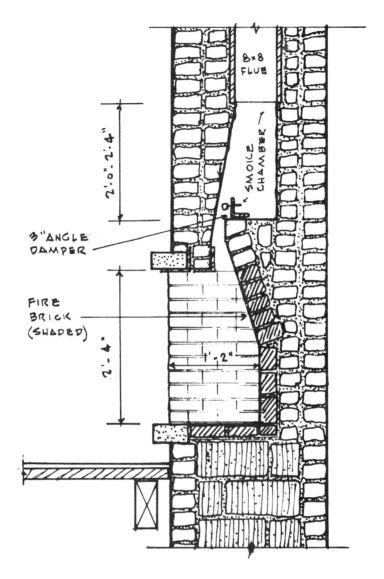

8×8 FLUE

SMOKE CHAMBER

2'-0"-2'-4"

3" ANGLE DAMPER

FIRE BRICK (SHADED)

2'-4"

1'-2"

Small Rumsford fireplace reminiscent of the one in my grandfather's living room.

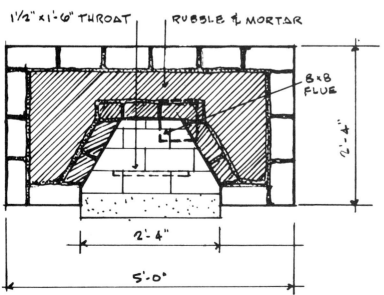

1½"×1'-6" THROAT

RUBBLE & MORTAR

8×8 FLUE

2'-4"

2'-4"

5'-0"

Mr. Vivian's book is excellent for basics of wood heating but his material on stoves and stovepipe installation is weak and in some cases dangerous. For new installations I recommend *The Wood Burners Encyclopedia* by Jay Shelton.[*]

The second fireplace design is a giant which has an opening 4 feet wide and 4 feet high. This one was designed by David Howard for use as a primary heat source for his open-plan houses. Make sure that for any fireplace, old or new, you provide an outside air intake in the hearth. This way the fireplace won't suck valuable room air up your chimney. Provide a positive means of closing off both the air intake and the fireplace throat when it's not in use. Since the old Rumsfords were used all of the time, they never had dampers. Indeed, modern dampers won't fit, so a special closure has to be devised. This can be a steel angle, a plate, or just a cover over the front of the fireplace opening.

Building a fireplace is tricky and not usually a job for a beginner. However, finding a mason who won't tell you you are crazy for building a Rumsford can be a major obstacle. Most masons build the firebox "to the damper" which is how they have been trained. Since you will have no conventional damper, they have to work out the shape themselves with great care. If they insist upon using a conventional damper, look elsewhere for a mason. I have heard of two masons who know how to do these fireplaces; both are from Massachusetts—John Hilly of Eastham and Jim Doud of Harwick. There must be others.

Coal stoves are generally smaller than woodburners and, of course, coal burns hotter, so they put out more heat. Also coal burns for a very long time. If you do not have access to reasonably priced wood or the time to cut it yourself, you should certainly consider a coal stove. Good coal stoves are all made of cast iron and have a firebrick liner to absorb the intense heat of the coal. My favorite is the Lange Model 6304RA. It also has a small cooktop for extra cooking space.

Cookstoves Another prime source of heat for a small house is the combination fuel cookstove. These units have been constantly refined over the last century and will provide a superior source of heat. They can be bought new from the Malleable Iron Range Company[†] for about $800. They are available in coal-wood-gas, coal-wood-oil, or coal-wood-electric versions. They are of simple modern design and are substitutes for a conventional range and furnace. If you want to save money and have a more interesting range, shop for a used one. Magic Chef and Monarch have made these ranges for many years. Most of their offerings will be wood-coal-gas in rather modern cabinets. For a truly fine range which is also aesthetically pleasing, try to find an old Glenwood. These ranges came in a bewildering variety. Of the 20 or so examples which I have seen, no two were ever alike. Frequently they come in a nice soft grey with white panels. Some are black cast iron; others come in beige, brown, cream, and light green. Glenwood is noted for the accurate, uniform heat of their ovens (either gas or wood-coal) and their two-stage burners which allow economical control of gas. Unlike most modern

[*] Jay Shelton, Porter Street, Williamstown, MA 01267.

[†] Monarch Ranges, Malleable Iron Range Company, Beaver Dam, WI 53916.

ranges, the pilot lights on the Glenwood do not have to burn constantly and waste all that fuel. If you have a house with a central chimney and an open living-dining-kitchen area (as illustrated in many of the designs in this book) you can use one of these ranges as the prime source of heat for your house. Add some south-facing windows and maybe an electric heater in the bathroom and you have a fine heating system which will cost very little to operate. Remember that with this system you are saving extra by using the source of cooking heat as room heat as well. The final bonus is that you also have a fine-quality cookstove which will do a much better job than any modern junkpile.

Another possibility is to use a wood cookstove such as Patsy Hennen's (shown here). In this case, you will probably want a secondary cooking unit for hot weather. My grandmother had a "summer kitchen" to keep

Nothing cooks quite like a woodstove. This beauty is Patsy Hennen's.

the heat of the woodstove out of the main house. Most of the wood cookstoves available in this country are antiques, or newly reproduced versions made from old dies. For good, efficient stoves with modern combustion principles, one has to go to imported models. Tyrolla makes a crisp, modern cookstove, while Jøtul makes a colorful porcelain-enamel unit of Norwegian style. Both will do double duty for cooking and heating. Lange makes a very large stove which is primarily intended as the main heat source for a house, but has an oven and burners on top of the range proper (the cooktop will be a bit high for some). House Number 24 uses this stove as its heat source and as a backup for a gas cookstove.

For an arrangement which doesn't permit a central cookstove, or just in case you don't want to try to learn the rather special technique of cooking with wood, you should keep an eye peeled for an old gas range. My old Glenwood cost only $25 and I wouldn't swap it even for a new $500 range. The Rolls-Royce of gas ranges is the Chambers. The oven is so well insulated that you heat it up to desired temperature, shut it off, and let the stored heat do the cooking. Everything on the stove is of the very highest quality. Aesthetically, it is a thing of great beauty. The design is unusual and exquisite 1930s modern. These ranges came in shiny black, rich blue, fire-engine red, and, of course, white. The entire stove is made of cast iron and weighs nearly 700 pounds. When last sold in the 1950s the price had climbed to over $900. I nearly cried when I found the wreckage of one which had been run over by a bulldozer at our local dump.

Heating Stoves

The rest of the Hennen's heating system.
This stove heats their well-insulated house
with ease.

Wood-heating stoves could fill an entire book, but I will give you a quick rundown on what I consider to be the best available. The Scandinavian stoves are generally regarded as top quality. Jøtul, Tyrolla, Lange, and Mørso are the major brand names. High-quality cast iron is very difficult to manufacture. The Scandinavians have been at it for hundreds of years and their products show it. There is an Irish cast-iron stove, called the Reginald, which is identical to the small Jøtul and sells in kit form for about half the price of a Jøtul. Be wary of American attempts at stovebuilding. Stoves made of sheet steel are widely advertised as of "lifetime" construction. If you are buying a permanent major heat source for your home, it will pay to buy the best. There is only one American-made, cast-iron stove on the market with really sophisticated combustion chambers. It is called the Defiant.* It has openable front doors so that you can enjoy an open fire (the Jøtul Combi has the same feature). The Washington Stove Works† makes a dandy cast-iron galley stove for about $80. I have used this stove successfully as a sauna heater.

---

*It is manufactured by Vermont Castings, Incorporated, in Randolph, VT 05060.

†Box 687, Everett WA 98200.

The Defiant stove, a very high-quality American challenger to the Scandinavian imports.

If you do not have the money for one of the good cast-iron stoves, I would recommend one of the small, airtight sheet-metal stoves now on the market for about $30, or one of the airtight door kits for a 55-gallon drum. You can replace the drum every year and be sure of having a safe stove for very little money. Remember that all slow-burning stoves build up dangerous creosote deposits in the chimney and require frequent cleaning. Some of the more expensive stoves, particularly the Defiant, claim to have greatly reduced this problem, but it pays to check the chimney several times a year.

Increasing Heating Efficiency

There is a "grey" area between the cheap sheet-metal stoves and the expensive cast-iron imports. It is occupied by a couple of heavy sheet-metal stoves lined with firebrick. These are the Riteway and the Shenandoah. They cost less than $200 and offer relatively good value for the money. They are both rather ugly and tend to detract from the appearance of a room. The much-touted Ashley has become too over-priced to be seriously considered. The Riteway and Shenandoah are much more efficient and of vastly better quality for about the same price.

Before I leave the subject of wood heating, I want to discuss some devices which can be added to a conventional fireplace to improve its efficiency. Several such devices are described in the individual houses featured in the book, but I will mention them briefly here. Paul Sturgis, an engineer from Stone Ridge, New York, has devised an extremely efficient heat exchanger for use with ordinary woodstoves or a fireplace. In his system, the wood is burned at extremely high heat as in a kiln and then the hot gasses are diverted through the tubular exchanger providing considerable heat to the room. Several small fires a day are required to do this. Paul claims greatly improved efficiency, low wood use, and no creosote buildup as virtues of his system.

Inventor Paul Sturgis displays his soft touch by making some fine adjustments on his heat exchanger.

Numerous heat exchangers of the type placed right into the fireplace are on the market. Most offer too little improvement to be seriously considered.* If the fireplace is turned into a stove by installing airtight glass doors, some of these units work pretty well. Gregg Allan has recycled an old cast-iron radiator in a double-sided glass-doored fireplace in House Number 23. It is connected to radiant copper-piping coils buried in the floor.

*An excellent fireplace heat exchanger is available from Southeastern Solar Systems, 4705 J. Baker Ferry Road, Atlanta, GA 30336.

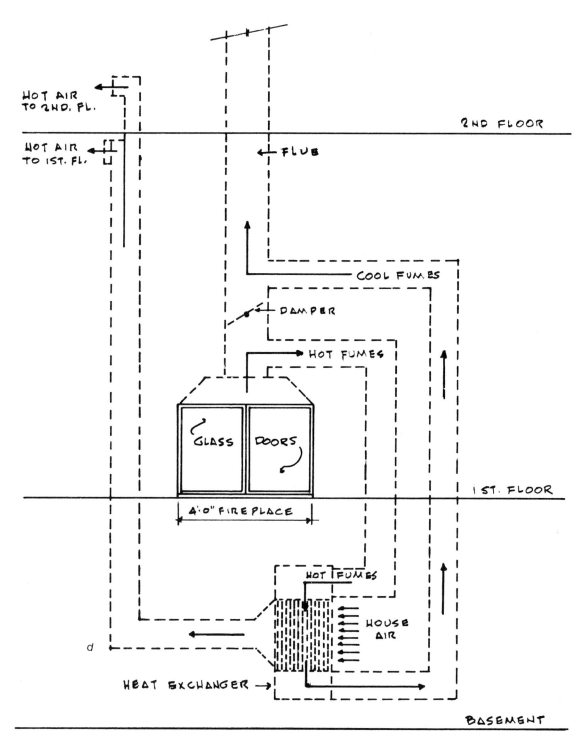

HOT AIR TO 2ND. FL.

HOT AIR TO 1ST. FL.

2ND FLOOR

FLUE

COOL FUMES

DAMPER

HOT FUMES

GLASS DOORS

1 ST. FLOOR

4'·0" FIREPLACE

HOT FUMES

HOUSE AIR

d

HEAT EXCHANGER →

BASEMENT

Schematic diagram of Paul Sturgis's heat-recovery fireplace. A fire is laid with well-seasoned kindling, newsprint, and wood. The damper is then placed in the open position, the fire lit, and the glass doors closed. When the fire is burning briskly and clean and the insulated chimney (which extends 24 feet above the hearthline) is well heated, the damper is closed tight. The negative pressure in the chimney sucks the fumes down to the basement, through the heat exchanger and back up into the chimney above the damper. Some 64 stainless steel tubes in the exchanger heat the surrounding house air around them, which is convected to the ceiling of the first floor and a register on the second floor. This heated air is sucked down to the basement through a register, insuring wide distribution throughout the house, and it continues to circulate without any fans, noise, or auxiliary power until the fire goes out. The damper is opened before opening the glass doors for refueling and then closed after the glass doors have been shut.

Gregg uses a heating method which has been a favorite of mine for many years now. Unless you have experienced the delight of being warmed by a gently heated masonry floor, you can't possibly understand. The ancient Romans used this technique by circulating heated air in ducts under their floors, thereby warming the floor. You'd think in all those years since we would have made some progress, wouldn't you? Heat can be supplied to floor coils from a variety of sources. Conventional systems which use a hot-water boiler have been the normal method until recently. Since the mass of the masonry floor is an excellent place to store heat, solar collectors can be hooked to this system. Gregg Allan lets the floor itself absorb heat from the sun during the daytime and supplements the heat with a fireplace heat exchanger at night. In a small house the coils can also be fed by an oversized domestic hot-water heater of 80 to 120 gallons fueled by either gas or oil. An oversized heater can also be hooked to a few feet of baseboard-type hot-water radiation heaters. This can be thermostatically controlled and used as a backup in kitchen and bathroom areas to keep pipes from freezing when your house is unoccupied and if you are using a heating system which requires frequent attention, such as wood or coal.

These radiant floor systems are rarely used for two reasons. The first is that the mechanical engineers who usually design heating systems are terrified of it because the system doesn't fit into their standard heating tables. Also, since it is buried in concrete, if they make a goof (which they usually do) it is permanent and they can't go back and modify the system. The second and quite valid reason is worry about leakage or freeze-ups under a floor slab. Jackhammers are expensive. I have solved this latter problem by installing the coils in a bed of sand which is in turn covered with brick pavers. The system doesn't transmit quite as well this way, but it is easy to get to if anything goes wrong. In order to work well, the floor must be well insulated. I recommend 3 inches of polyurethane or 6 inches of Zonolite.

A closeup of the heat exchanger. Hot air from a stove or fireplace is ducted to the heat exchanger through the pipe at the lower right, and then passes through the heat exchanger through the pipe at the chimney at the upper right. Room air is taken in through the spaces around the heat exchanger tubes and is exhausted to the room by the pipe at the far left. Gravity does the whole thing, and it's very effective.

Depending upon their size, locations, and configuration, the houses in this book require small heating systems ranging from 10,000 to 50,000 Btu's. The above units would be suitable for most of them. Ironically, your major consideration may not be keeping warm but getting around the "bank problem." Bankers are notorious for being behind the times, and none of them have any technical background. One prime rule ingrained in the banking system is that a house must have "central heating" before it can be considered for a loan. All of the sad people who have tried in vain to buy a beautiful old house know this line well. What does one do if faced with this problem? Since the power companies have successfully bought off the banks, electric heat has to be considered. Most bankers are totally ignorant of such things as heat load and unit sizing, and you can usually pull the wool over their eyes with a few cheap electric heaters scattered around on the walls. Of course, you don't actually want to *use* them. One friend even acquired a batch of burned-out heaters, repainted them, and screwed them to the wall (without wiring, of course). A typical banker came and looked (in the summer) and approved the project without question. The minute he left, the heaters were unscrewed and taken back to the dump where they belonged.

If you live in an area of reasonable electric rates, there are some little-known electric heating systems which are more efficient than fossil fuels. The foremost example of these works upon the radiant principle which I mentioned earlier. This is a rather unusual-looking flat plate of tempered glass with a heating element fused to its back surface. The glass heats up and radiates heat to the occupants. These units* work very nicely when installed on a sloping ceiling or set high on a wall and angled down toward the occupants of the room. These heaters have been on the market for years yet have sold poorly until recently. The reason is that mechanical engineers insist upon rating them by standard convection heating methods by which they are no more efficient than standard electric heaters. One of the large 1,500-watt units will warm the occupants of a large room in a well-insulated house. The units are rather expensive but work very well and are over 30 percent more efficient than standard electric heaters making them competitive with oil in many areas.

One of the few promising contributions, if not the only one, from the commercial heating industry is the heat pump. Since it doesn't use any fuel to actually make heat it can be wonderfully efficient, provided it is used under just the right conditions. The heat pump is essentially a large version of a refrigerator with reversible action. In the winter it refrigerators the outside air—or perfectly some other mass—and in the summer it refrigerates the inside of your house. It is actually pumping heat from one place to another; hence its name. Conventional commercial heat pumps are best suited for moderate climates since conventional air-conditioning units are more efficient at cooling than heat pumps. However, there are many ways to improve upon their efficiency. If you have a source of running water that doesn't freeze, the heat pump will extract heat from it in winter and exhaust heat to it in summer at a considerable savings in operating costs.

Heat Pumps

The ambient temperature of the earth (52°F. several feet down) can be used to make the heat pump very efficient. The coils must be buried at about five feet and the installation costs can be quite expensive. If the coils ever have to be dug up, you run into more expense. However, this system works beautifully, is fully automatic, summer and winter, yet is cheap to operate. Design of these systems is complex and requires professional help. The average heat pump dealer will not be of much help.[†]

One obvious way to improve the efficiency of a heat pump is to supply extra heat to the outdoor coil by means of solar heat. In fact, this is probably the most suitable application for solar heat today as it can eliminate much of the complexity and expense of these systems. Since it is not a "pure" solar system, it doesn't appeal to many of the gadget-happy solar engineers. This system is so promising that the U.S. Department of Commerce has out a large book just on that subject. If you

*The heaters can be purchased from the Continental Radiant Glass Heating Corporation, 24–26 216th Street, Bayside, Long Island, NY 11360, or Aztech International, Albuquerque, NM 87100.

[†] One mechanical engineering firm that specializes in energy efficiency is Flack and Kurtz, 29 West 38th Street, New York, NY 10001. Paul Sturgis is one of the few engineers who is very familiar with this system. If you should need his help he lives in Stone Ridge, New York.

are interested, it is well worth its $8 price.* It presents many exciting ideas on how to combine solar energy with the heat pump.

Central Heat Systems   If, when you reach the bottom line, you or the bank still want a conventional furnace, what is available? You will find that the regular plumbing-heating dealer only has large furnaces which are much too large for your well-insulated house. They are also expensive. There is a readily accessible alternative. Several companies make small, efficient and generally well-constructed furnaces for house trailers. These units run about $225 new and about half that as rebuilt units. A word of warning here: make sure that your house *is* compact and very well insulated; if not, the furnace will run all the time and use lots of oil or gas. Otherwise, they can serve as a fully automatic primary heating system or as backup to wood/solar heat.

If you choose a boiler, connect it to an efficient distribution system such as the underfloor coils which I mentioned earlier. If you use radiators, insulate the outside walls, windows, and doors well and then place the radiators on the *inside* walls in as compact a layout as possible. This way, they will heat you and your house, not the outside world. This directly contradicts what your heating contractor has been taught, so you will have to fight to get the system installed this way.

Similarly, if you use a system that requires ductwork, make sure that it is centrally located with as short runs as possible from the furnace. For an example, see the Blumes' house in chapter 12. In this case, we had to get a roofer to install the ductwork because the heating contractor said everyone was crazy. Crazy or not, there was a savings of over $3,000 in installation costs alone. I had the Blumes install a humidifier, which you should always do on a ductwork system.

An easy, efficient method to combine the simplicity of a simple central woodstove with the even heat of a so-called "central" heating system is to use some electric fans. They can be just simple surplus fans set so as to distribute heat from a warm area above a stove to a cooler corner of the room. If you have a really remote space or a room which you frequently close off from the central heated space, there is an excellent fan available. It is an axial-type fan which slips right into standard-size round ductwork making the installation a snap for the do-it-yourselfer. It comes in various sizes for 5-, 6-, and 8-inch ductwork. The large size will move enough air to heat a large room. [†]

Air will tend to stratify with the heat rising to the top of a high-ceilinged open space. An old-fashioned paddle-bladed fan hung from the ceiling will help push the heated air back down to the floor. Make sure to buy one of the multispeed fans, as you will want to use the slowest speed in winter. These fans set at higher speeds can also help with summer

*It is available from the National Technical Information Service, 5285 Port Royal Road, Springfield, VA 22151. It is document number C0025601.

†These fans are available from Airtrol Corporation, 203 West Hawick Street, Rockton, IL 61072.

cooling. The two major brands are Hunter and Emerson. The Hunter is the traditional old-fashioned kind while the Emerson is nondescript modern. Both can be ordered wholesale from any of the Rosetta Electric stores in New York City. (Rosetta is also a good source of supply for all electrical supplies.)

If you have extremely hot, humid summers, you should use air conditioners rather than a heat pump. Heat pumps, if used exclusively for cooling, are less efficient than other methods of cooling. If the temperatures are moderate, you should learn to cool your house by natural means. A well-designed and properly sited house will not need artificial cooling except in the most extreme southerly climates. If the house is designed to take advantage of prevailing breezes and has properly placed windows; it will be easy to keep cool. See House Number 29 for an example of a house specifically designed for a southern climate. Remember that open planning and compact overall shape will make your task easier. Design your house so that the house itself acts as a chimney. A small house of two or three levels with generous vents placed at the highest point and intakes at ground level will readily cool itself. Again, make sure to place the vents so that the natural breezes provide forced circulation.

Cooling

Moving air will make a person feel 7 to 10°F. cooler. Residential air conditioning systems use thousands of watts, while whole-house fans use hundreds.

John Felter, President of
the American Ventilation
Association

A Plexiglas window, hinged with a piano hinge, provides light and ventilation at the peak of the house. Even though the ceiling height is less than five feet at the ridge, the loft inside this window makes a nice place for a double bed.

Pat Hennen's version of the same window as the one on the preceding page has an insulating flap which can be adjusted with a rope, giving easy control of air flow.

Safety Precautions   As a final thought, I will leave you with one of the most important considerations for your heating system: *safety.* There are some dangers involved with the use of wood heat and there are simple, easy safety precautions which should be taken to combat them. The first one should be taken whether or not you use wood heat. Provide *fire extinguishers;* it is amazing how few people have them in their homes. A short indoor garden hose, hooked up and ready to go could also be helpful. *Do not* however, apply large quantities of cold water to a very hot metal surface. It will immediately rupture, causing disaster. Equip your hose with a misting nozzle. This can do double duty as a fire safety device and provide extra humidity. Fire extinguishers should be provided near every heating device and in the kitchen. Everyone in the household should know how to use them.

The second very important safety consideration is *oxygen.* This is necessary for any type of combustion. If you have an airtight structure and build a fire with no outside air intake, *you will die!!!* The fire will use up the available oxygen and then the humans will expire. Most people don't really believe this, but it can and does happen. Fireplaces, furnaces, wood cookstoves, and the like should all be provided with a small duct to supply outside air to their combustion chamber. A piece of 3-inch or 4-inch plastic pipe buried under the floor will usually do nicely. Be sure to screen the outside intake to prevent an invasion of rodents, insects, etc. The inside end should have a damper to be closed when the heating device is not in use.

The final precaution involves chimney safety. Burning wood produces creosote which is highly volatile. It will build up inside a chimney or stovepipe for months or years and then catch fire with explosive violence. The majority of people in this generation are inexperienced in the use of wood as a fuel. They don't know that flues have to be cleaned regularly. The fuel burned and the type of stove are also important factors. Most of the thermostatically controlled, "airtight" stoves burn wood very slowly at the expense of considerable creosote buildup. Combination-fuel cookstoves, which were primarily designed to burn coal, also contribute when used with wood. Metal stovepipe can literally explode when the creosote liner ignites. If you plan to use a wood device either as a primary or secondary source of heat, read *Wood Heat* carefully and make sure that you have an adequate oxygen supply, a clean chimney, and a handy fire extinguisher.

Chapter 10

Natural and Artificial Lighting, and Wiring

We are not only now faced with wildly escalating costs for electricity, but also the likelihood of serious shortages in the near future. In the long run, technology will probably solve the electrical-power supply problems, but for the next few years rationing, reduced voltages, and reduced hours of electrical use will probably be the norm.

Wind Generators

In selecting the site for your new house, you should consider the possibilities of wind or water power. A small Honda generating plant might also be a possibility. Sometimes land can be acquired very cheaply because commercial power lines are so far away that running lines to the property would be prohibitively expensive. Most alternate-power supply sources provide rather limited amounts of power, so be prepared to conserve electricity and use only the minimum amount actually required. Water-powered generating plants are desirable if you have a constant source of water from a stream. Winter freeze-ups are a very real possibility, but an expensive battery storage system is not otherwise required.

Wind generators are romantic, beautiful sources of power. Although much research is being done, the machines which are commercially available at the moment leave much to be desired. The very weak link in wind generating plants is the lack of economical battery systems to store the wind power. Since the wind blows intermittently, a good storage system is vital to having sufficient amounts of power. Sadly, the cost of a storage and control system can exceed the cost of the wind machine itself. And this is for a very small system which would be barely adequate for a typical household. Our whole country runs on electrical power. Inefficient industrial plants consume vast amounts of power. For instance, it takes enough electricity to heat 10 houses for a year just to convert one ton of aluminum ore into raw metal. Intense competition for short supplies will force the costs of electrical power up rapidly.

The United States, once the leader in wind power, has lagged far behind the rest of the world in development of wind plants. We can hope that this lag will soon be rectified. In the meantime most commercial plants are manufactured elsewhere. The best known are Dunlite of Australia,* Elektro of Switzerland,† and Aerowatt of France.** Kedco of the United States shows promise of developing very well-designed machines. †† Their first model is a bit too small to be used for anything except a cabin or emergency backup. A larger model is due to be marketed soon which should be competitive with the foreign models. Grumman Aerospace Corporation has introduced a very big, very expensive, machine which appears to be very well designed. Considering the extravagant price, the future for this machine seems dim. I can only hope that some of the technology will rub off onto smaller, more sensible firms.

Before power lines became common in rural America, home wind plants were the norm. Several firms have started reconditioning Jacobs wind machines.§ Although not quite up-to-date technologically, these units are famous for their durability. If you are interested in having a good, time-tested American unit for a reasonable cost, this is the way to go. *Wind Power Digest*,§§is a fine source for up-to-date listings on firms offering reconditioned generators, units for private sales, and general information on developments in wind power.

Nothing seems to tickle the fancy of the home tinkerer quite so much as building his own wind generator and cutting free of the public utility companies. Unfortunately, these machines are not as easy to build as most people think. Improperly constructed machines tend to self-destruct in a high wind. Even getting them to work properly in the first place can be quite a chore. If you do have the determination and are prepared for the possibility of failure, I think building your own power plant is a wonderful project. Michael Hackman of Earthmind,★ is one of the foremost experts on building your own. He has written two books, *Wind and Windspinners* (1975) and *The Homebuilt, Wind-Generated Electricity Handbook* (1977). Earthmind also rebuilds wind machines, so you might be able to buy a reconditioned one from them. *Wind Power Digest* says that these plans are the best ones out for a homebuilt unit.

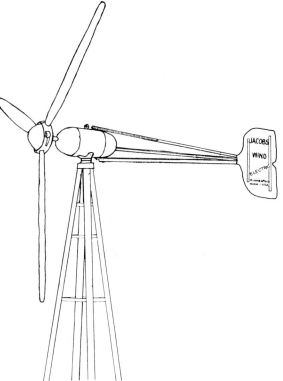

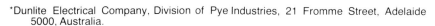

*Dunlite Electrical Company, Division of Pye Industries, 21 Fromme Street, Adelaide 5000, Australia.

† Elektro G. m.b.h., Winterthur Street, Gallerstrasse 27, Switzerland.

**Aerowatt S. A., 37 rue Chanzy, 75 Paris lle, France.

††Plans for the well-designed, moderate-power Kedco generator originally known as Helion are available from Helion, Box 4301, Sylmar, CA 91342. This unit should cost around $600. Kedco, Incorporated, is located at 9016 Aviation Boulevard, Inglewood, CA 90301.

§One I know of is North Wind Power Company, Box 315, Warren, VT 05674.

§§*Wind Power Digest*, 54468 CR31, Bristol, IN 46507.

★Earthmind, Josel Drive, Sagus, CA 91350. The books are $8 each postpaid.

Lighting

The fluorescent light fixture is suspended about a foot from the ceiling. A V-shaped baffle conceals the fixture and bounces indirect light off the ceiling.

Whether you are planning to use a low-output alternate power source or still use commercial power, it is very important to save energy. One area of very high waste is artificial lighting. Until recently, electricity was so cheap that few people gave any thought to lighting efficiency. Excessive levels of lighting became commonplace. This development was largely the doing of a subversive organization called the Illuminating Engineering Society. The IES successfully lobbied for and got excessive lighting levels written into law in many places. They publish a list of recommended levels for various uses which is used in many codes. Guess what? The IES turns out to be funded by your loveable local power company who wants you to use just as much power as possible. Unfortunately, people get used to the excessive levels at work and at school and then overlight their homes. With careful planning, you can light your home more effectively while using less energy. It can also reduce your initial costs for wiring your house.

To begin with, daylight is free. There should be no excuse for using artificial lighting in the daytime. Plan the locations of windows and skylights so that you provide natural illumination for all frequently used work surfaces.

Use efficient sources of artificial light and place them carefully. Most commercial houses come with an ugly, useless ceiling light in the center of each room with outlets for portable lamps scattered around the perimeter. In a well-planned home, localized lighting is provided for specific tasks. Most lamps and lighting fixtures waste light output through shades and diffusers. These are necessary because most light bulbs have such a bright surface intensity that they need to be shielded with globes or shades to be used. There is an easy alternative. Use a globe-type G-40 bulb. It is about 6 inches in diameter and comes in several wattages, the 40- or 60-watt sizes are both of such low surface brightness that they can be used as an exposed light source.

A simple strip of fluorescent lighting is tucked under open shelves to light a kitchen counter. From normal viewing angles, the light is hidden by the baffle at the front edge of the shelf.

You can also save money on fixtures by using these bulbs in inexpensive wall-mounted porcelain sockets. If the bulb is used in this manner, the light will reflect off both the walls and the ceiling. Thus, the room itself is used as the reflector for the light bulb. Lighting fixtures built into the ceiling or covered with shades and globes can waste up to half of their energy input. If you try to buy G-40 bulbs at your local hardware store, you will find that they are very high priced and identified as "decorator bulbs." If you use several of them throughout your house, it will pay to buy them wholesale. Sylvania markets them at a reasonable price through large electrical supply dealers. You can also get them from the Durotest Corporation.* Don't be tempted to buy Durotest's long-life bulbs though. They use much more power than conventional bulbs because the filament is built heavier for durability.

Fluorescent lights also have a place in the household. They use much less power per lumen of output and are a low-brightness source well suited for use under shelving for lighting counters or concealed in lighting troughs to provide indirect lighting for a whole room. The trouble with fluorescent lights is color. The two major, widely distributed brands

*Durotest Corporation, 157 West 57th Street, New York, NY 10019.

are available only in ugly shades of blue which no one in their right mind would want in their house. The Durotest people, however, make their bulbs in over 40 different colors including an exact duplicate of incandescent light and an exact duplicate of natural daylight. Don't be fooled by the "daylite" or "warm-white" bulbs put out by General Electric or Westinghouse; they are just slightly better shades of ugly blue. The Durotest people make a delightful array of other warm shades which completely dispel the nasty, cold image of fluorescent lighting. It is too bad that giant companies produce such cold colors and have given this efficient light source such a bad name.

Use only fixtures which accept four-foot-long, 40-watt bulbs. This is the standard size and also the most efficient bulb. Short lengths are a poor buy as they are little more efficient than standard incandescent bulbs. Use incandescents for localized-point source lighting and fluorescents for wide-area diffuse light. One 40-watt fluorescent fixture can provide adequate lighting for a kitchen, bathroom, or general lighting for a living area. This picture is an example of a fluorescent light over a kitchen counter. Fluorescent lights should always be hidden behind a baffle. The direct light gives off a slight pulsation which affects some people adversely.

Bulbs with a built-in reflector similar to an automobile headlight are also an efficient light source, particularly if you want to concentrate light in a specific area. They come in both "spot" (narrow beam) and "flood" (wide beam) versions. If you do want to recess a light somewhere, make sure that you use this type of bulb to get the maximum output for the least energy.

For outside lighting, I suggest weatherproof versions of the reflector-type bulbs. Swivilier and Stonco make inexpensive swiveling sockets which accept these bulbs. You just set them to the desired angle and tighten a set screw. This makes a functional, weatherproof outside fixture. If you need to light a really large outside area, you should consider a quartz-iodine-type bulb. These are even more efficient than fluorescents. They are very powerful and if placed properly will light a large yard with ease.*

Electrical heating devices and equipment with large motors such as pumps, air conditioners, freezers, refrigerators, and the like are the real hogs in an electrical system. Try to cut their use to a minimum and make sure that they are all wired to use 220 volts if possible. Most refrigerators are wired for 110, but all of the other items are readily available in the higher voltage. The higher voltage allows a smaller wire size and reduces resistance thereby saving energy. This is why power companies transmit power at very high voltages over the main lines and then reduce it with a transformer at your house. Two-hundred-and-

The truth is, all energy-using devices have an energy-saving position on the controls. It is called OFF. There are no exceptions, for one minute, for one hour or one day. The laws of physics govern and no amount of wishful thinking will change them.

Fred M. Niel, Energy Management Department, Memphis Light, Gas, and Water Division, Memphis, Tennessee

---

*One economical unit is marketed by the L. E. Mason Company under the trade name Mighty Light. It comes with a 250-watt quartz bulb and sells for less than $30. Swivilier, Stonco, and Mighty Light fixtures are normally available from most lighting fixture supply stores.

twenty volts has long been standard for all wiring in many foreign countries. Many commercial buildings in this country are wired this way now. Future shortages may create a push for full 220-volt installation in new housing.

Refrigerators and Freezers

The refrigerator usually stands out as the real energy hog in an efficient house. There are alternatives to most other heavy energy users, but refrigeration is vital to store food properly. There is room to drastically reduce the power consumption of the refrigerator, though. For six to eight months out of the year, the typical refrigerator is doing something silly. In the very hot summer months, it is taking heat out of the food and dumping it in the kitchen where you don't want it. In the winter it is taking a great deal of energy to try to combat your inside heating system to make the inside of the refrigerator as cold as the outside air. In our area, the old estates had ice ponds and icehouses. Ice was harvested from the ponds in winter and stored for the following summer. This made much more sense than our current wasteful practices.

There are a couple of other alternatives to the power-wasting conventional refrigerator. The first is the Servel gas refrigerator, which is of extremely high quality and has no moving parts, making it quite durable. It is very efficient and runs on a tiny gas flame. Servels are highly prized in areas where there is no electric power and by owners of small wind machines. Of course, there *are* problems with the Servel. Who knows how long gas will be available at any sort of reasonable price? Also, they have not been made for several years, so they are getting very scarce. No domestic manufacturers still make gas-fired refrigerators, although several foreign companies still do. A catalog from Lehman Hardware and Appliance* lists several sizes of both refrigerators and freezers which run on gas and kerosene. Generally the units are expensive, but they still may be a lot less than a ½-mile power line or a larger wind generator.

The other alternative is a small, efficient European refrigerator. Some of them can be had in 220 volts and are much smaller and hence require less power to operate. The drawback here is that Americans have become used to using the refrigerator as a storage space for all sorts of things not really requiring refrigeration. Or, all the dinner leftovers are simply dumped into the refrigerator, platters and all, wasting more space. I tried one of these small refrigerators in the summerhouse and have had constant complaints. For one or two people, though, I think it would be ideal.

Let's assume that you opt for a conventional, large, electric-powered refrigerator. What can be done to reduce the load it places on your electrical system? In the case of a battery storage system, you could save thousands of dollars by using a smaller-size wind machine. Basically, the typical refrigerator consists of a moderately well-insulated box with the hot evaporator coils which dissipate the heat fastened directly to the back of the box. The coils are placed where they get rather poor air circulation and are so close to the box that they actually

*Box 41, Kidron, OH 44636.

tend to reheat the contents. Fortunately, this disaster can be rectified. If you have the space, you might consider tilting the coils out from the box and applying 1 inch of polyurethane insulation to the back of the box. A small fan to cool the coils can also be installed. Some large boxes do have fan cooling, but its primary function is to stop the compressor from overheating. A small surplus fractional-horsepower fan will cost less than $5 and save you many times that amount in electricity costs. While you're at it, you should install the same insulation board on the sides, top, and bottom. If you build in the refrigerator, this can easily be done and will not show from the front. Make sure that you don't do anything to stop the air flow from the compressor or coils, though. If you don't have room to move the coils out very much, you can still help improve efficiency. Take some of the ¼-inch Styroboard which I described in chapter 7, laminate reflective Mylar or aluminum foil to both sides, and glue it to the back of the refrigerator. Space the coils out an extra ¼-inch or install a fan to maintain air circulation. The same material can be applied to other surfaces of the box and noticeably boost its efficiency.

Three of the houses in this book have refrigerators designed for outside venting so that the hot exhaust can be vented outside in the summer and the coils can be cooled by outside air in winter. A good refrigeration mechanic can also remotely mount your coils outside if you desire. The compressor of the refrigerator cannot be exposed to freezing temperatures while operating or it will burn out.

More obvious tips for refrigerator efficiency involve defrosting so that ice does not insulate the coils inside the box. *Never* buy a "frost-free" refrigerator or one with a heating element on the door gasket. These can use more than twice as much electricity as conventional models. Virtually everything on a refrigerator is replaceable, so an old box in good condition may be worth fixing up with a new compressor and remote coils. Check the door to see that the gasket fits tightly on any refrigerator, old or new. Most gaskets can be replaced and worn gaskets are a prime source of cold loss. Keep dust cleaned off the coils and make sure that nothing interferes with air flow around them. Finally, don't store anything in a refrigerator which isn't absolutely necessary and keep door openings down to a minimum.

All of the above comments apply equally well to a food freezer, and then some. First, buy a chest-type freezer, not an upright. Simple laws of physics should tell manufacturers not to build these monsters, but they still do. If you are relying on wind power, you may wish to consider using just a food freezer and an ice chest. Both should be extremely well insulated with polyurethane. In this fashion, the freezer becomes a storage unit for excess power from the wind. In very windy periods, the freezer can freeze extra ice for the ice chest. This type of arrangement requires care and attention and would not be suitable for careless people or those who are absent from home for long periods. Very heavy insulation, much more than the stuff which comes from the factory is essential to use this storage method. Also, I would only recommend it in northern sections of the country.

Wiring   Planning ahead will help you save money on your wiring installation. If you think through your lighting needs, you can eliminate many useless switches and outlets. An easy way to eliminate switches is to use wall-mounted, pull-chain light fixtures. Each switch can cost $50 or more installed, so the elimination of just a few can save a substantial amount of money. While you are at it, plan the location of your convenience outlets. How many times have you crawled under a bed or moved a chest because the outlet was poorly placed? it is usually better to place them up at 48 inches above the floor to make them accessible without moving the furniture.

Order both your switches and outlets in plain smooth white. They are more attractive than the pale yellow things with dirt-catching grooves normally sold. The white ones *are* standard and cost almost exactly the same as the yellow ones. Don't believe anyone who tells you otherwise. They are probably trying to sell you premium-priced "decorator" devices with square push buttons. Electric supply houses will not want to make a special order for just one or two items, so get your whole order at once.

Electric wiring is one of the easiest places in the house to save money by doing the work yourself. Virtually all places in the country have electrical inspectors who have to check the wiring before the power company will connect your house to their mains. The National Electric Code provides that the homeowner can do his own wiring, so you should be able to do it yourself. H. P. Ricter's periodically updated book, *Wiring Simplified* (31st ed., 1974),* is the standard bible here. Follow him carefully for the technical aspects of wiring and you should have no trouble passing the inspection.

If you are using a windmill waterwheel, or your own generator, you usually would not need to get an inspection. You can also cut your electric service back to a sensible 30- or 60-amp. main service from the wasteful 100-amp. one required by the power companies.

An electrical contractor will charge between $1,000 and $1,500 for a small house. The materials for a small house should run between $300 and $400. Your savings will pay for a solar water heater. Think about that as you do your own wiring. Also, you can make sure that you get all of those carefully planned lights and outlets in the right place. Actually being there and placing them yourself may cause you to rethink some of your earlier planning. Being confronted with the decisions in the field never hurt anyone.

Electrical Safety Tips   1. Study the code. Know what you are going to do before you start. Read H. P. Ricter thoroughly and make sure that you understand the requirements of your job. Wiring is very easy, but it can also be very dangerous if you make a mistake.

2. If you are a beginner, have someone knowledgeable check your work. As a general rule, the power company will require inspection before they connect your service. In cases where you are not connecting to a commercial source of power you should still have your work checked.

*Available from Park Publishing, 1999 Shepard Road, Saint Paul, MN 55116.

3. Don't use aluminum wire ever except for a main service cable. Aluminum has less current-carrying ability than copper and also can break from metal fatigue and burn down your house. Main service cables are frequently unavailable in anything but aluminum, so you may not have a choice. Anti-oxidizing compounds should be applied to the cable before connecting the wires to the terminals. Since the main cables are heavy there is little danger of breakage as there is with lighter wire for wiring circuits. Make sure the screw terminals are *tight*.

4. Loose connections can cause arcing and fires. All connections should be well made. If you are uncertain of your ability to twist wires together tightly, get the special two-piece wire nuts which have a screw-type terminal inside. These have a plastic cap which screws onto a brass body, making a very safe and secure connection. You may have to special order these connectors.

5. Never break the ground (white) wire. It is there for safety. The black wire should always be the one that is switched. When running wires through outlets (receptacles) be sure to follow the markings on the outlets. Reversing the wires could cancel out the protection of the ground wire and give someone a lethal shock. The bare neutral wire is a safety backup for the ground; use similar care in making sure that it is not interrupted.

6. Install "ground fault eliminators" for all exterior and wet areas. This is an extra circuit breaker which immediately cuts power in case of a live wire or shorted appliance. It is an expensive, but good safety item. The cheaper variety is installed right at the outlet. Better units take the place of a circuit breaker in the main panel. The advantage of the latter unit is that a whole circuit can be connected to them.

Chapter 11

Restorations—Remodel to Save Energy

After a whole book talking about designing and building new houses, I must candidly admit to an overwhelming preference for old houses. Give me the choice, and I will work to save something that already exists rather than build something new. This is the untimate solution to saving both resources and money.

When I was about four years old, I asked my father how much more it cost to buy a car than to build a house. Up until that time, I had considered the automobile to be the supreme pinnacle of engineering. When I was told that the house cost much more than the automobile, I was transformed into an avid house explorer. It has been a lifelong passion. If my father had gone on to explain that houses were inefficiently hand-built and cars machine-made and that I was correct in my value judgement, I might be an automotive engineer today.

In earlier days, houses were less well insulated and usually heated with wood. Consequently, the designs tended to be efficient and compact. The plague of sprawling ranchhouses has left many nice small houses behind, abandoned to the ravages of vandals and weather. Frequently these houses were built with heavy, braced timber frames. This is fortunate for the old house hunter as these structures will withstand exposure to weather much better than the "modern" flimsy 2 × 4-framed ones. Another development which has caused many solid structures to be abandoned is the development of the interstate highway system. Many times, interstates have cut right across county road systems, isolating one or two houses at the end of a road. These properties are rarely listed with realtors, so you will probably have to look on your own.

If you are lucky, you may find a solid shell of a building which has never been touched. It is much better to start with a shell which has never been wired or plumbed. In this way, you are not paying for work which will probably have to be redone in order to make it efficient and workable. Pay careful attention to the orientation of the old house. Frequently they were sited to take advantage of the weather, but not necessarily. They should have one sizeable south-facing wall which you can open up with windows to admit the sun. If the shell is small enough and decrepit-looking, you may find that the owner doesn't regard it as having a commercial value and will sell you the property just for its own value. Be sure to encourage such a line of thinking and don't appear too interested in the building in front of the owners.

Since such properties are rarely listed, they are difficult to locate. My favorite way to find them is to buy U.S. Geological Survey topographical maps and go exploring. These maps are available from a big map company such as Hammonds, or from your state university geology department. These maps are great in that they actually show abandoned houses.

Occupied houses are shown as tiny black dots; unoccupied ones as open squares. Look for a trail going off into the woods (shown as a dashed line on the maps). These may have a nice house at their end. Also, try to find the intersections between old local roads and new superhighways. One flaw with these maps is that they may be wildly out of date; the usual map was made 10 to 15 years ago. They are constantly being updated, however, so there may be any date on the map from 1942 to 1976. After you find your house, you may have trouble locating the owner. Try neighbors and any nearby stores, bars, post offices, or restaurants first. If that doesn't produce results, you will have to go to the local tax assessor's office and track the owner down that way. Sometimes, the tax officials don't like to cooperate, so be prepared to give them a story about a lost relative as a reason for trying to locate the owner of the house.

Maybe the prospect of living way off the beaten path or your job or profession won't permit such a rural solution. Many cities have rundown areas with very nice old small houses. Some progressive cities have instigated programs for selling these old buildings for a token sum to people who are willing to rehabilitate them. In olden days, before the trucking industry wiped out the railroads and waterways, really scenic areas of many cities were taken over by industry, making whole residential areas undesirable. Now many of these areas sit almost deserted, just waiting for someone with imagination to come along.

The picture here shows an extreme example of such a house. This one is fire-gutted, but the structure is still solid. In this case, the sellers are actually willing to *deduct* a bit from the purchase price of the property in order to sell it, the theory being that you will have to pay to tear down the house. Since the size and shape of this house is fairly typical of a small row house, I have included a plan for remodeling it to demonstrate how the same principles which I apply to a new house can be applied to an old one. Since I really love this style of house, I have in-

This small house is considered worthless by its present owners because of fire damage. Most of the damage is to the interior plaster which should be removed anyway.

A solar greenhouse is to be added to the south face of the house. See the plans in chapter 12 for further details.

Many old houses can be made quite spacious by removing partitions. Structural support must be provided if you remove bearing walls. Note the beam in this picture.

cluded plans at the end of the book for this one to be built as a new house.

The front of this house faces north and has a nice view of the Hudson River. It had the very typical three-window facade with two windows and a front door downstairs. In this house, the stairhall forms an entrance vestibule and isolates cold winds from the northwest from the livingspace. I have added a small solar greenhouse to the south-facing rear wall. Even though this house sits as a detached unit, it was obviously built from a set of plans for a townhouse as it does not have windows on either side. Sometimes, small urban lots turn up which would be ideal for such a house. To squeeze just a bit more space into this house, I have added a small penthouse bedroom right in the middle of the roof. This has several advantages aside from adding livingspace. It allows positive natural ventilation through all of the house. Since it is above the roofline, it permits forced ventilation to be directed through any part of the house simply by opening windows in the downstairs rooms and leaving all of the penthouse vents open. It also gives a shaft of light right in the middle of the upstairs and further permits visual space to be borrowed between the two levels.

The small, two-flue chimney near the middle of the house is ideal for a back-to-back installation of a wood-coal kitchen range and a small woodstove for the living room. In this case, the floors span the entire distance from wall to wall, so there is no need for intermediate supports if you wish to leave the space undivided. The photograph shows how rooms can be opened up by removing a wall so that the living, dining, and kitchen areas flow together into one seemingly large space. The actual area may be rather small, but allowing all three spaces to become one makes the space seem larger. In this case, I installed a greenhouse-type window to brighten an otherwise dull room.

Notice how the upstairs of this house has been divided into a parents' bedroom and a childrens' suite. What makes this house really work is that I am able to steal an extra level of space from the attic area. The steep roofs of old houses make ideal sleeping lofts, especially if you add a skylight to provide some extra daylight. If you cut away part of the second-floor ceiling, both areas will seem larger. Examine your house to see if there is a ridge board (a common feature of these old houses). If there isn't, the second-floor ceiling joists are tying the walls together and supporting the roof. If so, be very careful about removing anything structural. Sometimes these houses also had collar beams about halfway up the rafter, tying the rafters together, thoroughly disrupting any other attic use.

The picture here shows how I solved the problem in one house. If you want to do something similar, it would pay to check with an architect or engineer as each house is different and yours might require more reinforcement. Even if you can't take out all of the second-floor ceiling, you should be able to open up a sizeable section so that light from a skylight can reach to the second floor. Proper organization of the sleeping spaces can save a lot of space. Built-in beds are a real winner in this category. Try lots of sketches of your sleeping area to see if you can squeeze in extra bed space without adding to the house. Don't forget that space up in the peak of the roof. If you can visually relate to the rest of the second floor, a tiny loft just big enough for a bed will be quite comfortable. Four feet of headroom is adequate, particularly for kids. Make sure that you insulate the roof heavily and provide an operative window in the loft or it will be hot in summer.

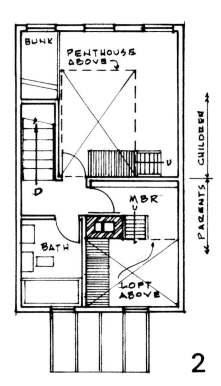

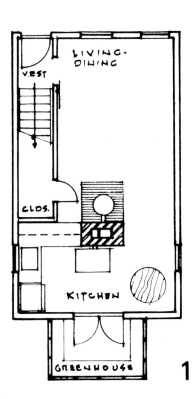

Ceiling and partitions were removed from this second floor, and tie beams were replaced by the box beam just above the skylight. The ladder at upper right leads to sleeping loft.

Efficient use of space makes an old house livable.

An example of a good plastering job done by completely inexperienced homeowners. This is the Mackey house.

Since I mentioned insulation, I should stress it one more time. As I have said throughout the book, the best way to save on heating costs is to reduce the requirements for heat. If the outside walls are in good shape, you may want to have urea-formaldehyde insulation blown into them. If they are cracked and rough, remove the plaster and insulate with fiberglass. Since old houses may have irregularly spaced studding, this will take a lot of work and may not be as thorough as it should be. My recommendation for this condition is to nail a 1-inch layer of Styrofoam over the inside face of the studs. This considerably boosts the insulating value of the wall and makes an excellent base for a variety of inside finishes. My favorite is rough grey plaster (see chapter 6). Another possibility is to apply Sheetrock to the Styrofoam, using construction adhesive. You will only need a few nails or some braces to hold the material in place until the adhesive sets.

Many contractors will charge you a fortune to refinish the inside of an old house because they don't know how to do the Sheetrock and will cut it to fit the existing studding. In the olden days when they didn't have 4 × 8 sheets of materials to deal with they just eyeballed the stud spacing. If you install some horizontal nailers over the studs in the wall before you apply the Styrofoam, you can install vertical paneling as an interior finish. Electrical wiring, if done to code, will almost totally destroy the plaster in an old house. If you can get away with your own generator, windmill, trailer service, or other source, you may be able to minimize the wiring and save the old walls. Otherwise, be prepared to lose them.

In all of your work with an old house, pay constant attention to air infiltration and leakage through window glass. Seal all cracks with a good-quality caulking such as Mono and check all of your construction details to make absolutely sure that you do not have any air leaks. Even if you can't afford storm windows for large or odd-shaped old windows, you can make simple insulating covers for the windows (see chapter 7). If necessary, add an entrance vestibule, either inside or out, to shut the winter winds out of your house.

Two tiny windows were replaced with an expanse of south glass and a deck at low cost.

Strongly resist the temptation to add to an old house. Heat bills are going to go nowhere but up. If you spend your effort reorganizing the spaces within the existing shell, you will be far ahead in the long run. If the space still seems too crowded, consider adding a deck or a solar greenhouse. The picture shows a small bungalow which has had a nice south-facing deck added. The deck makes the house seem much larger inside and out; the south-facing glass lets in winter sun (note the insulating drapes). There are even some conveniently placed decidious trees which shade the deck and the glass in the summer. This deck cost less than $600 and adds a great deal to the value of the house. A conventional addition would have produced dark interior spaces and cluttered up the exterior. It would also have cost several thousand dollars and added to the heating bill instead of reducing it.

The corner steps give this deck an interesting touch.

The *Old House Journal** is a monthly publication chock-full of nice ideas and sources of materials devoted to restoring and maintaining the old house. The editors seem to be primarily interested in restoring old buildings to their original condition and are not necessarily interested in low cost or energy efficiency. *Old House Journal* readers Kay and Edward Blair are curators of a museum where they came across the 1900-era picture of their present house. When they tried to find the house in the photograph, they realized it was across the street, covered with asbestos. These pictures accompanied an article in *Old House Journal* and show the various stages of the house.

Kay comments, "The work was hard and it took us a whole summer to accomplish, but we did it all ourselves with no previous experience to bring to the job and our 2½-year-old son was a part of the project as well. Children can be very useful when it comes to cleaning up the mess and even our toddler found it fun to load the truck. The feeling of pride and accomplishment is most rewarding at the end of the job and we felt our project was doubly successful when two other neighborhood

**Old House Journal,* 199 Berkeley Place, Brooklyn, NY 11212.

The house right after completion in 1900.

(facing page)

The restored house is painted dark gold with blue trim to articulate its features.

homeowners painted the trim on their houses to make them stand out and give some contrast. Rarely a week goes by that someone doesn't stop and point and look at the house or photograph it. It has been a rewarding experience and we join the ranks of homeowners who find the charm and history of an old house far outweigh the problems or inconveniences."

As it looked when the Blairs bought it.

(facing page)

A Case History   To show just what can be done with an old house, I will give you a case history of one. Howard and Kay Blume came to me and asked that I look at an old house for them. The house had been abandoned for several years, but the owner had painted and repaired it in an effort to sell it. It consisted of a very old (circa 1800) center hall farmhouse with a large expensive stone addition very skillfully attached to the back. If all people made additions this skillfully, our countryside would be considerably improved. The house was for sale for a very low price considering its close proximity to New York City. I enthusiastically encouraged the purchase of the house.

Now, the fun begins: banks. The first banker refused to get out of the car: "We couldn't loan money on that. The driveway only goes as far as the barn and there's no way to drive right up to the house." The second banker actually got out of the car and made it to the front door. Since it was very wet and the door stuck, he couldn't get into the house. Kay hiked back to the car to get some tools, leaving the banker on the front porch. He decided to kick the front door open, thereby enraging a colony of bees who lived in the wall next to the door. When Kay returned, she found the second banker trying desperately to take his pants off to get at some of the bees. The third banker, an elderly gentleman, said, "Oh yes, the Hanks house, a fine place. We'd be delighted to loan money on it. Do give me a call when you get finished, I'd like to come see it."

While the Blumes were shopping for a bank, they also checked some other prices. The house had a monster coal furnace which had been converted to oil in the basement. Unfortunately, the ductwork had been disconnected and the furnace discharged all of its heat through a grille into the front hall. Obviously, something had to be done with the furnace. A local plumbing-heating contractor gave them an estimate of $5,500 just to replace the furnace. The Blumes nearly fainted. He had been planning the biggest boiler possible with "baseboard radiation" running around the outside walls in all of the rooms, nicely heating the whole outdoors. A typical incompetent performance from a commercial heating contractor in this country. I can't believe that any of this is intentional; it's just that the contractors have no proper background in designing the systems and just "do it the way we always have done it." I explained that the money would be much better spent insulating the walls and installing storm windows and doors. Then they could install a small, efficient heating system. All of the old ductwork, except for the actual connection to the furnace, was still in good shape. We put in a very small forced-air furnace which uses most of the original ductwork and saved over $4,000. Urea-formaldehyde insulation for all of the walls of the house cost $1,100. Custom storm windows and screens were another $1,200.

Each room of the house had its own fireplace. Those in the old part had been rebuilt, but were in need of more attention. The massive central chimney in the new addition was in fine shape. I instructed the contractor how to rebuild the fireboxes to conform to a Rumsford shape. In the case of the newer central chimney, I added a two-sided fireplace. These are usually notoriously inefficient. In this case, we installed a sloping panel of tempered glass to approximate the Rumsford shape and narrow the throat. From the dining room side, the fire is only viewed through the glass, but is actually in the room. The mason constructed a marvelous arched opening through the chimney (see the before and after pictures). Then he went on to rebuild the fireboxes of all the other fireplaces in the house. All of them were very skillfully done and looked as though they had always been Rumsfords. Since the contractor had been given the contract to build the Perlberg house, I took a moment to congratulate the mason and tell him how happy I was that I would have him around to build the massive chimney with all of its special features. He looked slightly embarrassed and said, "Alex, there's something you should know. I'm a carpenter, not a mason. I had just done a little bit of masonry work before and volunteered to help with the masonry since Ben didn't have a mason." Like I said, it's very hard to get a professional mason to build a Rumsford, but now the Blumes have efficient wood heating in every room of the house. It's nice to think about when the next oil shortage comes along.

Many people would have thrown out the old plumbing fixtures. We recycled them. The old wooden toilet tank which was high up on the wall and encrusted with years of paint was taken to the local paint-stripping shop and turned out to be walnut. The huge cast-iron tub was repositioned and enclosed in a curved cedar surround. An old shower with a large fine-spray head from a junk shop was installed with the tub.

The tiny maid's room behind the bathroom was eliminated. Its space was added to the bathroom and used to accommodate a cedar sauna and a washer and dryer. The sauna was built as a freestanding unit which stopped short of the ceiling so that the feeling of space was maintained. On the wall of the sauna, we installed an European-style instantaneous-type water heater. Since the Blumes are all away in the daytime, it didn't make sense to have a large tank of hot water sitting there wasting energy. This type of heater is only turned on when needed and the flow of water through the unit actuates the burner. I was lucky and found this gem in an abandoned apartment building. It is a Junkers* unit and miraculously even has an American Gas Association seal of approval. Since the American appliance companies have conspired to keep these heaters out of this country, it is very curious that this one got here. Although it consumes the same amount of gas per hour of continuous operation as a standard 30-gallon American heater, it only uses gas when it is actually being used. The American type uses the energy regardless. Also, as soon as the 20 gallons of really hot water is taken off the top of the American heater, cold water rushes in and cools off the remaining 10 gallons so that it is unusable. The Junkers puts out a steady stream of hot water as long as you need it. The major drawback is that it will only serve one faucet at a time due to the restriction on volume through the unit. Since the European countries tend to have minimum plumbing systems like the ones I advocate in this book, this makes the instantaneous heaters ideal for their use.

Back in the attic, we came upon a very strange metal-lined wood tank. It had double walls and was insulated with sawdust. Several sets of pipe

*Available from Junkers & Company, GMBH, Wernau Neckar, West Germany.

Before renovations, the kitchen was almost in its original 1914 condition.

The cabinets in the new kitchen are all handmade from #2 pine. The butcher-block island provides extra counterspace.

A small, dark pantry occupied space in the middle of the downstairs.

By removing the wall flanking a brick chimney and cutting through the double-sided fireplace, the pantry becomes a bright dining area.

led off into the gloom. Everyone was quite mystified as to its function. When I came home that night, I found some new books in the mail. Actually, they are reprints of old books which were advertised in the *Old House Journal*. The books are *Palliser's New Cottage Homes* (1887) and *Victorian Architecture* (1873).* The specifications in the back of Palliser's immediately cleared up the mystery. The carpenter was instructed to "build an insulated tank" in the attic and the plumber was instructed to "provide piping, lead lining, and a force pump to push water up to the tank—an early system for providing running water. At first, we were going to convert the tank to a bathtub, but then we decided that the old cast iron was too nice to discard. So we moved it outside and made a hot tub out of it. Heat for the water is provided by means of a solar hot-water heater. It has been reinsulated and an insulated cover is provided to keep the heat in. The solar water heater has diverter values so that it can be used for hot water for the house when not in use for the tub.

Since the Blumes now live in a large old Victorian house, they have gotten used to lots of space. My next challenge was to give them lots of space without extending the house. In two of the bedrooms, we ripped out most of the ceilings and installed loft beds. In the master bedroom suite, this gave them a lower level sitting room with a cozy fireplace and a separate dressing room. Upstairs is an ample sleeping loft with a skylight looking out at a friendly tree. At the head of the bed is a window which overlooks the front stairhall and another skylight.

This solid brick shell makes a nice start for a new house. Insulation should be applied on the outside of the brick.

A forest of happy plants hang from some of the original beams which sail across the stairhall. These beams were part of the roof of the original farmhouse and were covered over by the roof of the extension. They make excellent hangers for the plants and also are a nice place to put some steps to get to the roof hatch. The roof hatch is original; we just replaced the solid cover with a Plexiglas one. Several sheets of Plexiglas were bought wholesale and used for the skylights and to construct the small greenhouse in the bathroom. One large south-facing window in the bathroom was removed to make room for the greenhouse, and a section of the wide roof overhang was removed and glazed with Plexiglas as a roof for the greenhouse.

Try very hard when working with an old house to install only those windows and doors which are in keeping with the feeling of the original structure. If all of the windows and doors are tall and narrow, wide horizontal windows would be totally out of place. So-called "picture windows" which have one badly proportioned pane in the middle flanked by an operating window on either side are always out of place in any structure.

Many old houses are made of masonry. Masonry houses have their own special problems. Masonry absorbs large quantities of heat or cold very readily. This means that a masonry wall almost has to be insulated if you live in a northern climate. The old standby method of insulation was to build a wood-stud wall inside or face the inside of the wall with Styrofoam and then install Sheetrock. This was in the pre-energy-crisis

*They have been reprinted by The American Life Foundation and Study Institute, Watkins Glen, NY 14891.

era, but unfortunately, the construction industry learns very, very slowly—a world-famous newspaper recently recommended this method in their homeowner's column. Of course, the insulation does work on the inside, but by insulating this way you don't get to take advantage of the heat-absorbing qualities of the masonry. I would recommend leaving the brick exposed on the inside and applying insulation to the outside of the brick wall.

Frequently an old brick house has weathered badly on the outside and will need expensive repointing and even replacement of brick to restore it. I recommend spraying the north, east, and west walls with 3 inches of polyurethane insulation and then covering it with cement stucco. The urethane will thoroughly seal the brick surface and even has a good bit of structural reinforcement value. Also it's very quick, if a bit expensive. It will have to be installed by a professional contractor, but you can apply the stucco yourself. Make sure that you cover it right away with the stucco, as the urethane is quite flammable. In this way, you can expose much of the brick inside where it can absorb heat and reflect it back to the occupants. In order not to cover all of the old brick on the outside, I recommend insulating the south wall on the inside. If you don't want to go to the trouble of framing out the wall, you might have the insulation contractor spray the inside of this wall with polyurethane. Then you could cover the inside with plaster, again, a do-it-yourself job.

The final results will be a structure with one south-facing inside wall with smooth plaster and the rest of the walls of exposed brick. If this is a bit too much brick , consider reversing an insulation to the inside wall on the east side. The west and north walls should definitely be insulated on the outside if you are to get the most out of your insulation.

Old houses have a charm which is almost impossible to duplicate today. Tradesmen just don't exist who can do the ornate wood and masonry work that was found in the last century. Even if much of the original work is missing in your house, old woodwork from a salvage yard that could be out of place in a new house will fit right into the old one. In many cases, the sort of workmanship which one finds in these buildings would be unaffordable today, even by a millionaire. By saving an old building, you are preserving a part of our heritage. Also, you can save energy by not using all of those new materials.

Chapter 12

Estimating Costs
and Preparing Plans

The most urgent consideration for most people who build a house is: How much will it cost? If you are a wise consumer and shop carefully, plan thoroughly, and take the time and trouble to search out wholesale outlets and used materials, you can reduce your house cost to a very reasonable minimum. Costs can vary widely in different areas of the country. The heavily industrialized Northeast, particularly the Boston area, is the high-cost champ. Since Massachusetts has the most repressive building codes in the country, I wouldn't recommend that anyone build there, anyway. Certain parts of the rural South where lumber is plentiful have abnormally low construction costs. The costs which I cite leave out such extremes and give a range which should be readily achievable in most parts of the country.

The following costs are based upon a unit price per square foot of area. They assume that you will use the basic methods of design and construction which I describe in this book. Obviously, if you build a sprawling house with many bathrooms and much waste, these figures will not hold. For labor costs where figures for complete houses are cited, I make the assumption that you will use a small non-union crew and act as your own coordinator. Hiring your labor directly can save well over half of the normal costs of dealing with a contractor. But here I am not counting the value of your time which may be a major factor. If you don't have the time or inclination to direct the job yourself, try to find a very small one- or two-man construction firm to do the job for you. Be very cautious with money, though. Small contractors are notoriously poor businessmen. Try to pay for materials directly or arrange to reimburse the contractor immediately upon delivery. Do not turn him loose with a large advance for materials or a charge account at a lumberyard. Both approaches could lead to disaster.

If you are willing to do your own labor, you can deduct about 40 percent from the figures below.

Approximate building costs:

Shell for an on-grade house . . . .$ 6–$10/square foot
Complete on-grade house . . . .$18–$22/square foot
Complete buried south-facing house . .$28–$32/square foot

Before you get too elated about how much money you are saving, remember that you have to add utilities such as well and septic system and miscellaneous costs such as a road and clearing your site. These costs can vary from virtually nothing for an urban lot with city services to many thousands of dollars for a rural site. Later on I give an exact current breakdown for a small house using recently quoted (spring 1977) figures for rural upstate New York.

One good way to control costs is to have accurate drawings for your house. In this way, expensive changes and corrections can be avoided. The drawings will also be necessary for dealing with the bank and the building inspector. You may have to cheat a bit on your drawings for both of these purposes. Banks are very big on three bedrooms. If you plan a study or a sleeping loft or some other space, you may want to change the labels for the bank to read "Bdrm. #1, Bdrm. #2, and Bdrm. #3. The building inspector can be a bit more tricky, as he will actually inspect your house. In his case, you may have to go the opposite direction and leave out rooms which you actually plan until after he has made his final inspection. This is because there are some very repressive regulations in the so-called "Uniform Building Code" which regulate room sizes. The intent was obviously to prevent unscrupulous contractors from building tiny unpleasant rooms, but the code overlooks the possibilities for efficient use of space with built-in bunks and the like. Generally, the codes restrict the smallest dimension of any room, except the bath, to a minimum of 7 feet, 0 inches and the minimum area per room is 80 square feet. A further stipulation is that no area of the room with a ceiling area of less than 5 feet, 6 inches high can be counted toward the minimum area for the room. The easy way around this is to label the space in question *storage*. Of course, the same space on the bank's drawings may have to be labeled Bdrm. #3 in order to get your loan. In case all of this sounds a bit devious, there are actually professional "expediters" in New York City who work full-time advising architects and building owners on how to present fake documents to the building department to get approval. In the good old days these same people greased appropriate palms to make sure that the plans were approved in less than the usual two or three years. Fortunately, New York City has clamped down and none of this happens anymore, or so we are told.

One final trick if you plan to do all of the work yourself is to draw the plans to metric scale. Metric is actually much simpler to work with, but the odds of either the bank or the building inspector have a metric scale and being able to figure out actual sizes are pretty dim. In general, make the plans neat and clear, but provide the least amount of information actually necessary. In *Low-Cost, Energy-Efficient Shelter* I gave checklists for exactly what information should be shown on plans. Look over those lists before making your drawings.

Contracts   If you hire a contractor to do a major portion of the work on your house, it will pay to sign a contract. I recommend the AIA contract form number A111 "Owner-Contractor Agreement—Cost Plus Fee." It is available from your local chapter of the American Institute of Architects for a nominal fee. At best, the owner-contractor relationship teeters on the brink of hostilities. There is just no way possible to spell out beforehand all possible situations which might arise. If difficulties do arise, the legal profession is ill-equipped to handle them. Any solution involving lawyers and courts is likely to take years. I strongly recommend that you insert the following paragraph in any contract that you make with a contractor:

> Any controversy or claim arising out of or relating to this contract, or the breach thereof, shall be settled by arbitration in accordance with the Construction Industry Arbitration Rules of the American Arbitration Association, and judgment upon the award rendered by the Arbitrator(s) may be entered in any court having jurisdiction thereof.

Forms for arbitration proceedings may be obtained from:

American Arbitration Association
140 West Fifty-first Street
New York, NY 10020

Outline Specifications   Here is a sample of the outline specifications that I prepared for the bank since these are rather different than those for a conventional house.

Passive Solar-Heated House for
Mr. and Mrs. Eric Perlberg:

The accompanying design is for a self-sufficient, energy-saving house which is capable of storing large amounts of heat from the sun and reradiating it to the occupants. Backup heating consists of radiant glass panels (electric) and a woodstove. The basic principles involve using extra-heavy insulation, large masses of masonry inside the structure and insulating covers for glass areas to trap stored heat in the building.

EXCAVATION

The site shall be sufficiently cleared for working purposes only in the immediate area necessary for construction. All trees shall be properly protected from damage. Remove all topsoil and loose rock from top of ledge rock. Architect to inspect before machinery is removed from site.

FOUNDATION

Poured-concrete-grade beam pinned to ledge rock as directed by architect. Concrete to be 3,500 psi (pounds per square inch); reinforce with 2-#6 top and bottom. Intermediate piers and chimney foundation to be reinforced with #6 at 6 inches on center each way.

FRAMING

Structural frame of the building shall be heavy-braced timber type. Material shall be construction-grade Douglas fir or L. L. yellow pine. Members shall be pegged together as detailed. Vertical and horizontal members to be overlapped to provide moment connection between floor and wall. Hardwood pegs must be used.

SHEATHING

Shall be ⅝-inch CDX exterior-grade plywood. Attach with construction adhesive and nails in accordance with UAPA specifications. Note that studs are spaced 24 inches (O.C.) so that more nails will be required. Studs are placed horizontally between posts to receive vertical siding.

INSULATION

Components of the building shall have a minimum R factor as follows: walls, 30; roof, 42; floor, 15. Wall insulation should consist of 6 inches of urea-formaldehyde or construction giving equal insulating value. Roof insulation should be 12 inches fiberglass or equivalent. Floor should be insulated with 3 inches polyurethane or equivalent. Grade beams to be insulated to same value as floor. Thermal shutters to be constructed of 2-inch closed-cell polystyrene (open-cell polystyrene is *not* acceptable).

ROOF

Roof for all sloping areas to be standing-seam terne. Install in strict accordance with directions of Follansbee Steel Company. Material to be prime-painted before installation. Flat deck to have 20-mil Hypalon traffic deck as manufactured by Gates Engineering Company, Wilmington, Delaware. Material to be applied over AC plywood deck in strict accordance with manufacturer's directions. Exception; fiberglass tape to be used over plywood joints.

FLOORS

Grade-level floor shall be brick set in standard sand bed. Minimum 3-inch sand cover over insulation. Flooring for upper levels and living room to be kiln-dried pine planks, 12 inches wide, set with cut nails. Vapor barrier to be installed under all grade level floors.

DOORS AND WINDOWS; SKYLIGHTS

Sliding-glass doors for solar greenhouse shall be double-glazed with ⅝-inch tempered insulating glass. Finish to be baked enamel; dark brown. Areas of fixed glass shall be ⅝-inch tempered. Skylights and special windows shall be ¼-inch Plexiglas. Stained glass windows shall be double-glazed with ⅛-inch Plexiglas. All operating sash shall be weather-stripped with compression-type weather stripping and equipped with cam-action handles. Exterior doors shall be cavity type filled with insulation.

PLUMBING

Provide submersible pump complete with pressure tank, controls, well piping (Goulds or Meyers). Interior piping to be Type L copper supply. PVC waste lines. Connect to septic system by others. Hot water to be supplied by solar water heater of "Breadbox" design by Steve Baer. All outlets to be equipped with flo-control valves to save water.

ELECTRIC

Provide 200 amp. overhead electrical service. Provide backup heating system of radiant heat panels as manufactured by Continental Radiant Glass Heating Company, Long Island City, NY 11101. Since these units use 30 percent less energy than other electric heaters, substitutes will not be considered.

FINISHES

All exterior woodwork to be finished with clear Cuprinol. Interior woodwork to have stain finish as desired. Floors and cabinetwork to be finished in satin polyurethane. Sheetrock to be finished in three coats of flat latex.

GUARANTEE

All systems and workmanship to be guaranteed for one year from date of completion.

**Working Drawings—
A Solar House**

Here are working drawings for House Number 24, the Perlberg House. This is one that I designed to bring together the principles of solar-tempering with post and beam construction. Don't worry too much about how neat or professional your plans may look. It is the *information* on them that is important. Do make sure that they are accurately to scale. Real disasters can result when something is not drawn to scale and a major piece of equipment won't fit into the final house. There is an easy way for the amateur designer to help himself avoid this problem—use a product called Deitzgen Quickdraft. It comes in a pad of 48 sheets which have a nonreproducible grid printed on them. The pad is Catalog No. PG-197-M87 and costs about $10. A metric scale pad is PM-197-M1. Draw your plans at a scale of ¼-inch to 1 foot. This means that ¼-inch of space on your plan represents an actual size of 1 foot. The guidelines on this paper are ideally spaced for this scale. Each small square on this paper represents 6 inches. If you follow my advice and use 6-inch-thick exterior walls, you can simply follow two parallel adjacent lines for each of your exterior walls. By using this paper, you can eliminate virtually all drafting tools. As a bare minimum, use just a straightedge and a No. 2 pencil with an eraser. All dimensions can be worked out by counting the squares and the lines printed on the paper will keep your drawing straight and accurate.

After you make your first-floor plan, study it carefully to see if it uses space efficiently and does what you want it to do. Usually, you will want to sketch up several alternatives. A quick way to do this is to take some sketch paper and a felt-tip pen and do a number of quick overlays right over the original drawing. Get your family members involved; maybe they can add some good ideas.

The elevations of the house should be drawn at the same scale as the plans. Study your window placements very carefully. Go to your building site and look at what you will actually see through the windows of the house. Will they shut out winter cold, but admit summer breezes? Think about it.

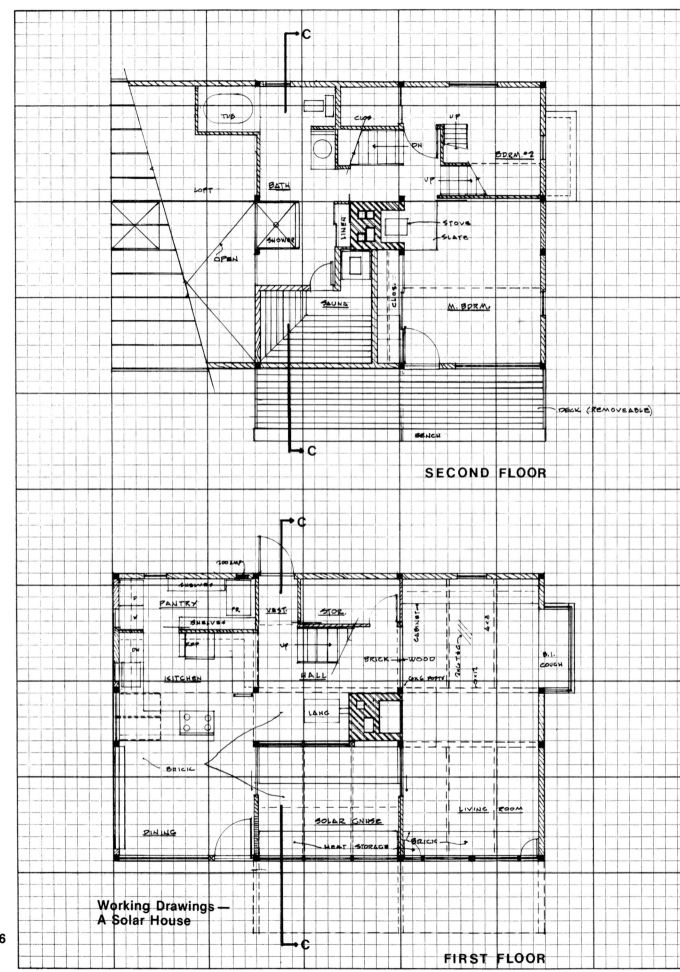

C

TUB

CLOS.

UP

DN

UP

BDRM. #2

LOFT

BATH

LINEN

STOVE
SLATE

SHOWER

OPEN

CLOS.

SAUNA

M. BDRM.

DECK (REMOVEABLE)

BENCH

C

SECOND FLOOR

C

100 AMP

SHOWER

PANTRY

PR

VEST.

STOR.

D

SHELVES

CABINET

4x8

W

REF

UP

BRICK → WOOD

B.I.
COUCH

6x6 POSTS

DN

KITCHEN

HALL

10x10

LANG

BRICK

LIVING ROOM

DINING

SOLAR GNHSE

HEAT STORAGE

BRICK

**Working Drawings—
A Solar House**

296

C

FIRST FLOOR

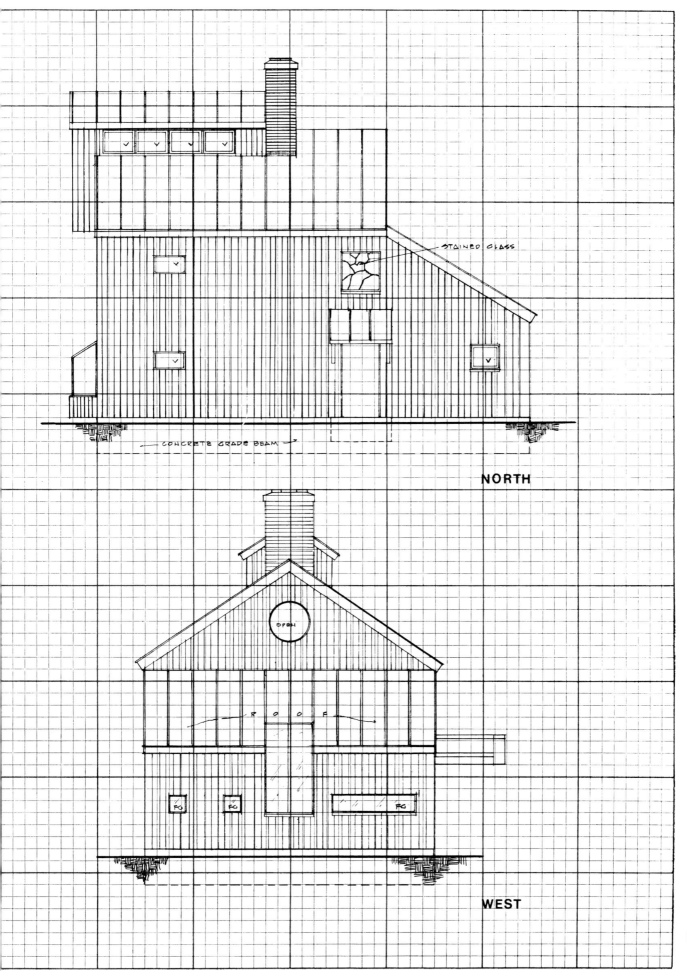

STAINED GLASS

CONCRETE GRADE BEAM

NORTH

OPEN

R O O F

FG   FG   FG

WEST

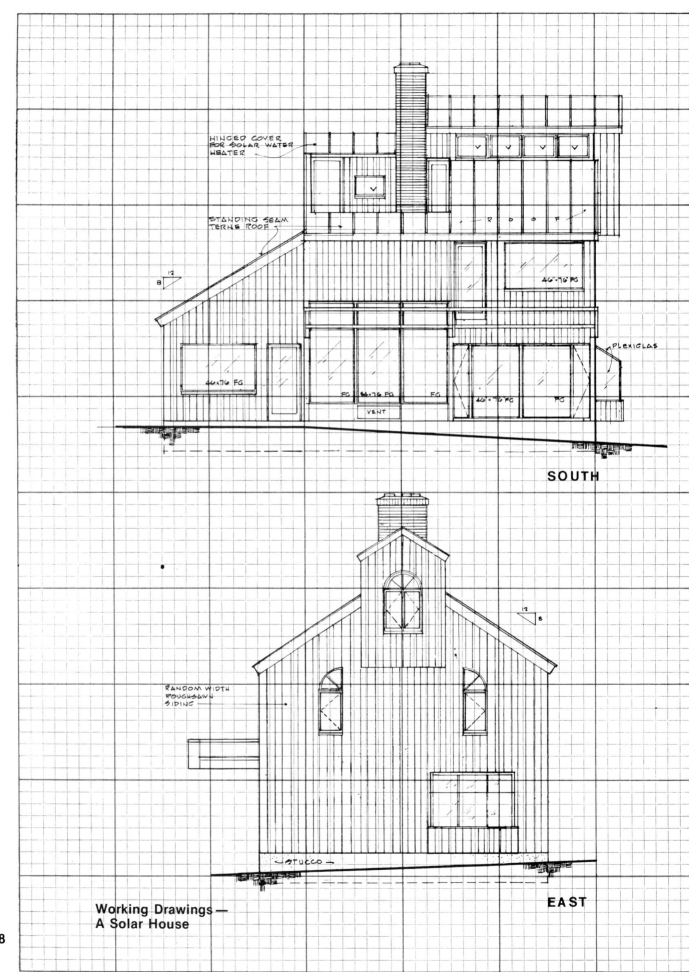

HINGED COVER
FOR SOLAR WATER
HEATER

STANDING SEAM
TERNE ROOF

R O O F

12
8

46"×76 FG

PLEXIGLAS

46×76 FG

FG 54×76 FG FG 46"×76 FG FG

VENT

SOUTH

12
8

RANDOM WIDTH
ROUGHSAWN
SIDING

STUCCO

EAST

**Working Drawings—
A Solar House**

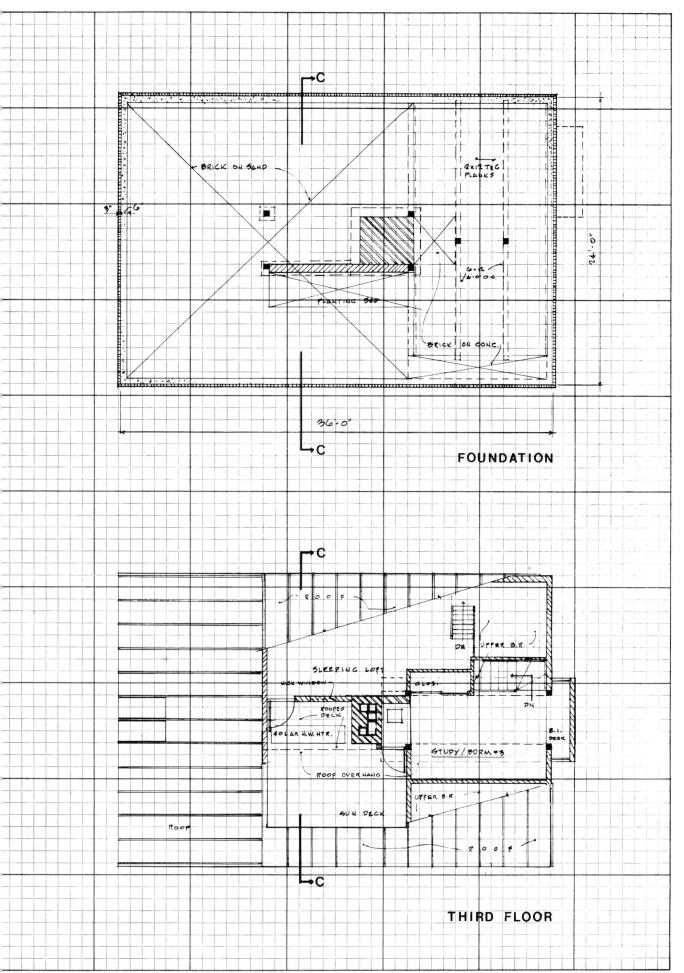

FOUNDATION

THIRD FLOOR

299

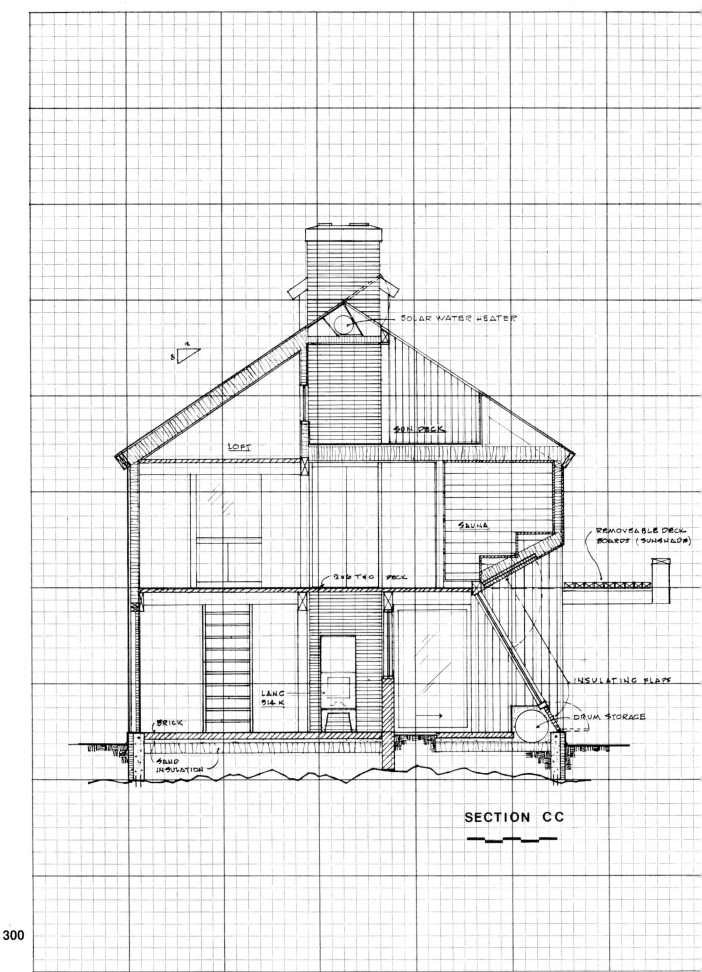

SOLAR WATER HEATER

LOFT

SUN DECK

SAUNA

REMOVEABLE DECK BOARDS (SUNSHADE)

2 x 6 T & G DECK

INSULATING FLAPS

LANG 314 K

DRUM STORAGE

BRICK

SAND INSULATION

SECTION CC

Based upon the information contained in the preceding plans and specifications, the contractor submitted the following proposal for the construction work for the Perlberg House:

PROPOSAL

House for Mr. and Mrs. Eric Perlberg
Riverby-Whittenburg, New York

SUBMITTED BY:

Benjamin Bromiley Carpentry and Cabinet Shop
Red Hook, New York

The following price includes foundation, frame, sub-siding, siding, insulation, finished walls, fireplace, Lange stove, chimney, stairs, finished floors, shelves, sauna, standing-seam roof, exterior doors and windows, interior doors, paint (two coats), plumbing, electrical wiring (including fixture allowance, antenna system, and lightning rods), temporary electrical service, and interior and exterior trim.

NOT INCLUDED:

Well, septic system, road, and landscaping.

These prices were arrived at from blueprints and specifications furnished by Alex Wade, Architect. We believe these prices to be a true and accurate figure at this time, however we reserve the right to change them prior to contract should it be made necessary by increased material costs, changes in specifications, or should probable savings be discovered in future conferences with Mr. Wade.

As delays in plumbing and electrical work can result in longer delays in construction, we reserve the right to final selection, with the owner's approval, until an approximate starting date is submitted.

All necessary insurance forms and/or waivers to be submitted prior to start of construction.

TOTAL CONSTRUCTION PRICE:

All items above listed: Twenty-nine thousand, eight hundred and forty-five dollars and 00/100 cents. [$29,845.00]

Should further information be desired, please feel free to call or write.

Thank you for your consideration.

Benjamin Bromiley   24 March, 1977

Available House Plans

For those who do not feel capable of drawing their own plans or who particularly admire some of the plans in this book, I have selected 12 houses for which I offer working drawings. These drawings are available for $25 per set from Smallplan, Box 43, Barrytown, NY 12507.

I have not included plans for many of the houses in this book either because they were designed for very special conditions or they were the owner's private personal design. I will be happy to provide additional information for any of the other houses in this book if you wish. Additional photographs of these houses are available from Neal Ewenstein RD1 Elizaville, NY 12503.

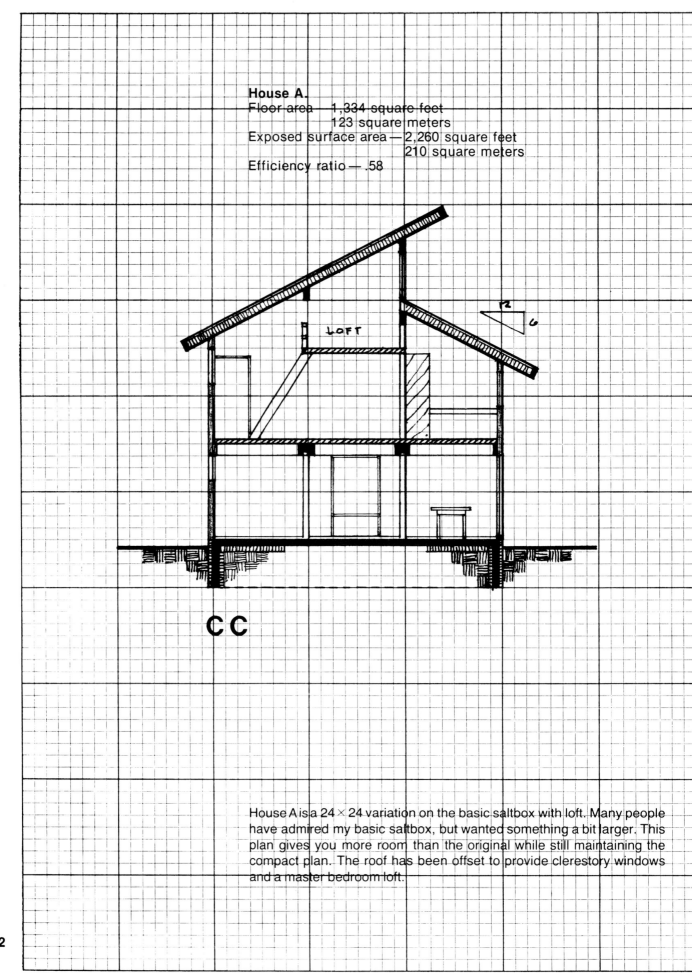

House A.
Floor area — 1,334 square feet
123 square meters
Exposed surface area — 2,260 square feet
210 square meters
Efficiency ratio — .58

LOFT

12
6

C C

House A is a 24 × 24 variation on the basic saltbox with loft. Many people have admired my basic saltbox, but wanted something a bit larger. This plan gives you more room than the original while still maintaining the compact plan. The roof has been offset to provide clerestory windows and a master bedroom loft.

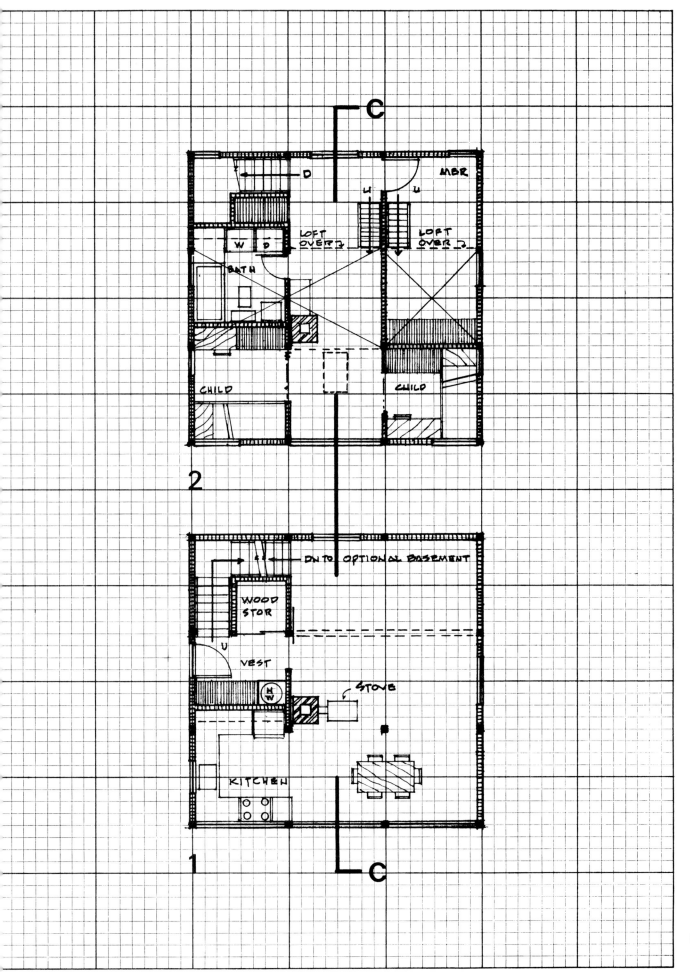

C

D

MBR

LOFT
OVER 2

LOFT
OVER 2

W   D

BATH

CHILD

CHILD

2

DN TO OPTIONAL BASEMENT

WOOD
STOR

VEST

STOVE

KITCHEN

1

C

30 Energy-Efficient Houses

House B is a duplex version of the basic 20 × 24 saltbox. Will Robertson is building this one in Nashville, Tennessee. He plans to rent out the one side of the house to pay off his mortgage. The plan has been reworked to provide a large master bedroom on the second floor and a full bedroom on the loft level reached by a stair instead of a ladder. This plan can readily be used with the basic saltbox if you desire.

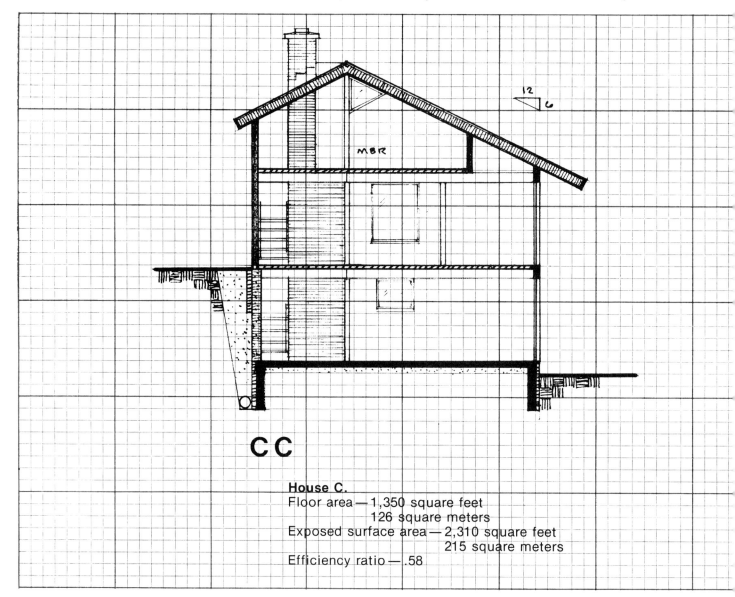

CC

House C.
Floor area—1,350 square feet
126 square meters
Exposed surface area—2,310 square feet
215 square meters
Efficiency ratio—.58

House C is a hillside version of the saltbox. In this case, you enter on the living-dining-kitchen level and go down a flight to the children's suite. The parents have a large bedroom-loft which overlooks the living room.

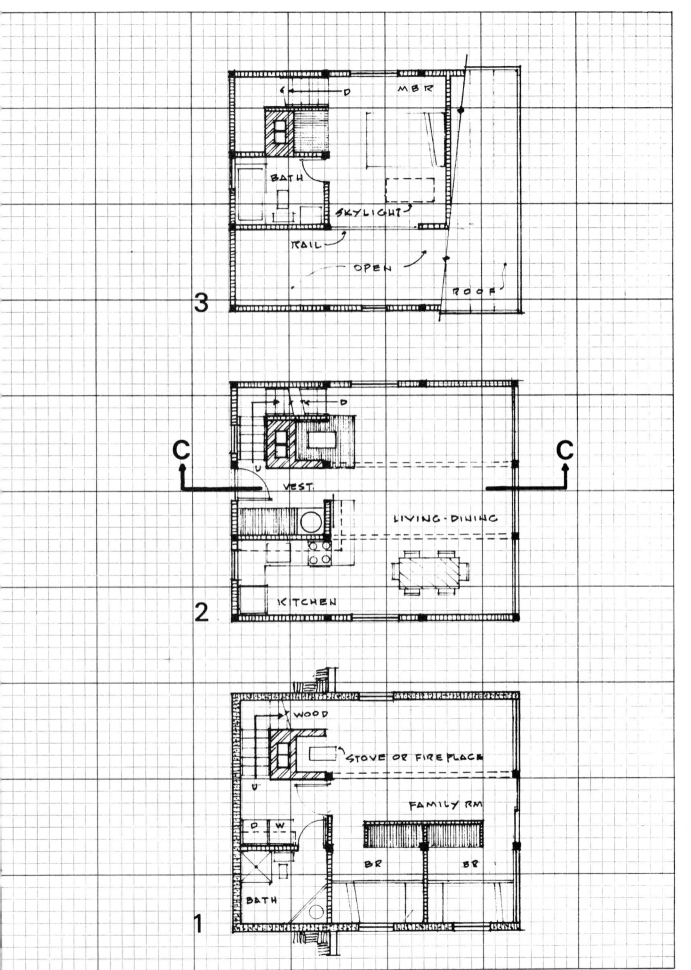

30 Energy-Efficient Houses

House D is Eric Replogle's buried house (see House Number 22). It has many unusual features such as a sod roof. I would advise checking soil conditions with a local engineer before deciding on this house. Also beware of rock. Blasting is very expensive.

House E is my "Volkswagen" house. It is designed to provide a basic small family house for the very least money. Construction is basically conventional except for the floors. I have deliberately omitted my usual post and beam structure so that you can hire a conventional Joe Blow contractor to erect the shell and not have any hassles about unfamiliarity with post and beam framing methods. The house has also been designed with an eye to banks and building inspectors. It can meet most building codes with ease. This house was not designed by me. One of the readers of *Low-Cost, Energy-Efficient Shelter*, Jim Velez of New York City, carefully followed all of my design principles, sketched up this design, and asked me to prepare working drawings and find a contractor to put up the shell of the house for him. To give you an idea of the costs which you might expect for a small house, I give you a list of

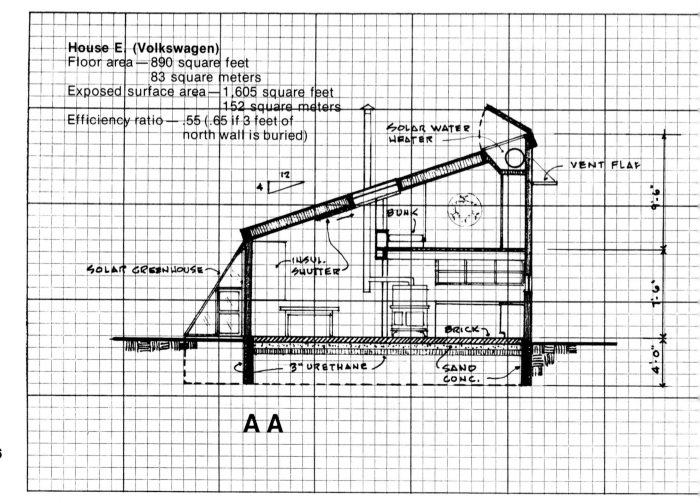

House E. (Volkswagen)
Floor area — 890 square feet
83 square meters
Exposed surface area — 1,605 square feet
152 square meters
Efficiency ratio — .55 (.65 if 3 feet of north wall is buried)

SOLAR WATER HEATER

VENT FLAP

BUNK

SOLAR GREENHOUSE

INSUL. SHUTTER

BRICK

3" URETHANE

SAND CONC.

9'-6"

7'-6"

4'-0"

A A

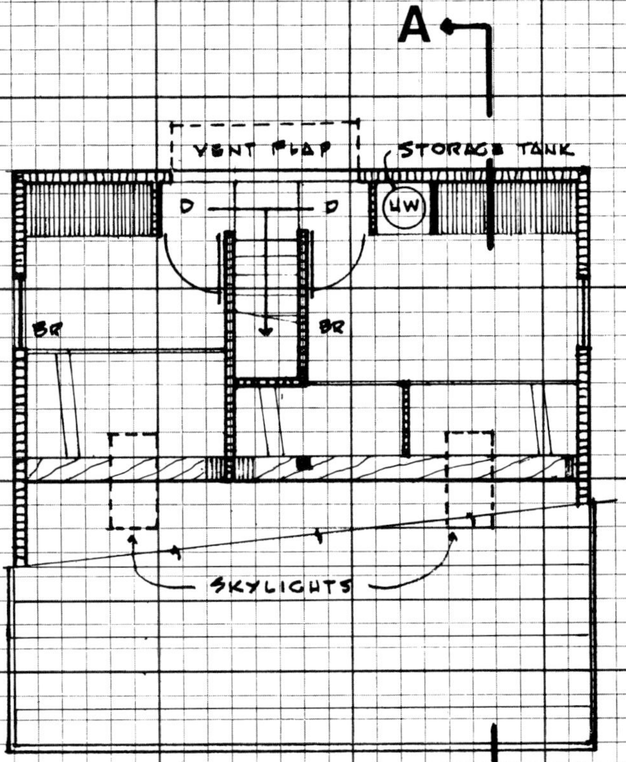

A

VENT FLAP   STORAGE TANK

D   D   HW

BR   BR

SKYLIGHTS

2

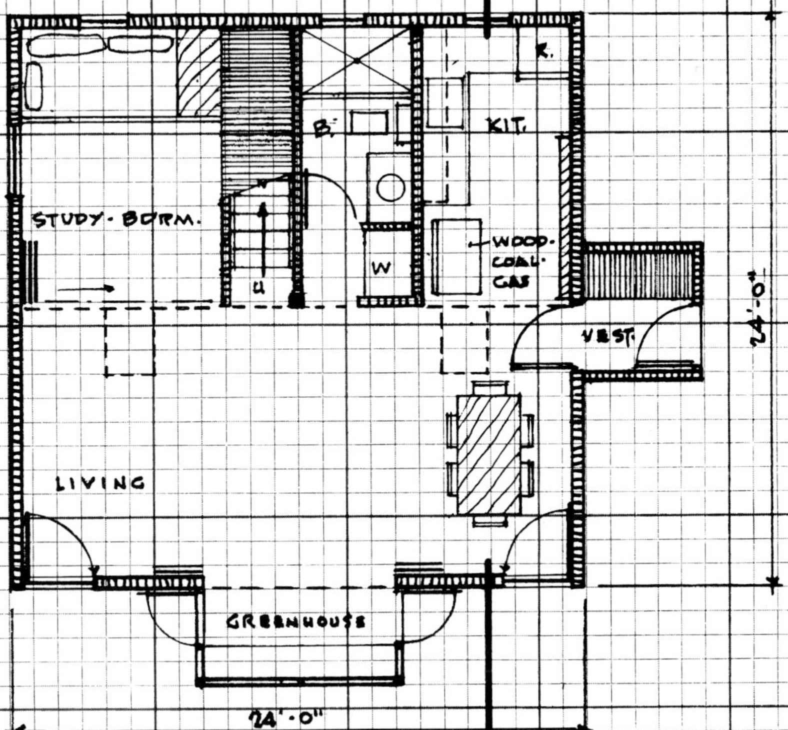

R.

B.   KIT.

STUDY·BDRM.

WOOD·
COAL·
GAS
W

VEST.

LIVING

24'-0"

GREENHOUSE

24'-0"

1

A

actual costs and quotations for materials for this house:

Shell of house erected with second-floor balcony	$6,300
Septic system (1,000 gallons)	900
Well	850
Road (gravel) 300 feet long	550

The above items were contracted and included labor. Jim plans to do the rest of the work himself. Estimated costs for other materials are enumerated below:

Brick (used) and sand for floor	$70
Used windows and doors	85
Insulation (foundation insulation included in shell price)	160
Sheetrock	130
Roughsawn siding	220
Paint and stain	80
Electrical supplies (100 amp. service)	375
Plumbing, including pump (used fixtures)	520
Barrel stove and chimney	85
Miscellaneous hardware and trim	120
Used kitchen appliances	65

If you salvage materials carefully and do all of your own work, you can easily cut the cost of this house to under $5,000 and have a very pleasant dwelling place. Even fully contracted, it could be built for less than $15,000. The method that Jim took, outlined above, strikes a happy medium between these extremes.

House F is the schoolhouse. These plans show how a similar structure might be built new and are also useful for renovating an old one-room school, small church, or similar building.

House G is a small townhouse for those who like traditional architecture. It is simple and unadorned. It would be ideal for recycling old windows and architectural woodwork. See page 279 for plans and pictures.

House H is not in the book. It is somewhat similar to the Barnett house on page 43 except that it is a bit smaller and has an added loft and solar greenhouse. It is a pole-type house designed to be built on a steep south-facing slope. While I do not recommend this type of construction generally because of heat loss and insulation problems, some sites may have too much rock to make digging into the hillside economical. This house still lets you use a south-facing slope, even a steep rocky one.

House I is another pole-type structure. This one is designed for southern climates and is particularly designed to take advantage of natural air circulation for cooling. It is the Pergola house, Number 29, shown on page 197.

House J is the basic shed-type, four-post house described under House Number 30. It is adaptable for a wide variety of sites. It can be built as a pole house first like the two preceding houses. In this version, it would be ideal as a vacation house or southern house. The plans show a small basement for the center area which would also be a possible solution for a steep rocky site. The third variation shows a slab-on-grade design. This is an ideal house for the do-it-yourselfer because of its very simple design. If codes are likely to be a problem, try House E which is of similar design but of conventional construction.

House K is a larger version of the four-post house. This one is designed with a built-in solar greenhouse and a masonry wall to store heat. It has small bedrooms with a large, open livingspace. This house is capable of storing much heat from the sun. It also has provisions for a built-in solar hot-water heater which is a modified version of Steve Baer's famous "Breadbox" design. See Perlberg Working Drawings, page 196, for details of this hot water heater.

House L is a still larger version of the same basic four-post design. In this case, it is designed for a sloping site and can accommodate an active solar collection system installed at basement level. John Lundquist reworked my design to provide a large master bedroom and a semidetached kitchen which was requested by his wife. The original idea was to use a solar-assisted heat pump for heating and cooling, as the Nebraska location has both very hot summers and cold winters. Note that even though the ground-level dimensions are exactly the same as House K, the two houses are completely different in design.

In case you want to contact any of the other architects mentioned in the book, their addresses are as follows:

David Howard
Box 295
Alstead, NH 03602

Mike Ondra
New Tripoli, PA 18066

David Wright
Sea Ranch, CA 95497

Gregg Allan
Stella Rural Route 3
Amherst Island
Ontario, Canada

Jedd Reisner
2 Innis Avenue
New Paltz, NY 12561

Some contractors who have worked with energy-efficient designs in various parts of the country are:

Benjamin Bromiley Carpentry Shop
Feller-Neumark Road
Red Hook, NY 12571

Aarhaus Construction
Box 311
Creston, IA 50801

Columbia Construction and Renovation Company
1108 Rangeline
Columbia, MO 65201

Dennis Kuntz
Box 207A
Bainbridge Island, WA 98110

Lea Poisson
Box 119
Harrisville, NH 03450